HOME HEALTH CARE NURSING

Administrative and Clinical Perspectives

Contributors

RONALD ATWOOD, A.A., R.N.
Clinical Specialist
Northern California Regional
  Spinal Cord Rehabilitation Center
Santa Clara Valley Medical Center
San Jose, California

WILLIAM H. BOOTHE, B.S.ED.,
  M.P.H.
Executive Director
Visiting Nurse Association of
  Johnson County
Iowa City, Iowa

JOY E. BUEHLER, B.S.N., R.N.
Rural Home Nurse
Butte Valley/Tulelake Rural
  Health Projects
Dorris, California

MICHAEL PARKER CASHMAN,
  A.S., A.A., B.S.N.
Clinical Specialist
Northern California Regional
  Spinal Cord Rehabilitation Center
Santa Clara Valley Medical Center
San Jose, California

LINDA G. CHERRYHOLMES,
  R.N.C., A.R.N.P., M.S.
Nurse Practitioner
Occupational Health and Safety
Northern Telecom Electronics
West Palm Beach, Florida

Formerly, Nurse Consultant
Forest Terrace Home Health
  Agency
Tampa, Florida

JUDITH L. ELKINS, R.N., B.S.N.
Supervisor
California Health Professionals
  Home Health Agency
Chico, California
  and
Instructor
Butte College
Oroville, California

VIRGINIA C. HAGGERTY, M.S.N.,
  R.N., J.D.
Formerly, Executive Director
Florida Nurses Association

JUDY WILLINGHAM HANSEN,
  R.N.
Home Health Home Care
Mobile, Alabama

SANDRA M. HILLMAN, B.S.,
M.S., PH.D.
Samuel Merritt College of Nursing
Oakland, California

NAOMI MARCO-MANELIS, B.S.,
R.N.
Formerly, I.V. Nurse
Woodland Memorial Hospital and
O.P.T.I.O.N. Care
Chico and Sacramento, California

JOYCE B. MARVAN-HYAM,
B.S.N., P.H.N., M.P.A.
Staff Nurse
Kaiser Home Health Agency of
Kaiser Foundation Hospital
Oakland, California

JOANNE MEANY-HANDY, R.N.,
M.S.
Associate Executive Director
Visiting Nurses Association of
San Francisco
San Francisco, California

SHARON T. O'MALLEY, R.N.,
B.S.N.
Nurse Consultant
Office of Medical Director,
Division of Medical Assistance
Washington Department of Social
and Health Services
Olympia, Washington

STEVEN ROSENBERG
Rosenberg Associates
Bolinas, California

KATHI SANTORO, R.N.,
Respiratory Nurse Clinician
Account Representative
Foster Medicals
Orange County, California

PATRICIA S. WATTERS, B.S.N.
N.T. Enloe Memorial Hospital
Hospice Program
Chico, California

JULIE K. WERNIG, B.S.N.,
R.N., M.A.
Co-owner
California Health Professionals,
Inc.
Chico, California

NANCY WICKENS, B.S.N., R.N.
Training Manager
Upjohn HealthCare Services
Tampa, Florida

HOME HEALTH CARE NURSING

Administrative and Clinical Perspectives

Edited by
Sandra Stuart-Siddall
California State University at Chico
Chico, California

AN ASPEN PUBLICATION®
Aspen Systems Corporation

1986

Rockville, Maryland
Royal Tunbridge Wells

Library of Congress Cataloging in Publication Data

Main entry under title:
Home health care nursing.

"An Aspen publication."
Includes bibliographies and index.
1. Home care services. 2. Home nursing. I. Stuart-Siddall, Sandra. [DNLM: 1. Home
Care Services. WY 115 H7655]
RA645.3.H648   1986   362.1′4   85-15812
ISBN: 0-87189-245-6

Editorial Services: Ruth Bloom

Library of Congress Catalog Card Number: 85-15812
ISBN: 0-87189-245-6

Printed in the United States of America

1 2 3 4 5

This book is dedicated to those people who influence my life in the most positive of ways. They offer their love, counsel, and moral support to me unlimitedly.

Mother
Thomas
Brian
Michael
Gaye

I also acknowledge the tremendous professional and personal support that I receive from **Jean and Pam.**

Table of Contents

Foreword

An important new specialty is emerging in nursing. Home health care nursing, historically recognized as an original component of community health nursing, has received attention as a unique and significant type of community-based nursing practice. The editor of this book has successfully compiled current information about the major, common, management, and clinical issues in home health care nursing. In addition, *Home Health Care Nursing* will serve as a part of the essential cornerstone for the development of this new community-based nursing specialty with unique conceptual and theoretical bases and practices.

Modern community health nursing originated in England during the mid-nineteenth century. William Rathbone, an English philanthropist, was so impressed with the private-duty, home nursing care his wife received during an illness that he instituted an organized nursing service to care for the sick poor in their homes. The first community health nursing service was established in Liverpool and became so successful that, shortly afterwards, a formal education program was instituted in England to prepare nurses for the practice innovation and the concept of community health nursing expanded to other countries, including the United States.

During the first half of the twentieth century, home health nursing in the United States was largely provided by visiting nurse associations and the nursing divisions of governmental health agencies—usually city and county health departments. Public health principles and practices as well as the notions of family and community care were integrated into home health nursing services with community health nurses performing roles as generalists, providing both preventive services to individuals, families, and communities as well as nursing care to the sick.

The organizational structures and philanthropic orientation of home health care remained stable until the mid-1960s when Medicare legislation was passed. This legislation provided a major source of third party payment for home health care services, and the types and numbers of home health agencies have increased rapidly. In addition to sources of reimbursement, several other factors stimulated the growth and demonstrated the importance of what has become the home health care industry. These events include rapid growth, both in absolute numbers as well as percentage, of the elderly population, and the emphasis on health cost containment, especially through reductions in in-hospital lengths of stay.

Currently, the home health care industry is characterized by diversity and change. Home health nurses provide care through the auspices of various types of agencies, representing diverse structures and philosophies. Treatments that were experimental in hospitals ten years ago are commonly being performed in homes. Patients and their families have increasing significant responsibilities for their recuperation and therapy; substantive needs for teaching, guidance, and assistance with coping; and increased needs for community support systems to assist with resultant problems and needs.

Despite the major changes in the home health care field, one factor has remained constant—the essential and predominant component of home health care is nursing care. Because home health care is largely nursing care, the adequate preparation for and continuing education of nurses currently practicing in the field are important. However, only a handful of books specifically focused on home health care nursing have been published. This book, therefore, is a relevant and welcome pioneer in an important and expanding component of the nursing literature.

The book is organized into two parts. Administrative aspects of home health care are emphasized in Part I, and clinical aspects are the focus of Part II. This dual focus is not intended to encourage a bipartite approach to practice, but rather to assist the reader to understand both the context and the content of practice. The practicing nurse must understand both the resources as well as the constraints of the home health care system in order to provide creative, professional care to individual clients and families in addition to participating in the development of systems of home health care and supportive services. Content on reimbursement, competition, marketing, and planning is very timely and relevant to all home health nurses— especially those who hold managerial and other leadership roles in home health agencies.

The clinical topics for the chapters in Part II were well chosen. The chapters include comprehensive, readable, and well referenced discussions of current patient management issues. These chapters can be used as a source of basic information for students and beginning home health nurse practitioners, reference and review material for nurses in practice, and orientation information for nonnurses in the field.

Collectively, the authors have succeeded in capturing the state of the art in home health care nursing. They have contributed to the compilation of information not previously found in one book and have made a number of unique contributions to the nursing literature. This book will likely be a classic in home health nursing for some time. Because of the growth of this nursing specialty, other complementary and competing books are likely to emerge. The editor and the authors of this book have provided a creditable base for building and comparison.

Violet H. Barkauskas, Ph.D., R.N.
Associate Professor and Chairperson
Community Health Nursing
School of Nursing
The University of Michigan
Ann Arbor, Michigan
November 1985

Part I

Administrative Aspects of Home Health Nursing

Chapter 1

Start Up of an Organization: From an Administrative Viewpoint

Julie K. Wernig

Because of Medicare legislative and regulatory changes, home health care has grown dramatically since the 1970s. It is an industry that has attracted much governmental and private sector interest. The estimated number of Medicare-certified home health agencies has increased by 64 percent from 1972 to 1981 and by 17 percent from 1981 to 1983. Six hundred new agencies were established over the latter two years, compared with 1,400 over the previous ten years (Williams, Gaumer, and Cella 1984). In light of the changing demographics of our aging population, coupled with the national swing toward home health care, it is anticipated that the home health care industry will continue to expand at a tremendous rate. The implications of this growth are significant to both administration and nursing personnel.

Home care services can be delivered by any individual, service group, organization, or agency with the desire to provide services to the ill, disabled, or frail elderly. Consequently, the quality of services rendered, the type of personnel used, and the standards of care and sources of funding vary widely.

In an attempt to ensure the delivery of safe quality care to the public served, the federal government has set forth regulations governing the home health care industry, as specified and described in the Health Care and Safety Code, Social Security Act and Title 22, chapter 6, Sections 74600 to 74749. These regulations outline the requirements for establishing and operating a licensed home health agency and must be adhered to if an agency chooses to use Medicare as a funding source for the care rendered to eligible, homebound Medicare recipients. Although some states do not require licensing of home health agencies, compliance with Medicare regulations is required for Medicare certification.

Agencies that do not participate in the Medicare program are not subject to federal regulation of services and have only to contend with local and state regulation of business practice and consumer demands. This type of agency frequently provides homemaker aide and private duty nursing services.

It is the intent of this chapter to focus on administrative issues that are of concern to the organization contemplating licensure as a home health agency. Specific administrative guidelines are presented, based on the assumption that an established business is operational and has adequate financial and administrative capabilities for the provision of home health care services. A number of components that require understanding, forethought, and planning before the establishment of a home health agency are addressed. Areas of concern include (a) licensing requirements and guidelines, (b) capital outlay and projections for cash flow, (c) bookkeeping requirements, (d) quality assurance measures, and (e) policy and procedure development.

LICENSING

A basic understanding of the terminology used in the regulations to describe home health agency activities is essential for an agency's assessment of its ability to comply with licensure requirements.

1. *Home Health Agency*: A "public agency, private organization or subdivision of such an agency or organization which is primarily engaged in providing skilled nursing and other therapeutic services on a part-time or intermittent basis to patients in a place of residence used as the patient's home under a plan of treatment as prescribed by the attending physician, which meets the requirements of Titles XVII and XIX, P.L. 93-603." (Health Care and Safety Code, Sections 1727-1734)

2. *Public Agency*: An agency operated by the state or local government subject to all federal, state, and local regulations. This type of agency is frequently restricted in flexibility and ability to diversify or to respond to the impact of increasing competition.

3. *Private Agency*: A nonprofit or proprietary agency that is not operated by a state or local government. A nonprofit agency is exempt from federal income taxation under 26 USC 502(c)(3). A proprietary agency is subject to all federal income taxation requirements. Private agencies, particularly proprietary ones, have a great deal more flexibility for diversification which enables them to respond more quickly to industry changes.

4. *Subdivision*: A component of a health agency, such as a home care department within the hospital or the nursing division of a public health department, that meets all licensing requirements (Health and Safety Code, Sections 1727 and 1734).

5. *Part-time* or *Intermittent Care*: The provision of services less than eight hours a day and less than a total or forty hours a week. Care is provided based on a reasonable expectation that the patient's condition will change within a limited time frame. The patient may need to be seen daily for dressing changes or every 90 days for a catheter change.

6. *Plan of Treatment*: The proposed plan of care for the patient while at home. The plan is written by a nurse and must be signed and approved by the attending physician. The plan of treatment (POT) addresses the following points:

   • a description of the types of services to be provided
   • the frequency and duration of treatment
   • the diagnosis
   • any functional limitations
   • extent of homebound status
   • describes medications and diet
   • needed medical supplies
   • descriptions of the expected outcome of treatment

7. *Skilled Nursing Service*: Nursing care provided under the direction of a registered nurse according to the plan of treatment that has been authorized by the physician responsible for the patient. The score of services must be skilled in nature and may include catheter changes, dressing changes, wound care, IV therapy, medical administration, and patient and family teaching.

8. *Fiscal Intermediary*: The organization authorized by the Health Care Financing Administration (HCFA) to reimburse providers for health care services rendered. Blue Cross and Blue Shield are examples of insurance companies that have been given authority to administer Medicare reimbursement to home health agencies rendering home services to eligible Medicare recipients.

9. *Physical Therapy*: Patient treatment provided for specific physical problems by a registered physical therapist. Therapy may involve gait training, exercises to increase muscle strength, diaphragmatic breathing, training to use a walker or other assistive devices, patient and family education, or rehabilitative treatment to restore mobility and independence.

10. *Occupational Therapy*: A specific type of patient treatment provided by a registered occupational therapist. Therapy may involve teaching skills that will assist the patient in the management of personal care, including bathing, dressing, and cooking/meal preparation. The

occupational therapist helps to improve the individual's functional abilities, teaches adaptive techniques for activities of daily living, and works with upper extremity exercises.

11. *Medical Social Work*: Social services performed by a licensed medical social worker. It involves helping the individual with social and emotional problems that may impede the progress or stability of the patient's medical condition. Medical social workers frequently assist the patient and family members through counseling and coordinating referrals to social service agencies.

12. *Speech Therapy*: A specific type of patient treatment provided by a registered speech therapist for various speech disorders. Therapy is primarily indicated after a stroke to help patients with comprehension and speech difficulties. Speech therapists provide restorative therapy, diagnostic and evaluation services and therapeutic services.

13. *Homebound Status*: The health status of a patient with impeded mobility away from the home environment. The patient may be unable to go shopping, attend church, visit the doctor, or leave the home without the assistance of another individual, supportive device, special transportation, or significant physical difficulty. Absences from a home must be infrequent and only for a short duration. A patient may be considered homebound due to physical disabilities or a lack of mobility caused by a variety of physical problems.

14. *Activities of Daily Living (ADL)*: Activities generally performed by an individual on a daily basis such as bathing, dressing, feeding, personal hygiene, mouth care, etc. Impaired individuals may have difficulty performing their basic essential activities.

The federal government has authorized each state to regulate the issuance of home health agency licenses. Although states may vary in their control over the number of licenses issued (such as requiring a certificate of need), regulatory requirements are similar.

In California, home health agency licensure is regulated by the State Department of Health Services. The regulations and guidelines are specifically identified by Title 22, chapter 6, article 2, which clearly states that no agency can present itself as a home health agency without being licensed by the State Department of Health Services.

To obtain a license to operate a home health agency a number of requirements must be met. The process generally takes a minimum of six weeks, depending on the level of expertise within the organization applying for the license, access to home health agency policy and procedure manuals, and availability of experienced personnel or consultants, as well as availability of State Department staff to monitor the agency requesting a license.

Application for License

The application for licensure evaluates the compliance of a number of pertinent components and examines such things as the legality of the entity (partnership, corporation, individual, etc.), the types of service to be delivered, and the location of the office. The location is important for two reasons: (1) It is the basis for classification as a rural or urban agency as defined by the Federal Register and will ultimately affect the rate of Medicare reimbursement for services rendered. (2) Services must be delivered within a 50-mile radius from the home health agency office.

In addition, the application seeks information concerning the administrator as well as the identity of all individuals having responsibility for the operation of the agency. Evidence may need to be provided demonstrating "reputable and responsible character" (Title 22, Section 74661).

Information regarding the organization's financial stability is required to ensure fiscal responsibility of a sufficient magnitude to operate a home health agency. The state also requires a copy of a current organizational chart as evidence of appropriate company structure and a financial disclosure statement of owner and principal stockholder interest in other entities or facilities licensed by the department.

Fingerprint cards may be requested for the owners, administrator, or other officers or employees as the Department of Social Services deems necessary for the purpose of "conducting a criminal record review" (Title 22, Section 74661). A license may be denied if any of these individuals has a felony conviction or has committed any other crime that may provide evidence that she or he is unfit to provide home health services. The department will make exceptions if documentation can be provided to demonstrate that the individual in question has been rehabilitated and is of good moral character.

Licensing Regulations

All agencies applying for licensure must meet the requirements set forth by the state with the exception of those in rural areas in which no other licensed provider exists and a lack of service could constitute a hardship for the residents of that community. The state can then issue a license for a specific period. This type of situation most commonly occurs in rural areas that have limited access to local personnel who are capable of meeting experience or educational level requirements.

A license may be denied by the state for a number of reasons: noncompliance of the laws and regulations, suspended or revoked home health agency license within the previous 24 months, inability to establish that the premises, management, bylaws, equipment, staffing, standards of care and services are adequate and appropriate to the operation of a home health agency (Title 22, Section 74669). This clause is subject to wide interpretation and is discussed in greater detail later. If an application for licensure is denied, the applicant may petition for a hearing by the department in accordance with Chapter 5, Part I, Division 3, Title 2 of the Government Code, Section 11500.

The license must be renewed yearly, along with the filing fee (currently $850 in California), 30 days before expiration. The license cannot be transferred to a new owner or entity. Therefore, any change in ownership would necessitate a new application for licensure. Branch offices and subunits must each be licensed separately from the parent agency, even though they may be operating under the same management.

Once the application for licensure as a home health agency has been submitted and tentatively accepted, a representative from the state will make an agency visit to evaluate compliance with the regulations for the provision of services. Although the guidelines are specific, there is some interpretive latitude given, which will vary with individual reviewers. It is highly recommended that the agency under review provide a comfortable, quiet, cooperative environment for the reviewer.

The purpose of the on-site review is to evaluate an agency's compliance with the regulations and its capability to provide home health care services as described in the regulations. The review process generally includes (1) an interview with the administration, (2) review of home health agency policy and procedure manual, (3) review of related personnel files, (4) review of a sample chart, (5) review of ownership documents, (6) review of contracts, (7) inspection of the premises, (8) an exit interview with administration. If the reviewer approves the agency for licensure, services may be rendered effective on that date.

The agency will be reviewed again 30 to 60 days later to determine whether the agency is actually complying with the regulations in the provision of home health care services. This review will involve an evaluation of (a) any deficiencies noted earlier, (b) patient care documentation, (c) qualifications of personnel rendering services. Recommendations will be made for deficiencies or for more efficient methods of documentation.

If the reviewer finds the agency in compliance of the regulations, then the license will be issued and the fiscal intermediary notified of acceptance of the agency for Medicare reimbursement. The requirements for services rendered and specific personnel qualifications are discussed in the Policy and Procedure section. Once the actual license is received, the original or a copy must be displayed in an area accessible to public view. State representatives will review all home health agencies yearly to ensure continued compliance with licensing regulations.

CAPITAL OUTLAY

The start up of a home health agency can be an expensive proposition and should be considered carefully before diving into the home health care industry. As with any business, a substantial amount of capital is required to set the wheels in motion, and consistent informed management is essential to the solvency of the organization.

In this section the reader is introduced to key financial issues that must be considered in the development of a home health agency. Areas to be addressed include funding sources, reimbursement rates, reimbursement mechanisms, anticipated expenditures, budgeting process, cash flow projections, and implications of cost reporting on cash flow and reimbursement.

Once it has been established that a need exists in the community, adequate referral resources are secured, the type of patient population to be targeted is identified, and the various funding sources are examined. In general, Medicare is the primary funding source for most home health care agencies. It is an attractive funding source, since it pays 100 percent of Medicare charges for appropriate home health care services. However, denials and bureaucratic delays can seriously impede cash flow. Medicare intermediaries exert the greatest control over an agency's operations in exchange for the Medicare dollar.

Medical/Medicaid also reimburses for home health care but at a lesser rate for services and requires prior approval for services to be rendered. Private insurance carriers are increasing their coverage for home health care services in response to rising costs of medical care, whereby home health care is a less expensive alternative to hospitalization. Their requirements for reimbursement are less stringent, but they have been known to create substantial delays in payment for services rendered. Patients may pay for services privately, but the cost can be quite prohibitive in comparison with charges for private duty nursing services offered by nonMedicare-certified health care services.

Fee schedules for Medicare reimbursement are somewhat restricted in terms of the cost caps set forth by the federal government. A variance in cost caps is related to the wage index and rural or urban classification described in the federal register. Medical/Medicaid also restricts the amount reimbursed for home health care services. A business cannot charge different prices for similar services to different buyers. Consequently, the same charges will be billed to insurance, Medicare, and Medicaid; however, the reimbursement rate will differ with each funding source.

The reimbursement mechanism differs among funding sources and is closely regulated by Medicare to prevent fraud and abuse. Briefly, an agency may bill for services rendered once the intermediary has authorized eligibility for care. The process may take from one week to six months, depending on delays in billing, desk review by the intermediary for appropriateness, incomplete paper work, and so forth.

Agencies may elect to use the Periodic Interim Payment (PIP) method, which allows for more frequent and regular reimbursement by Medicare. This method eases cash flow problems for the agency with fluctuating utilization. It is inadvisable to use this method if tremendous growth is anticipated, as regular incoming payments will not increase with elevated expenditures directly related to growth. An agency would then have to secure an additional funding source to cover temporary cash lags. With respect to delays in reimbursement, substantial cash should be secured before start up of the agency to cover all initial expenses related to service provision. Conceivably, an agency may not see its first Medicare dollar until six months after start up.

In anticipation of a delay in reimbursement, it is imperative that an agency project expenditures, develop a budget, and project cash flow to determine the amount of capital required to support the agency. Anticipated expenditures may include:

- Personnel wages and benefits
- Operating expenses:

	telephone	duplicating supplies
	training	membership/subscription
	travel	advertising/marketing
	insurance	equipment depreciation
	postage	legal/accounting services
	medical supplies	office supplies

- Occupying expenses:

	rent	depreciation
	utilities	facility license
	housekeeping	insurance
	maintenance	

Once potential expenditures have been identified, a budget needs to be developed. Expenses should be classified as either fixed or variable and extended over a one-year period. Irregular budget items, such as salary/wage increases, variable payroll expenses, consultants, travel out of town, audit fees, legal fees, convention expenses, and back-up wages for staff substitutes, should be identified and included in the projected budget. Revenues are projected based on the number of billable visits anticipated for each discipline provided. Salaries for contract services and wages paid per visit are variable and should be reflected in projected revenues and variable expenses. Developing a budget will help the agency to plan for the growth required to cover all fixed and variable expenses. It is an essential tool that can be carefully scrutinized to determine an agency's viability.

A cash flow budget should be projected to identify monthly cash and total capital needs over a one-year period. Items to be included are:

- beginning cash balance
- total expenditures
- depreciation
- projected revenue collection
- amortization
- fixed asset purchases.

Cash flow budget projections should take into consideration cost report reconciliations. A new agency may have difficulty complying with the regulations because of a general lack of experience with home health care reimbursement mechanisms and requirements. As a result, it may find itself with a high percentage of visit denials and delayed payments. Hence these variances should be anticipated in the planning process.

BOOKKEEPING

Accounting records vary considerably among the different home health agencies, depending on their size, availability of expertise, and automation ability. Medicare regulations require an agency to maintain fiscal records using generally accepted accounting methods; however, an agency's ability to maintain accurate, consistent traceable records often depends on the capabilities of the personnel employed by the agency.

It is recommended that all agencies prepare monthly financial statements, balance sheets, and statements of financial position and fund balance. If the bookkeeper cannot prepare such documents, an outside resource should be procured. Agencies frequently run into audit problems when the disbursement journal and general ledger are not properly maintained and expenses cannot be tracked.

The market has become flooded with a number of automation packages that can assist in accurately maintaining home health agency records, particularly payroll and billing functions. Many sophisticated packages are available that feed all data directly into the cost report, which helps to ensure accurate reporting and reduce the incidence of costly errors. A new agency needs to evaluate the pros and cons of ease and accuracy versus the cost factors involved in the acquisition of an automated system. Caution should be taken when purchasing a system that does not address updates and changes in Medicare requirements and reimbursement.

One of the single most important aspects of accurate record keeping is its relation to the annual cost report. A new agency may eliminate problems in the future if it enlists the services of an accountant or consultant who is experienced in home health reporting procedures to assist in setting up the agency's books. If the records are kept properly, information can easily be extracted for cost reporting purposes.

In addition to fiscal records, a log for Medicare billings should be maintained. Items to include in the log are patient name and number, dates admitted and discharged, number of visits by discipline, charges for each service, and diagnosis. The log can be reconciled to the patients' charts, Medicare payment summary, and billings. By using a three-way cross reference system, errors of omission can be detected more easily and the incidence of lost reimbursement can be reduced.

QUALITY ASSURANCE

As the governmental belt around the Medicare dollar tightens, fiscal intermediaries will attempt to gain more control over reimbursement to home health agency providers. Consequently, it is inevitable that fiscal intermediaries will narrow or change their interpretations of agency compliance of the regulations to minimize expending unnecessary Medicare dollars. A keen understanding of Medicare's quality assurance audits, as well as the development of internal auditing procedures, is essential to the future survival of any home health agency.

External review refers to "the fiscal intermediary's and/or state licensing agency's methods of reviewing compliance with conditions of certification or licensure" (Williams, Gaumer, and Cella 1984). Such reviews are generally provided by fiscal intermediaries, state licensing or Medicare certification reviewers, and HCFA regional surveyors, each focusing on a different aspect of operations. Fiscal intermediaries are interested primarily in use and costs of services provided and attempt to measure compliance through fiscal audits, compliance audits, and alternate review. State licensure surveyors determine whether or not an agency is complying with the requirements under Medicare's conditions of participation. At this point in time an agency is only required to conduct quarterly clinical reviews of open and closed cases by a multidisciplinary team. HCFA examines an agency in terms of its compliance with the conditions of participation; however, it focuses on evidence documenting the performance of quality assurance audits. It is not their intent to render judgment concerning agency standards on quality of care.

Medicare compliance audits are conducted by the fiscal intermediary at least once a year and are theoretically intended to educate the provider. However good the intentions may be, in reality the compliance audit has become a dreaded ordeal to many home health agencies because of interpretation inconsistencies by the reviewer. In theory, the practice of reviewing client charts for accurate documentation, medical necessity, and compliance with the regulations is reasonable and can provide useful feedback to the provider. What could be considered an educational process has turned out to be an expensive lesson in the merits of accurate record keeping for the agency, which must pay back to Medicare any money previously earned on visits that are reviewed retroactively and denied at the time of the audit. The problem seems to suggest that an agency is frequently uninformed regarding the rules used by the intermediary to evaluate compliance. This is partially due to (a) limited access to the regulations concerning compliance audits, which are located in HIM-13, Section 2300, and (b) reviewer disposition and temperament, which can vary, influencing interpretation of the regulations.

The purpose of the compliance audit is threefold, as described by Medicare:

1. To detect agencies that are billing for noncovered care so that corrective action can be taken by the intermediary. Such corrective actions may include putting a particular agency on intensive prepayment review or revising intermediary medical review methodology (which slows down reimbursement).

2. To detect fraud and abuse of the home health benefit

3. To indicate in which areas of home health coverage educational efforts should be aimed (Section 2300, Transmittal No. 258, Nov. 1981).

The reviewer must give the agency 24-hour advance notice of a visit (HIM 13, Sec. 2300.3). Twenty beneficiaries currently or recently served by the agency are preselected for review. At least 100 visits are examined, covering three months of billings within the previous six months. The auditor should have the authority to deny claims at the time of the on-site review unless there are special circumstances requiring physician consultation. If the reviewer is not authorized to make denials, then the audit should be protested to the intermediary and HCFA.

The following points will be evaluated by the compliance audit:

• Is the patient homebound?
• Are services delivered in the patient's residence?
• Were services furnished under a plan of treatment?

- Was the plan initiated in writing in a timely manner?
- Is the plan complete?
- Were changes or extensions made in accordance with policy?
- Were visits counted correctly?
- Were duration and frequency of aide visits reported accurately?
- Were evaluation visits billed appropriately?
- Were any excluded services provided?
- Is there evidence of physician certification?
- Were the services medically necessary?
- Were the visits classified appropriately?
- Were medical supplies and appliances ordered and supplied?
- Were the data provided sufficient to substantiate original payment?

Although the regulations do provide reviewers with specific guidelines, it is evident from the evaluation criteria that there is some latitude for judgmental decisions. The key to minimizing compliance review denials is documentation. If a patient's clinical needs are known and service is provided for a purpose, then it must be explained and justified. From Medicare's standpoint, if the documentation is not present, then the visit was not made or ordered, and therefore, it is nonreimbursable.

The auditor may choose to visit five beneficiaries in their homes. It is recommended that the visit be accompanied by agency personnel to help clarify any misinterpretations and witness any interaction between patient and reviewer. The criteria used to select patients appropriate for homesite visits include:

- service of six months or longer
- three or more disciplines involved
- questionable need for continued home health services
- received seven or more visits a week
- received less than four visits a month.

The auditor must hold both an entrance and an exit interview with agency administration. The purpose of the entrance interview is to explain the scope and purpose of the review and answer questions. It is recommended that the auditor be treated courteously and provided a quiet and comfortable environment to review records. The exit interview provides the opportunity to discuss the rationale for denied visits. The agency has one week to rebut denials and submit additional information to substantiate its case. The agency will be notified two weeks later, in writing, of the audit outcome.

The alternative review audit is similar to the compliance review in terms of its evaluation criteria. The primary difference is that 30 charts are reviewed from the start of care to the end of care, as opposed to a specific three-month billing period. The purpose of the audit is to ensure that agencies that have been reimbursed for all claims submitted without intermediary desk review are complying with the regulations. It is intended to minimize overpayment for services technically and medically not necessary or provided.

Internal audits are essential in developing a quality assurance program within an agency. The sophistication and complexity of the audit vary, depending on the size and needs of an agency. The most common methods used are record audits, supervisory review, and peer review (Williams, Gaumer, and Cella 1984).

The current trend in quality assurance is an approach that focuses on a "process-outcome" evaluation of services. This method evaluates what services are provided in what order and the end result of care (mortality, morbidity, disability, social functioning, and patient satisfaction).

Medicare requires that internal audits address the following:

- a review for appropriateness of care for all patients at least every 60 days
- a sampling of closed and current clinical records to be reviewed quarterly by a multidisciplinary team
- a professional advisory group review of policies, procedures, and clinical care
- an annual report evaluating the total program of services provided.

Documentation of all audit results and methods is required for review by Medicare or the state and can provide a useful tool for an agency to evaluate its effectiveness and appropriateness.

Quality assurance programs can be sophisticated and costly for use in a small home health agency; however, numerous methods are available that are easily adaptable, inexpensive, and effective tools to be used in the development of a quality assurance program. In addition to Medicare's requirements for quality assurance programs described earlier, effective internal evaluation tools include:

- monthly statistical analysis of patients serviced
- monthly random chart audits
- monthly chart review for documentation of all patient services billed to Medicare
- review for technical errors before submitting billings
- admission review of all new patients by the nursing supervisor

- discharge chart review for all necessary documentation, appropriateness of care, signatures, etc.
- biweekly nursing staff meetings
- biweekly case conferences
- questionnaires sent regularly to referring physicians and patients
- personnel evaluations
- communication system to alert therapists and nursing staff of the rationale for denied visits.

Developing an internal quality assurance program is essential to maximize reimbursement and provide quality care. An agency will survive the Medicare squeeze better if it is cognizant of the rules and regulations of Medicare reimbursement and maintains accurate and appropriate documentation of all activity.

POLICIES AND PROCEDURES

The purpose of the policy and procedure manual is to document and describe how the agency will operate to provide home health care services. The manual must be specific and include all aspects of operations. It is an essential tool used in the education and orientation of personnel and provides the necessary documentation of regulation compliance as required by the state for licensure. The primary intent of this section is to introduce the reader to the regulations governing service provision and personnel requirements. Additional suggestions regarding format and policy and procedure development are presented.

A home health agency must provide part-time or intermittent skilled nursing services and at least one additional service, such as physical therapy, speech therapy, occupational therapy, medical social services, or home health aide services. Diet counseling, medical supply, and medical appliances also may be provided. The most frequently used disciplines are skilled nursing, physical therapy, and home health aides. All personnel used must be currently licensed, registered, or certified as required by the state for the services provided.

The home health agency may employ all personnel or contract with other providers as necessary for the delivery of services. Small agencies may find contracting for therapy services a more cost-effective and efficient means of using personnel. Contract arrangements should be specific and address the following elements:

- requirements for licensure, certification, or registration. Proof that the appropriate requirements are met must be submitted.
- scope of services to be provided
- documentation requirements
- provisions for method of payment
- responsibility to attend necessary meetings, such as patient care conferences, utilization review, etc.
- provision for mileage reimbursement
- evidence of worker's compensation and malpractice insurance coverage
- evidence of a negative tuberculosis test and physical examination indicating that the individual is free of communicable disease and able physically to perform the work required
- supervision specifications.

The home health agency must have a governing board to adopt bylaws, a charter, and an official statement of objectives. The objectives must describe the services provided and stipulate that the agency does not refuse service or employment or discriminate against any person because of race, color, or national origin (Title 22, Section 74717). In addition, the governing board is legally responsible for all home health agency operations and oversees the management of fiscal affairs. The board appoints the administrator of the agency and an alternate to cover in the absence of the administrator.

The administrator for the home health agency may be a supervising physician, a director of nursing, or other individual who has had either a minimum of one year of supervisory experience in home health care or related service or preparation and experience in health services administration (Title 22, Section 74717). The primary responsibility of the administrator is to organize and direct all home health agency operations. General duties include:

- assisting with effective communications among the governing board, the professional personnel, and the staff
- maintaining good public relations
- developing and implementing effective budgeting and accounting procedures
- developing and implementing comprehensive agency policies and procedures governing general operations and health care services
- ensuring that appropriate personnel policies are enacted
- arranging and maintaining contracts when outside providers are used

- monitoring accounting and billing systems to ensure accuracy and compliance with Medicare regulations.

The director of nursing (DON) is frequently the central figure in the management of a home health agency and is responsible for directing all nursing and therapeutic services. The qualifications and regulations governing the position of DON are specifically outlined in Title 22, Section 74703, and address the following points:

- The DON must be employed 40 hours a week.
- If the DON is absent more than 20 consecutive days, the state must be notified in writing of the registered nurse who is temporarily assuming the responsibilities of the DON.
- Any DON vacancy must be filled within 60 days.
- The qualifications for the DON position are designed to ensure adequate management expertise to provide effective and efficient home health care services. The requirements for the position are:
  - registered nurse (RN) with a master's degree in nursing administration or supervision from an accredited NLN program or a public health administration program and two years' administrative experience in community health or related service within the past five years
  - RN with a baccalaureate degree in nursing and three years of supervisory experience in community health service within the past six years
  - employed as a DON in a home health agency at the time the regulations were enacted.

Rural areas have experienced some difficulty in recruiting qualified individuals to fill DON positions. However, state reviewers have on occasion broadened their interpretation of the regulations and accepted less qualified individuals for the DON's position. California reviewers have begun to accept acute care hospital experience as "related experience."

Additional staff requirements include the nursing supervisor, who must be an RN with a baccalaureate degree in nursing and two years' experience in community health (or related field) within the past five years. Staff RNs must have at least one year of nursing experience, or possess a public health nurse certificate, or hold a baccalaureate degree in nursing from an NLN-accredited program. Licensed vocational nurses must have at least one year of professional nursing experience and work under the supervision of an RN. Home health aides must be certified by a state-approved home health aide training program.

Physical therapy, speech therapy, and occupational therapy services must be provided in accordance with the plan of treatment (POT). The policy and procedure manual should contain detailed job descriptions of expected duties to be performed for each discipline used by the agency. Duties may include:

- providing patient treatment as ordered by the attending physician
- documenting and evaluating the individual's level of function
- continually updating the POT
- documenting all observations of the patient's condition on the patient's health record
- advising, consulting, and teaching family and agency personnel important aspects of the patient's therapy program
- assisting with the training of agency personnel as needed
- providing home evaluations with recommendations for change when appropriate
- participating in inservice education and patient care conferences.

Besides the personnel qualifications and responsibilities outlined here, the policy and procedure manual should contain the following elements:

- table of contents for easy, quick reference
- organizational goals and objectives
- geographic area to be serviced
- organizational chart
- description of the primary functions and services to be provided
- definitions of services and terminology
- policy regarding preventive treatment and rehabilitative services
- job descriptions and guidelines for skilled nursing services and referrals
- home health aide job description and qualifications
- description of the basic home health aide certification training program
- job descriptions and guidelines for therapy services and referrals
- medical supply and appliance policies and procedures
- provision for referring patient to other service providers when unqualified for home health agency services
- supervisory statement and description assuming responsibility for all employees and contract personnel functions
- job descriptions for all personnel, including qualifications, responsibilities and conditions of employment, hours of work, wage scales, vacation and sick leave provisions

- governing board statement of purpose, responsibilities of members, minutes, resolutions, and bylaws
- professional advisory committee purpose, responsibilities, and members
- administrative policies
- annual budget and policy
- policy regarding the limitations of service, including a description of specific conditions or situations that render an individual unqualified to receive home health agency skilled nursing services such as custodial care, chronic brain syndrome, chronic disease, not homebound, nonintermittent care, limited services provided by the agency, such as chemotherapy, etc.
- criteria for admission to home health agency services
- referral process
- admission procedure identifying each element in the process and including the initial nursing evaluation, client profile, plan of care, and homebound status
- plan of treatment, including initial orders, certification of need, and pertinent diagnosis, and generally include a description of the patient's mental status, types of services and equipment required, frequency of visits, prognosis, rehabilitation potential, functional limitations, activities permitted, nutritional requirements, medications and treatments, safety measures, instructions for timely discharge or referral, statement of treatment goals, and instructions to the patient and family
- physicians' orders and changes in orders
- communication with the physicians
- readmission to service
- administration of medications and treatment
- IV therapy policy and procedure
- lab work procedures
- tracheostomy care policy procedure
- plan of care, purpose and policy regarding completion
- medical policies and emergency medical orders
- clinical records containing pertinent past and current findings; plan of treatment; appropriate identifying information; name and phone number of physician; drug, dietary, treatment, and activity orders; signed and dated clinical and progress notes; copies of summary reports sent to the physician; discharge summary
- field files, purpose and policy, sample file
- clinical record-retention policy

- copies of forms used
  — intake form
  — patient consent form
  — bill of rights
  — initial evaluation form
  — treatment and medication list
  — nursing base line data
  — nursing notes
  — nursing care plan
  — physician order sheet
  — nursing summary discharge
  — patient discharge summary
  — medical treatment plan
  — letter terminating services
- policy regarding notification of noncovered care to beneficiaries of home health services
- Medicare claims review guidelines
- sample contracts
- criteria for discharge
- program evaluation plan
- quantitative program evaluation
- utilization review process
- annual report
- statistics, methodology, and policy
- team conference policy
- general policies regarding reportable injuries, child abuse, adult abuse, rape of client or family member, rape of staff employee, battered female, client expiring at home, illegal drugs in the home, meetings and conferences, department meetings, inservice education, safety precautions, incidents and accidents, infection control, nursing bag, CPR, transportation, expense report, general office policies and procedures
- personnel policy, including criteria for hiring and firing, nondiscrimination statement, orientation plan and checklist, inservice education, job descriptions, salaries, benefits and personnel file, dress code, employee evaluations, and health examination requirements.

The policy and procedure manual must be updated continuously and should be accessible to all staff members for review. It is recommended that the new home health agency contemplating licensure attempt to use another home health agency's manual as a guide to expedite the tedious and timely process of policy and procedure development.

SUMMARY

The primary issues of concern to the organization considering developing a home health agency have been addressed in this chapter. Specific licensing requirements are discussed to assist the organization in assessing its own capability of successfully complying with the regulations before funds are expended unnecessarily. Guidelines for capital outlay and projections for cash flow are described to provide the organization with some basic tools to be used in assessing its financial stability and resources available to operate a home health agency properly. Several bookkeeping methods are discussed to emphasize the crucial significance of accurate, Medicare-acceptable standards of record keeping. Quality assurance measures are discussed, with suggestions for internal auditing programs as well as guidelines for the development of a policy and procedure manual.

REFERENCES

Department of Health and Human Services. *Medicare Intermediary Manual*, pt. 2, Audits, Reimbursement, Program Administration, Transmittal No. 328, December 1984.

Elkins, Carolyn Pinion. *Community Health Nursing: Skills and Strategies.* Bowie, Md.: Robert J. Brady Co., 1984.

Hoffman, Janet. "Compliance Audit." *Home Health Journal*, September 1984, p. 21.

Holloway, Vonicha McClenny. "Documentation: One of the Ultimate Challenges in Home Health Care." *Home Health Care Nurse*, January/February 1984.

Lee, Nancy. *Elementary Accounting.* New York: Dryden Press, 1983.

Roeder, Bonnie. "Diagnosis-specific Home Care: A Model for the Future." *Caring*, December 1984.

Williams, Judith Lavor, Gary Gaumer, and Margot A. Cella. *Home Health Services: An Industry in Transition.* Cambridge, Mass.: Abt Books, 1984.

Chapter 2

Reimbursement Issues

Sharon T. O'Malley

In this day of rapidly increasing health care costs and the recent implementation of Medicare's hospital prospective reimbursement system—diagnosis-related groups, or DRGs—the home health care delivery system is on the front lines as an effective alternative health care delivery system.

Home health care is a complex system, however, not easily understood by the industry, much less the general public. The types of agencies in existence, the existing reimbursement sources, the cost reporting process, and current trends in the industry are discussed in this chapter.

TYPES OF AGENCIES

The term home health agency refers to a variety of public and private agencies that participate in the federal health insurance programs of Medicare and Medicaid. (A more specific definition is found in the federal Conditions of Participation; Home Health Agencies [C.F.R. 405.1201, Appendix 2–A]). These agencies, regardless of type, must comply with all applicable federal, state, and local laws and regulations, as well as be certified by the state-certifying body designated by the federal government.

In some states, home health agencies must also obtain a "certificate of need" or licensure before opening for business. Once the certificate of need is received and the agency has been in operation for 60 days, the agency may apply to the state-certifying body for certification. However, the agency cannot bill the federal health insurance programs until certification is received. A survey will be conducted on a regular basis to ascertain that all requirements of Section 1861 of the Social Security Act (Conditions of Participation) are met.

Before the enactment of Medicare (Title XVIII of the Social Security Act), in 1966, home health care was provided primarily by one of three sources:

23

Visiting Nurse Associations (services), nursing divisions of health departments, and hospital-based programs. But since the arrival of Medicare, the number and types of agencies have increased dramatically.

The Health Care Financing Administration (HCFA) of the Department of Health and Human Services currently classifies home health agencies as official, voluntary nonprofit, combination official and voluntary, private nonprofit, and proprietary. Home health agencies are classified further according to location and governing structure. Those that are not housed within another type of service delivery system or institution are defined as free-standing; conversely, agencies that are housed within another service delivery system are commonly grouped according to type of provider. As a result, skilled nursing facility (SNF)-based and hospital-based agencies are common terms within the industry.

Administrative Organization

Regardless of the type of agency or governing structure, most agencies have the same or similar organizational components. The federal Conditions of Participation mandate that each agency participating in the federal health insurance programs have a governing body (owner or board of directors), an administrator, a supervising physician or registered nurse, and a professional advisory group. Historically and currently, professional nurses are the backbone of home health care and the discipline primarily involved in the administration and management of home health agencies.

Official Health Agencies

Official health agencies are given their power through legislation and are one of the oldest types of home health care providers. State and local tax revenues are the primary funding sources, with occasional charitable donations.

Rarely is home health care the only service provided by an official health agency. Depending on the community's size, population, and geographic location, services can range from a single community (public) health nurse to a full range of services, such as preventive health care, communicable disease control, chronic illness care, and environmental health. Official home health providers are generally the nursing divisions of state and local health departments; however, if they participate in the federal health insurance programs, they must maintain separate cost centers. Therefore, most official home health agencies have found it easier to maintain separate staffs and, in some instances, separate buildings, while still maintaining the official agency name.

Voluntary Agencies

Voluntary agencies do not rely on tax revenues and have no legislative authority. Such agencies are financed totally with non-tax funds, such as United Way, cancer societies, and heart associations, and with third party payments from a variety of sources, such as Medicare, Medicaid, and private insurance. Typically, a voluntary agency is governed by a board of directors composed of interested individuals who live within the area it serves.

The majority of voluntary home health agencies, as well as the best known and oldest, are the Visiting Nurse Associations or Services, commonly known as VNA or VNS. Each VNA or VNS is autonomous and operates independently of other VNA or VNS agencies. Historically, the voluntary agency depended primarily on the visiting nurse for service delivery, but today most VNAs and VNSs have developed a comprehensive, coordinated multidisciplinary approach to the delivery of home health care services.

Combination Official/Voluntary Agencies

Combination home health agencies are administered jointly by a board of directors and governmental authorities involved in health care. These agencies evolved in an effort to decrease costs through eliminating duplication of services. However, the number of combination agencies has been steadily decreasing. This decline has resulted primarily because official health agencies have chosen to focus on programs other than home health care and no longer participate in the federal health insurance programs.

Private Agencies

Private agencies may be either nonprofit or proprietary. Private nonprofit agencies are tax exempt under Section 501 of the Internal Revenue Code. Proprietary, meaning profit making, agencies are ineligible for tax exemption and before 1982 could not participate in the federal health insurance programs in states without licensure laws.[1]

The entrance of private home health agencies, both nonprofit and proprietary, into the home care industry has been marked with controversy. Critics argue that such agencies have entered the market primarily for monetary gain and that little difference exists between those designated nonprofit and those designated proprietary except that legal maneuvers have circumvented proprietary status. Also, private nonprofit agencies contend that they are providing a needed service in otherwise underserved areas.[2] The debate and controversy continue both within and outside the industry.

Either type of private home health agency may be owned by an individual or a corporation. Owners may or may not administer the agency. Many proprietary agencies are corporate owned, and some are available on a franchise basis.

Many private home health agencies do not participate in the federal health insurance programs. Rarely do such agencies offer a full array of home health services. Instead, most offer private duty nursing and homemaker/home health aide services that are more extensive than those available through Medicare and Medicaid. Services are generally offered in 2- to 24-hour "shifts." Reimbursement to these agencies is usually private payment for homemaker/home health aide services and private insurance for licensed care. There is a great deal of concern in the industry regarding the lack of mandated minimum standards for the operation of this type of private agency. Recently, however, there has been an increase in the joining together of these private agencies with certified agencies providing intermittent services. Thus minimal standards as outlined in the federal Conditions of Participation are ensured, and the realm of home health care is broadened.

Other Agencies

Hospital- or SNF-based home health agencies may be official, voluntary, private nonprofit, or proprietary, depending on the corporate structure of the facility. Home care agencies based in hospitals or nursing homes generally cite good continuity of care between the institution and home as their chief advantage.[3]

Some health maintenance organizations (HMOs) have entered the home health care field primarily as agencies accepting Medicare and Medicaid patients. Services covered totally by the patient's prepaid health plan are usually limited; therefore, the federal health insurance programs are the primary sources of reimbursement for HMO agencies.

CURRENT TRENDS

The number and types of home health agencies have increased dramatically since the enactment of the federal health insurance programs. Since 1982, when they were permitted to participate in Medicare and Medicaid in states without licensure laws, proprietary agencies have proliferated and currently account for the largest number of newly certified agencies.

The following statistics show the recent growth of the home health industry:

Summary of Home Health Agencies Certified from October 1983 Through March 1984

Overall Total

Free-standing voluntary	12	Hospital-based nonprofit	67
Free-standing official	13	SNF-based proprietary	20
Free-standing proprietary	114	SNF-based voluntary	3
Free-standing chain-based*		Private nonprofit	25
proprietary	66	Other**	2
Hospital-based proprietary	10		

*Includes franchisees and licensees.
**Includes one Indian nation and one SNF-based official.

Ranking by Auspice		Ranking by Type	
Proprietary	63%	Free-standing	70%
Hospital-based nonprofit	20%	Hospital-based	23%
Private nonprofit	8%	SNF-based	7%
Voluntary	5%	Other	—
Official	4%		
Other	—		
	100%		100%

Source: Reprinted from *Home Health Line* by permission of Karen Rak, editor and publisher.

SOURCES OF REIMBURSEMENT

Medicare

The potential for reimbursement of home health services comes from many sources, the largest being Medicare, Title XVIII of the Social Security Act (see Table 2–1). Before 1966 most patients paid cash for home health care services, and donations subsidized care for patients who could pay for only part or none of their care.[4] The HCFA is responsible for the management of the Medicare program.

Entitlement

Eligibility for Medicare reimbursement of home health services results only if the beneficiary is "entitled" to Medicare benefits. To be entitled the beneficiary must be 65 years of age *and* have paid into the Social Security or Railroad Retirement systems at one time or another. People under age 65 may also be entitled to benefits if they have been disabled for at least 24 months or have end-stage renal disease. Spouses of beneficiaries over age 65

Table 2-1 Sources of Reimbursement for Home Health Care

Source	Eligibility	Requirements	Coverage	Limitations (Not Covered)
Medicare (Title XVIII of the Social Security Act)	1. Over 65 and payment into the Social Security or Railroad Retirement system 2. Disabled at least 24 months 3. End-stage renal disease 4. Spouse of 1, 2, and 3	1. Homebound 2. In need of skilled care on an intermittent basis 3. Treatment plan established by a physician	•Skilled nursing care •Physical therapy •Speech therapy If at least one of the above is needed, coverage may also be provided for: •Home health aide •Occupational therapy •Medical social work •Medical supplies and equipment	1. Custodial care 2. Homemaker/chore services
Medicaid (Title XIX of the Social Security Act)	Persons meeting categorical and income requirements	1. In need of medically necessary care on an intermittent basis 2. Treatment plan established by a physician	Federal mandates: •Nursing care •Home health aide •Medical supplies and equipment At state's option: •Physical therapy •Occupational therapy •Speech therapy	Medical social work services
Older Americans Act (Titles III and VII)	Persons over age 60—special emphasis to those with low incomes	—	•Senior centers •Home-delivered meals •Transportation •Home repair •Information and referral	N/A
Social Services Act (Title XX of the Social Security Act)	Primarily based on financial need; exact criteria vary from state to state	—	Homemaker/chore service workers	N/A
Private insurance	Paid-up insurance policy with home health benefits	Generally, "in lieu of hospitalization"	Varies greatly	Depends on policy
Veterans Administration	Service-connected disability	Prior hospitalization at a VA facility	Usually the same as Medicare	Available only for service-connected disability; occasional coverage for veterans with no other funding source

and spouses and dependent children of those entitled because of disability or end-stage renal disease may also be eligible for Medicare benefits.

Eligibility

The Medicare program consists of two separate but coordinated insurance coverages known as Hospital Insurance (Part A) and Supplemental Medical Insurance (Part B). Part A of Medicare is the part that payment into the Social Security or Railroad Retirement system entitles a beneficiary to. Part B, however, is optional coverage that a beneficiary enrolls in and pays premiums for. Both coverages provide reimbursement for home health services. Until 1981, Part A covered home health services only after a three-day prior inpatient stay with a 100-visit limitation.[5] Part B also provided coverage for only 100 home health visits before 1981.[6] These restrictions no longer apply to home health coverage.

Home health services that are eligible for Medicare reimbursement must be medically necessary, of a skilled nature, intermittent, delivered to a home-bound beneficiary in his or her place of residence, under a plan of treatment established by a physician. In addition, the total home health plan must be reviewed by the physician at least every 60 days. Medicare cannot provide coverage for custodial care or homemaker/chore-type services. HCFA has spent a great deal of time and energy attempting to define the terms skilled and intermittent. The definitions are still unclear, but the result has been a severe restriction of the otherwise eligible Medicare population.

Primary qualifying services for Medicare reimbursement of home health care are skilled nursing, physical therapy, and speech therapy. If the beneficiary is in need of at least one of these, home health aide, occupational therapy, medical social work services, and medical supplies and equipment may also be provided in accordance with the physician's plan of treatment. Before 1981 occupational therapy was considered a qualifying service. Currently, however, a patient who has received a qualifying service but no longer requires one or more of those services but is still in need of occupational therapy may continue to receive home health visits for the purpose of occupational therapy.[7]

Medicaid

Medicaid, Title XIX of the Social Security Act, was enacted simultaneously with Medicare, in 1966. Every state is required to have a Medical Assistance (Medicaid) state plan and receives 50 percent in matching federal dollars to provide medical care and services to people meeting categorical and income requirements. Some health care services are mandated by federal regulation; others are provided at the individual state's option. Therefore, Medicaid health care services differ dramatically from state to state.

Home health care, however, is one of the mandated services for which all states must provide coverage. Minimal home health service includes nursing, home health aide, medical supplies, and equipment. Physical, occupational, and speech therapy services are covered at the state's option. Although reimbursable under Medicare, Title XIX does not make matching dollars available for medical social work services. Federal regulation requires states to reimburse for Medicaid home health care services only to agencies who meet the federal Conditions of Participation and are therefore Medicare certified.

Like Medicare, Medicaid home health services must be medically necessary and provided to an eligible recipient at his or her residence as part of a physician's order, including a written plan of care that is reviewed by the physician at least every 60 days. Nursing care, under Medicaid, does not have to be of a skilled nature, and any home health service offered by the states can serve as a qualifying service. Note that Medicaid does not have a homebound requirement. Medicaid federal regulations are purposefully broader than those of Medicare to increase the availability of home health care services to Medicaid recipients and to encourage their use as one alternative to institutionalization.[8]

In 1981, as a result of the Omnibus Reconciliation Act, home- and community-based care waivers were made available to the states under their respective Medicaid programs. These waivers allow for matching federal dollars for reimbursement of services not normally covered under the Medicaid program, for recipients who are in need of institutionalization at a skilled nursing or intermediate care facility. The services provided must be adequate to meet the recipient's needs and must cost *less* than institutionalization. Many states have chosen to participate in the home- and community-based waiver option, and a variety of innovative service delivery systems are made available.

Other Sources of Reimbursement

Titles III and VII of the Older Americans Act, enacted in 1965, have, on occasion, provided some limited funds for home health agencies. The main purpose of these funds, however, has been for elderly support services, such as senior centers, information and referral, home-delivered meals, transportation, and home repair services.

In 1975 Congress enacted the Social Services Act, Title XX of the Social Security Act, making a variety of services available to a whole new population. Eligibility for any Title XX service is based primarily on financial need, in contrast to Medicare, which is based on age and Social Security eligibility. Exact criteria for Title XX eligibility vary from state to state.

The most notable addition to home health care provided by this funding source was homemaker/chore services, which are separate from the home health aide services covered under Medicare and Medicaid. Homemaker/ chore service workers provide ancillary, in-home support services, such as housekeeping, laundry, and home repair. Home health aides, however, are employees of home health agencies who provide personal care services under the supervision of a registered nurse or licensed therapist as part of the physician's plan of treatment. Many home health agencies across the nation have elected to participate in the Title XX Homemaker/Chore Service program, thus broadening their available services.

The original intent of Title XX legislation was not to create a federal insurance program, but to supply states with time-limited funds for the establishment of various social services. Unfortunately, some states failed to follow through with funding some of these programs after federal dollars elapsed. Therefore, homemaker/chore service programs are not found in every state.

Many private insurance policies cover home health care in one form or another, but actual benefits vary greatly. Some policies cover intermittent home health care with few restrictions; however, coverage is primarily limited to individuals who would otherwise require hospitalization or institutional- ization. Increasing pressure from the home health industry has resulted in many state legislatures passing mandatory offering bills requiring private insurance companies to fund home health care as part of their benefit package. Most mandatory offering bills contain "in lieu of hospitalization" clauses, however, that allow reimbursement for home health services *only* when hospitalization would otherwise be required. It is doubtful that private insurance will ever be a major source of reimbursement for certified agencies because of these restrictions.

The Veterans Administration may also provide reimbursement for home health services for veterans after hospitalization at a Veterans Administration facility. This reimbursement generally is limited to service-connected disabili- ty veterans and occasionally those veterans with no other funding source. Also, many Veterans Administration hospitals have developed their own hospital-based care programs.

Unfortunately, there has always been and will always be a population in need of home health care who are uncovered by any reimbursement source. Many agencies have instituted a sliding fee scale to continue caring for this segment of the population. Private donations and endowments from charity organizations also assist agencies in funding "free" care.

ROLE OF THE FISCAL INTERMEDIARY

A fiscal intermediary is a public or private agency or organization designated by the federal government to process claims and monitor services delivered to federal health insurance clients. Public agencies, acting as intermediaries, are generally state agencies that enter into an agreement with the federal government to process medical insurance and home health agency claims and monitor services delivered to Title XIX (Medicaid) recipients.

Intermediaries processing Medicare claims, however, are usually private insurance companies. HCFA maintains a listing, by region, of insurance companies that are approved to act as fiscal intermediaries. Home health agencies may choose any company from that listing. Nationally, Blue Cross is the predominant private insurance company acting as fiscal intermediary for home health agencies. Before September 30, 1984, home health agencies had the option of participating directly with the federal government as intermediary through the Office of Direct Reimbursement (ODR) instead of a private insurance company. On September 30, 1984, the ODR was officially abolished.[9]

HCFA currently is responding to a Congressional mandate to reduce the number of home health intermediaries to ten, one in each region.[10] Congress believes that this reduction of intermediaries will result in more effective management of home health benefits.[11]

Regardless of what intermediary is used by home health agencies, its functions remain the same: to assist in the billing process, to act as consultant to providers, and to ascertain that providers remain honest in their fiscal relationship with the HCFA.[12]

THE COST REPORTING PROCESS

Intermediaries make payments to providers, but the amount of reimbursement to any provider is restricted to the lesser of the "reasonable cost" of the covered services and items or the "customary charges" with respect to such services.[13]

Reasonable cost, as defined by HCFA, includes the direct and indirect costs of providing services. Costs may vary from agency to agency because of scope of services, level of care, geographic location, and utilization.[14]

Customary charges are those uniform charges that are listed in a provider's established fee schedule. Federal regulations mandate that uniform charges be applied regardless of the type of patient or source of reimbursement.[15] Therefore, home health agencies are prohibited from charging fees that are based on the patient's ability to pay. An exception to this rule, however, is the sliding fee scale imposed by some agencies either as a result of a state or local government mandate or as a condition of a federal grant or loan. Some agencies feel that a sliding fee scale will affect their full cost reimbursement; however, there are provisions within the cost reimbursement formula that allow the full rate to remain unaffected.[16]

Most home health agencies elect to establish their customary charges based on actual costs using the federally mandated cost reporting form, HCFA 1728-80 (Appendix 2–B). The reader is cautioned, however, that indirect expenses are allowable as costs, thus contributing a certain amount of inflationary factors to the formula. Critics contend that this formula contains virtually no incentives for cost containment, thus contributing further to escalating costs. HCFA, in an effort to contain costs, does establish limits, or "caps," on the cost per visit of each discipline applied to the agency's total cost. The cost caps vary in different parts of the United States. Home health agencies may not receive reimbursement of their actual costs if those costs exceed the caps.

Home health agency cost reports are considered public documents under the Freedom of Information Act. Any member of the public may inspect or obtain a copy of any home health agency cost report.[17]

The entire Medicare reimbursement process is currently under close scrutiny by HCFA. 1983 brought the drastic change in hospital reimbursement known as DRGs. 1984 saw the nationwide freeze on physicians' fees. Home health agency reimbursement methodology is the big change for 1985.

The (proposed) new home health schedule of limits for cost reporting periods beginning on or after July 1, 1985 sets uniform limits by discipline. This is unlike the old methodology which established caps on the cost per visit applicable to the agency's aggregate cost. The new limits are set at 120 percent of the mean labor-related and nonlabor components of the per visit cost. Further reductions to 115 percent of the mean and 112 percent of the mean are proposed for July 1, 1986 and July 1, 1987 respectively.[18] Dramatic cost savings will result according to HCFA.

There are important implications for home health agencies. For the first time, the reimbursement methodology contains significant incentives for cost containment. Lower cost types of service will no longer be able to subsidize those disciplines whose costs exceed the caps. Agencies will be forced to closely scrutinize salaries, staffing levels, staff productivity, time on site per visit, and travel time and costs.[19] Agencies whose current costs exceed the limits may be forced to stop participating in the Medicare program. Thus, the potential for unserved beneficiary populations exists.

This new reimbursement methodology was announced in the May 14, 1985 *Federal Register*. The unusually short comment period ended June 13, 1985 and as of this writing, no further word from HCFA has been published. Historically, however, the home care industry has demonstrated a very strong lobby and has, on occasion, forced HCFA to "back-down" on new regulations. Actual implementation remains to be seen.

SUMMARY

This is an exciting time indeed to be involved in home health care. Many changes have evolved since the enactment of the federal health insurance programs, and many more are likely. The industry is currently caring for patients who are sicker, who come home from the hospital sooner, and who have more needs for advanced technological care and equipment than ever before. Health care providers of all types and the general public must be made aware of the benefits of home health care, and the industry must be united and prepared to meet the challenges.

NOTES

1. *Federal Register*, Vol. 47, No. 207, Tuesday, 26 October, 1982, p. 47389.
2. Jane Emmert Stewart, *Home Health Care* (St. Louis: C. V. Mosby Co., 1979), p. 36.
3. Ibid., p. 39.
4. Ibid., p. 96.
5. *Medicare Home Health Agency Manual*, U.S. Department of Health and Human Services, Health Care Financing Administration, HCFA Pub. No. 11, p. 16.5.
6. Ibid., p. 18.1.
7. Ibid., p. 14.
8. *Federal Register*, Vol. 41, No. 166, Wednesday, 25 August, 1976, p. 35847.
9. Karen Rak, " . . . Home Health Line," 10 December, 1984, p. 298.
10. " . . . Home Health Line," 10 July, 1984, p. 170.
11. Ibid.
12. Stewart, p. 108.
13. *Medicare Home Health Agency Manual*, p. 1-10.
14. *Medicare Provider Reimbursement Manual*, U.S. Department of Health and Human Services, Health Care Financing Administration, HCFA Pub. No. 15-1, p. 21-2.5.
15. Ibid., p. 26-4.
16. Ibid., p. 26-12.1.
17. *Medicare Home Health Agency Manual*, p. 32.2.
18. *Federal Register*, Vol. 50, No. 93, Tuesday, 14 May, 1985, p. 20178.
19. Ibid., 20189.

REFERENCES

Code of Federal Regulations. "Home Health Services," 440.70; 441.15.
Federal Register, Vol. 41, No. 166, Wednesday, 25 August, 1976, pp. 35847–35849.
Federal Register, Vol. 47, No. 207, Tuesday, 26 October, 1982, pp. 47389–47390.

Federal Register, Vol. 50, No. 93, Tuesday, 14 May, 1985, pp. 20178–20190.

Home Health Care-A Discussion Paper. League Exchange Number 113, National League for Nursing, 1977, Pub. No. 21-1689, pp. 43–46.

"Home Health Overview." National Association for Home Care, Research Division, June 1983.

Jarvis, Linda L. *Community Health Nursing: Keeping the Public Healthy.* Philadelphia: F. A. Davis Co., 1981, pp. 199–218.

Medicare Home Health Agency Manual. U.S. Department of Health and Human Services, Health Care Financing Administration, HCFA Pub. No. 11, pp. 1-10–32.2.

Medicare Provider Reimbursement Manual. U.S. Department of Health and Human Services, Health Care Financing Administration, HCFA Pub. No. 15-1, pp. 21-2.5–26-12.1.

"Medicare: Use of Home Health Services, 1978." Health Care Financing Program Statistics. Washington, D.C.: U.S. Government Printing Office, 1982.

"Medicare: Use of Home Health Services, 1980." Health Care Financing Notes. Washington, D.C.: U.S. Government Printing Office, 1983.

Rak, Karen, ed. " . . . *Home Health Line.*" 25 June, 1984, pp. 163–165; 10 July, 1984, p. 170; 10 December, 1984, p. 298.

Stewart, Jane Emmert. *Home Health Care.* St. Louis: C. V. Mosby Co., 1979, pp. 25–45, 96–124.

"Your Medicare Handbook." U.S. Department of Health and Human Services, Health Care Financing Administration, Pub. No. HCFA-10050, January 1984.

Appendix 2-A

Conditions of Participation: Home Health Agencies

Rev. 18 9-74 Regulations No. 5—Subpart L—Conditions of Participation; Home Health Agencies
Sec.
405.1201 General.
405.1202 Definitions.

(§§ 405.1203-405.1208 deleted, 39 FR 2251, Jan.17, 1974)

405.1220   Condition of participation: Compliance with Federal, State, and local laws.
405.1221   Condition of participation: Organization, services, administration.
405.1222   Condition of participation: Group of professional personnel.
405.1223   Condition of participation: Acceptance of patients, plan of treatment, medical supervision.
405.1224   Condition of participation: Skilled nursing service.
405.1225   Condition of participation: Therapy services.
405.1226   Condition of participation: Medical social services.
405.1227   Condition of participation: Home health aide services.
405.1228   Condition of participation: Clinical records.
405.1229   Condition of participation: Evaluation.
405.1230   Condition of participation: Qualifying to provide outpatient physical therapy services.

Subpart L—Conditions of Participation; Home Health Agencies
    Authority: Secs. 1102, 1842, 1862, 1870, 1871, 49 Stat. 647, as amended, 79 Stat. 309, 79 Stat. 325, 79 Stat. 331, 81 Stat. 846-847; 42 U.S.C. 1302, 1395 et seq.
    SOURCE: The provisions of this Subpart L appear at 33FR 12090, Aug. 27, 1968, as amended at 38 FR 18978, July 16, 1973, unless otherwise noted.

§ 405.1201 General.

(a) In order to participate as a home health agency in the health insurance program for the aged, an institution must be a "home health agency" within the meaning of section 1861(o) of the Social Security Act. This section of the law states a number of specific requirements which must be met by participating home health agencies and authorizes the Secretary of Health, Education, and Welfare to prescribe other requirements considered necessary in the interest of health and safety of beneficiaries. Section 1861(o) of the Act provides:

(o) The term "home health agency" means a public agency or private organization, or a subdivision of such an agency or organization, which—

(1) Is primarily engaged in providing skilled nursing services and other therapeutic services;

(2) Has policies, established by a group of professional personnel (associated with the agency or organization), including one or more physicians and one or more registered professional nurses, to govern the services (referred to in paragraph (1)) which it provides, and provides for supervision of such services by a physician or registered professional nurse;

(3) Maintains clinical records on all patients;

(4) In the case of an agency or organization in any State in which State or applicable local law provides for the licensing of agencies or organizations of this nature, (A) is licensed pursuant to such law, or (B) is approved, by the agency of such State or locality responsible for licensing agencies or organizations of this nature, as meeting the standards established for such licensing;

(5) Has in effect an overall plan and budget that meets the requirements of subsection (2); and

(6) Meets such other conditions of participation as the Secretary may find necessary in the interest of the health and safety of individuals who are furnished services by such agency or organization; except that such term shall not include a private organization which is not a nonprofit organization exempt from Federal income taxation under section 501 of the Internal Revenue Code of 1954 (or a subdivision of such organization) unless it is licensed pursuant to State law and it meets such additional standards and requirements as may be prescribed in regulations; and except that for purposes of Part A such term shall not include any agency or organization which is primarily for the care and treatment of mental diseases.

(b) The requirements included in the statute and the additional health and safety requirements prescribed by the Secretary are set forth in the conditions of participation for home health agencies.

§ 405.1202 Definitions.

As used in this subpart, the following definitions apply:

(a) *Administrator, home health agency.* A person who:

(1) Is a licensed physician; or

(2) Is a registered nurse; or

(3) Has training and experience in health service administration and at least 1 year of supervisory or administrative experience in home health care or related health programs.

(b) *Bylaws or equivalent.* A set of rules adopted by a home health agency for governing the agency's operation.

(c) *Branch office.* A location or site from which a home health agency provides services within a portion of the total geographic area served by the parent agency. The branch office is part of the home health agency and is located sufficiently close to share administration, supervision, and services in a manner that renders it unnecessary for the branch independently to meet the conditions of participation as a home health agency.

(d) *Clinical note.* A dated written notation by a member of the health team of a contact with a patient containing a description of signs and symptoms, treatment and/or drug given, the patient's reaction, and any changes in physical or emotional condition.

(e) *Nonprofit agency.* An agency exempt from Federal income taxation under section 501 of the Internal Revenue Code of 1954.

(f) *Occupational therapist.* A person who:

(1) Is a graduate of an occupational therapy curriculum accredited jointly by the Council on Medical Education of the American Medical Association and the American Occupational Therapy Association; or

(2) Is eligible for the National Registration Examination of the American Occupational Therapy Association; or

(3) Has 2 years of appropriate experience as an occupational therapist, and has achieved a satisfactory grade on a proficiency examination conducted, approved, or sponsored by the U.S. Public Health Service, except that such determinations of proficiency do not apply with respect to persons initially licensed by a State or seeking initial qualification as an occupational therapist after December 31, 1977.

(g) *Occupational therapy assistant.* A person who:

(1) Meets the requirements for certification as an occupational therapy assistant established by the American Occupational Therapy Association; or

(2) Has 2 years of appropriate experience as an occupational therapy assistant, and has achieved a satisfactory grade on a proficiency examination conducted, approved, or sponsored by the U.S. Public Health Service, except that such determinations of proficiency do not apply with respect to persons

initially licensed by a State or seeking initial qualification as an occupational therapy assistant after December 31, 1977.

(h) *Parent home health agency.* The agency that develops and maintains administrative controls of subunits and/or branch offices.

(i) *Physical therapist.* A person who is licensed as a physical therapist by the State in which practicing, and

(1) Has graduated from a physical therapy curriculum approved by

(i) The American Physical Therapy Association, or

(ii) The Council on Medical Education and Hospitals of the American Medical Association, or

(iii) The Council on Medical Education of the American Medical Association and the American Physical Therapy Association; or

(2) Prior to January 1, 1966,

(i) Was admitted to membership by the American Physical Therapy Association, or

(ii) Was admitted to registration by the American Registry of Physical Therapists, or

(iii) Has graduated from a physical therapy curriculum in a 4-year college or university approved by a State department of education; or

(3) Has 2 years of appropriate experience as a physical therapist, and has achieved a satisfactory grade on a proficiency examination conducted, approved, or sponsored by the U.S. Public Health Service except that such determinations of proficiency do not apply with respect to persons initially licensed by a State or seeking qualification as a physical therapist after December 31, 1977; or

(4) Was licensed or registered prior to January 1, 1966, and prior to January 1, 1970, had 15 years of full-time experience in the treatment of illness or injury through the practice of physical therapy in which services were rendered under the order and direction of attending and referring physicians; or

(5) If trained outside the United States,

(i) Was graduated since 1923 from a physical therapy curriculum approved in the country in which the curriculum was located and in which there is a member organization of the World Confederation for Physical Therapy.

(ii) Meets the requirements for membership in a member organization of the World Confederation for Physical Therapy,

(iii) Has 1 year of experience under the supervision of an active member of the American Physical Therapy Association, and

(iv) Has successfully completed a qualifying examination as prescribed by the American Physical Therapy Association.

(j) *Physical therapist assistant.* A person who is licensed as a physical therapist assistant, if applicable, by the State in which practicing, and

(1) Has graduated from a 2-year college-level program approved by the American Physical Therapy Association; or

(2) Has 2 years of appropriate experience as a physical therapist assistant, and has achieved a satisfactory grade on a proficiency examination conducted, approved, or sponsored by the U.S. Public Health Service, except that such determinations of proficiency do not apply with respect to persons initially licensed by a State or seeking initial qualification as a physical therapist assistant after December 31, 1977.

(k) *Physician.* A doctor of medicine or osteopathy legally authorized to practice medicine and surgery by the State in which such function or action is performed.

(l) *Practical (vocational) nurse.* A person who is licensed as a practical (vocational) nurse by the State in which practicing.

(m) *Primary home health agency.* The agency that is responsible for the service rendered to patients and for implementation of the plan of treatment.

(n) *Progress note.* A dated, written notation by a member of the health team summarizing facts about care and the patient's response during a given period of time.

(o) *Proprietary agency.* A private profit-making agency licensed by the State.

(p) *Public agency.* An agency operated by a State or local government.

(q) *Public health nurse.* A registered nurse who has completed a baccalaureate degree program approved by the National League for Nursing for public health nursing preparation or post-registered nurse study which includes content approved by the National League for Nursing for public health nursing preparation.

(r) *Registered nurse.* A graduate of an approved school of professional nursing, who is licensed as a registered nurse by the State in which practicing.

(s) *Social work assistant.* A person who:

(1) Has a baccalaureate degree in social work, psychology, sociology, or other field related to social work, and has had at least 1 year of social work experience in a health care setting; or

(2) Has 2 years of appropriate experience as a social work assistant, and has achieved a satisfactory grade on a proficiency examination conducted, approved, or sponsored by the U.S. Public Health Service, except that such determinations of proficiency do not apply with respect to persons initially licensed by a State or seeking initial qualification as a social work assistant after December 31, 1977.

(t) *Social worker.* A person who has a master's degree from a school of social work accredited by the Council on Social Work Education, and has 1 year of social work experience in a health care setting.

(u) *Speech pathologist or audiologist.* A person who:

(1) Meets the education and experience requirements for a Certificate of Clinical Competence in the appropriate area (speech pathology or audiology) granted by the American Speech and Hearing Association; or

(2) Meets the educational requirements for certification and is in the process of accumulating the supervised experience required for certification.

(v) *Subdivision.* A component of a multi-function health agency, such as the home care department of a hospital or the nursing division of a health department, which independently meets the conditions of participation for home health agencies. A subdivision which has subunits and/or branches is regarded as a parent agency.

(w) *Subunit.* A semi-autonomous organization, which serves patients in a geographic area different from that of the parent agency. The subunit by virtue of the distance between it and the parent agency is judged incapable of sharing administration, supervision, and services on a daily basis with the parent agency and must, therefore, independently meet the conditions of participation for home health agencies.

(x) *Summary report.* A compilation of the pertinent factors from the clinical notes and progress notes regarding a patient, which is submitted as a summary report to the patient's physician.

(y) *Supervision.* Authoritative procedural guidance by a qualified person for the accomplishment of a function or activity with initial direction and periodic inspection of the actual act of accomplishing the function or activity. Unless otherwise provided in this subpart, the supervisor must be on the premises if the person does not meet qualifications for assistants specified in the definitions in this section.

(§§ 405.1203—405.1208 deleted, 39 FR 2251, Jan. 17, 1974)

§ 405.1220 Condition of participation: Compliance with Federal, State, and local laws.

The home health agency and its staff are in compliance with all applicable Federal, State, and local laws and regulations. If State or applicable local law provides for the licensure of home health agencies, an agency not subject to licensure must be approved by the licensing authority as meeting the standards established for such licensure. A proprietary organization which is not exempt from Federal income taxation under section 501 of the Internal Revenue Code of 1954 must be licensed as a home health agency pursuant to State law. If no State law exists for the licensure of a proprietary home health agency, it cannot be certified for participation in the health insurance program.

§ 405.1221 Condition of participation: Organization, services, administration.

Organization, services provided, administrative control, and lines of authority for the delegation of responsibility down to the patient care level are clearly set forth in writing and are readily identifiable. Administrative and supervisory functions are not delegated to another agency or organization and all services not provided directly are monitored and controlled by the primary agency, including services provided through subunits of the parent agency. If an agency has subunits, appropriate administrative records are maintained for each subunit.

(a) *Standard: Services provided.* Part-time or intermittent skilled nursing services and at least one other therapeutic service (physical, speech, or occupational therapy; medical social services; or home health aide services) must be made available, on a visiting basis, in a place of residence used as a patient's home. A public or nonprofit home health agency must provide at least one of the qualifying services directly through agency employees but may arrange with another public or nonprofit agency or organization to provide the second qualifying service and any additional services. A proprietary agency, however, must provide all services directly, through agency employees.

(b) *Standard: Governing body.* A governing body (or designated persons so functioning) assumes full legal authority and responsibility for the operation of the agency. The governing body appoints a qualified administrator, arranges for professional advice (see § 405.1222), adopts and periodically reviews written bylaws or an acceptable equivalent, and oversees the management and fiscal affairs of the agency. The name and address of each officer, director, and owner are disclosed. If the agency is a corporation, all ownership interests of 10 percent or more (direct or indirect) are also disclosed.

(c) *Standard: Administrator.* The administrator, who may also be the supervising physician or registered nurse (see paragraph (d) of this section), organizes and directs the agency's ongoing functions; maintains ongoing liaison among the governing body, the group of professional personnel, and the staff; employs qualified personnel and ensures adequate staff education and evaluations; ensures the accuracy of public information materials and activities; and implements an effective budgeting and accounting system. A qualified person is authorized in writing to act in the absence of the administrator.

(d) *Standard: Supervising physician or registered nurse.* The skilled nursing and other therapeutic services provided are under the supervision and direction of a physician or a registered nurse (who preferably has at least 1 year of nursing experience and is a public health nurse). This person, or similarly qualified alternate, is available at all times during operating hours and participates in all activities relevant to the professional services provided, including the developing of qualifications and assignments of personnel.

(See Connecticut, Massachusetts, New Jersey, and Rhode Island Addenda in the Appendix.)

(e) *Standard:* Personnel policies. Personnel practices and patient care are supported by appropriate, written personnel policies. Personnel records include job descriptions, qualifications, licensure, performance evaluations, and health examinations, and are kept current.

(f) *Standard: Personnel under hourly or per visit contracts.* (1) If personnel under hourly or per visit contracts are utilized by the home health agency, there is a written contract between such personnel and the agency clearly designating:

(i) That patients are accepted for care only by the primary home health agency,

(ii) The services to be provided,

(iii) The necessity to conform to all applicable agency policies including personnel qualifications,

(iv) The responsibility for participating in developing plans of treatment,

(v) The manner in which services will be controlled, coordinated, and evaluated by the primary agency,

(vi) The procedures for submitting clinical and progress notes, scheduling of visits, periodic patient evaluation, and

(vii) The procedures for determining charges and reimbursement.

(g) *Standard: Coordination of patient services.* All personnel providing services maintain liaison to assure that their efforts effectively complement one another and support the objectives outlined in the plan of treatment. The clinical record or minutes of case conferences establish that effective interchange, reporting, and coordinated patient evaluation does occur. A written summary report for each patient is sent to the attending physician at least every 60 days.

(h) *Standard: Services under arrangements.* Services (see paragraph (a) of this section) provided under arrangement with another public or nonprofit agency must be subject to a written contract conforming with the requirements specified in paragraph (f) of this section.

[33 FR 12090, August 27, 1968, as amended at 33 FR 18647, December 18, 1968; 36 FR 7050, April 14, 1971; 38 FR 18979, July 16, 1973]

§ 405.1222 Condition of participation: Group of professional personnel.

A group of professional personnel, which includes at least one physician and one registered nurse (preferably a public health nurse), and with appropriate representation from other professional disciplines, establishes and annually reviews the agency's policies governing scope of services offered, admission and discharge policies, medical supervision and plans of treatment, emergency care, clinical records, personnel qualifications, and program evaluation. At least one member of the group is neither an owner (§ 405.-1221(b)) nor an employee of the agency.

(a) *Standard: Advisory and evaluation function.* The group of professional personnel meets frequently to advise the agency on professional issues, to participate in the evaluation of the agency's program, and to assist the agency in maintaining liaison with other health care providers in the community and in its community information program. Its meetings are documented by dated minutes.

(See New Jersey Addendum in the Appendix.)

§ 405.1223 Condition of participation: Acceptance of patients, plan of treatment, medical supervision.

Patients are accepted for treatment on the basis of a reasonable expectation that the patient's medical, nursing, and social needs can be met adequately by the agency in the patient's place of residence. Care follows a written plan of treatment established and periodically reviewed by a physician, and care continues under the supervision of a physician.

(a) *Standard: Plan of treatment.* The plan of treatment developed in consultation with the agency staff covers all pertinent diagnoses, including mental status, types of services and equipment required, frequency of visits, prognosis, rehabilitation potential, functional limitations, activities permitted, nutritional requirements, medications and treatments, any safety measures to protect against injury, instructions for timely discharge or referral, and any other appropriate items. If a physician refers a patient under a plan of treatment which cannot be completed until after an evaluation visit, the physician is consulted to approve additions or modifications to the original plan. Orders for therapy services include the specific procedures and modalities to be used and the amount, frequency, and duration. The therapist and other agency personnel participate in developing the plan of treatment.

(b) *Standard: Periodic review of plan of treatment.* The total plan of treatment is reviewed by the attending physician and home health agency personnel as often as the severity of the patient's condition requires, but at least once every 60 days. Agency professional staff promptly alert the physician to any changes that suggest a need to alter the plan of treatment.

(c) *Standard: Conformance with physician's orders.* Drugs and treatments are administered by agency staff only as ordered by the physician. The nurse or therapist immediately records and signs oral orders and obtains the physician's countersignature. Agency staff check all medicines a patient may be taking to identify possibly ineffective drug therapy or adverse reactions, significant side effects, drug allergies, and contraindicated medication, and promptly report any problems to the physician.

§ 405.1224 Condition of participation: Skilled nursing service.

The home health agency provides skilled nursing service by or under the supervision of a registered nurse and in accordance with the plan of treatment.

(See Connecticut, Massachusetts, and Rhode Island Addenda in the Appendix.)

(a) *Standard: Duties of the registered nurse.* The registered nurse makes the initial evaluation visit, regularly re-evaluates the patient's nursing needs, initiates the plan of treatment and necessary revisions, provides those services requiring substantial specialized nursing skill, initiates appropriate preventive and rehabilitative nursing procedures, prepares clinical and progress notes, coordinates services, informs the physician and other personnel of changes in the patient's condition and needs, counsels the patient and family in meeting nursing and related needs, participates in inservice programs, and supervises and teaches other nursing personnel.

(b) *Standard: Duties of the licensed practical nurse.* The licensed practical nurse provides services in accordance with agency policies, prepares clinical and progress notes, assists the physician and/or registered nurse in performing specialized procedures, prepares equipment and materials for treatments observing aseptic technique as required, and assists the patient in learning appropriate self-care techniques.

[33 FR 12090, August 27, 1968, as amended at 33 FR 18647, December 18, 1968; 38 FR 18978, July 16, 1973]

§ 405.1225 Condition of participation: Therapy services.

Any therapy services offered by the home health agency directly or under arrangement are given by a qualified therapist or by a qualified therapist assistant under the supervision of a qualified therapist in accordance with the plan of treatment. The qualified therapist assists the physician in evaluating level of function, helps develop the plan of treatment (revising as necessary), prepares clinical and progress notes, advises and consults with the family and other agency personnel, and participates in inservice programs.

(a) *Standard: Supervision of physical therapist assistant and occupational therapy assistant.* Services provided by a qualified physical therapist assistant or qualified occupational therapy assistant may be furnished under the supervision of a qualified physical or occupational therapist. A physical therapist assistant or occupational therapy assistant performs services planned, delegated, and supervised by the therapist, assists in preparing clinical notes and progress reports, and participates in educating the patient and family, and in inservice programs.

(b) *Standard: Supervision of speech therapy services.* Speech therapy services are provided only by or under supervision of a qualified speech pathologist or audiologist.

[33 FR 12090, August 27, 1968, as amended, at 36 FR 19250, October 1, 1971; 38 FR 18978, July 16, 1973]

§ 405.1226 Condition of participation: Medical social services.

Medical social services, when provided, are given by a qualified social worker or by a qualified social work assistant under the supervision of a qualified social worker, and in accordance with the plan of treatment. The social worker assists the physician and other team members in understanding the significant social and emotional factors related to the health problems, participates in the development of the plan of treatment, prepares clinical and progress notes, works with the family, utilizes appropriate community resources, participates in discharge planning and inservice programs, and acts as a consultant to other agency personnel.

§ 405.1227 Condition of participation: Home health aide services.

Home health aides are selected on the basis of such factors as a sympathetic attitude toward the care of the sick, ability to read, write, and carry out directions, and maturity and ability to deal effectively with the demands of the job. Aides are carefully trained in methods of assisting patients to achieve maximum self-reliance, principles of nutrition and meal preparation, the aging process and emotional problems of illness, procedures for maintaining a clean, healthful, and pleasant environment, changes in patient's condition that should be reported, work of the agency and the health team, ethics, confidentiality, and recordkeeping. They are closely supervised to assure their competence in providing care.

(See Connecticut and Oregon Addenda in the Appendix.)

(a) *Standard: Assignment and duties of the home health aide.* The home health aide is assigned to a particular patient by a registered nurse. Written instructions for patient care are prepared by a registered nurse or therapist as appropriate. Duties include the performance of simple procedures [such] as an extension of therapy services, personal care, ambulation and exercise, household services essential to health care at home, assistance with medications that are ordinarily self-administered, reporting changes in the patient's conditions and needs, and completing appropriate records.

(b) *Standard: Supervision.* The registered nurse, or appropriate professional staff member, if other services are provided, makes a supervisory visit to the patient's residence at least every 2 weeks, either when the aide is present to observe and assist, or when the aide is absent, to assess relationships and determine whether goals are being met.

(See Massachusetts Addendum in the Appendix.)

[33 FR 12090, August 27, 1968, as amended, at 33 FR 18648, December 18, 1968; 38 FR 18978, July 16, 1973]

§ 405.1228 Condition of participation: Clinical records.

A clinical record containing pertinent past and current findings in accordance with accepted professional standards is maintained for every patient receiving home health services. In addition to the plan of treatment (sec § 405.1223(a)), the record contains appropriate identifying information; name of physician; drug, dietary, treatment, and activity orders; signed and dated clinical and progress notes (clinical notes are written the day service is rendered and incorporated no less often than weekly); copies of summary reports sent to the physician; and a discharge summary.

(a) *Standard: Retention of records.* Clinical records are retained for 5 years after the month the cost report to which the records apply is filed with the intermediary, unless State law stipulates a longer period of time. Policies provide for retention even if the home health agency discontinues operations. If a patient is transferred to another health facility, a copy of the record or abstract accompanies the patient.

(b) *Standard: Protection of records.* Clinical record information is safeguarded against loss or unauthorized use. Written procedures govern use and removal of records and conditions for release of information. Patient's written consent is required for release of information not authorized by law.

§ 405.1229 Condition of participation: Evaluation.

The home health agency has written policies requiring an overall evaluation of the agency's total program at least once a year, by the group of professional personnel (or a committee of this group), home health agency staff, and consumers; or by professional people outside the agency working in conjunction with consumers. The evaluation consists of an overall policy and administrative review and a clinical record review. The evaluation assesses the extent to which the agency's program is appropriate, adequate, effective, and efficient. Results of the evaluation are reported to and acted upon by those responsible for the operation of the agency and are maintained separately as administrative records.

(a) *Standard: Policy and administrative review.* As a part of the evaluation process the policies and administrative practices of the agency are reviewed to determine the extent to which they promote patient care that is appropriate, adequate, effective, and efficient. Mechanisms are established in writing for the collection of pertinent data to assist in evaluation. The data to be considered may include but are not limited to: number of patients receiving each service offered, number of patient visits, reasons for discharge, breakdown by diagnosis, sources of referral, number of patients not accepted with reasons, and total staff days for each service offered.

(b) *Standard: Clinical record review.* At least quarterly, appropriate health professionals, representing at least the scope of the program, review a sample of both active and closed clinical records to assure that established policies are followed in providing services (direct services as well as services under arrangement). There is a continuing review of clinical records for each 60-day period that a patient receives home health services to determine adequacy of the plan of treatment and appropriateness of continuation of care.

§ 405.1230 Condition of participation: Qualifying to provide outpatient physical therapy services.

Section 1861(p) of the Social Security Act provides in pertinent part as follows:

(p) The term "outpatient physical therapy services" means physical therapy services furnished by a provider of services, a clinic, rehabilitation agency, or a public health agency, or by others under an arrangement with, and under the supervision of, such provider, clinic, rehabilitation agency or public health agency to an individual as an outpatient * * *

As a provider of services, a home health agency may qualify to provide outpatient physical therapy services if such agency meets the statutory requirements of section 1861(o) of the Act and complies with other health and safety requirements prescribed by the Secretary for home health agencies, and, additionally, is in compliance with applicable health and safety requirements pertaining to rendition of outpatient physical therapy services. The applicable health and safety requirements pertaining to outpatient physical therapy services are included in the conditions of participation in Subpart Q of this part. (See §§ 405.1719, 405.1720, 405.1722, 405.1724, and 405.1725.)

[38 FR 18978, July 16, 1973]

Appendix 2-B

Home Health Agency Cost Report

This report is required by law (42 USC 1395g; 42 CFR 405.406 /b/). Failure to report can result in all interim payments made since the beginning of the cost report period being deemed as overpayments (42 USC 1395g).

Form Approved
OMB No. 0938-0022

HOME HEALTH AGENCY COST REPORT	INTERMEDIARY USE ONLY	DATE RECEIVED
	☐ AUDITED	
	☐ DESK REVIEWED	INTERMEDIARY NUMBER

PART I — GENERAL

1.

NAME AND ADDRESS	PROVIDER NUMBER	DATE CERTIFIED
HOME HEALTH AGENCY		
	COST REPORTING PERIOD	
	FROM	TO

2.

AGENCY IDENTIFIER

1. ☐ COMBINATION OFFICIAL AND VOLUNTARY
2. ☐ OFFICIAL a ☐ Federal b ☐ State c ☐ City d ☐ City-County e ☐ County f ☐ Health District
3. ☐ VOLUNTARY NON-PROFIT a ☐ Church b ☐ Other Than Church
4. ☐ PRIVATE - NON-PROFIT
5. ☐ PROPRIETARY a ☐ Sole Proprietary b ☐ Corporation c ☐ Partnership

PART II — HOME HEALTH AGENCY — STATISTICS

		Title XVIII		Other		Total	
		Visits	Patients	Visits	Patients	Visits	Patients
		1	2	3	4	5	6
1	Skilled Nursing						
2	Physical Therapy						
3	Speech Pathology						
4	Occupational Therapy						
5	Medical Social Service						
6	Home Health Aide						
7	All Other Services						
8	Total Visits						
9	Unduplicated Census Count						
10	Home Health Aide Hours						

PART III — HOME HEALTH AGENCY — NUMBER OF EMPLOYEES (FULL TIME EQUIV.)

	Enter the number of hours in your normal work week ____	STAFF	CONTRACT	TOTAL
		1	2	3
1	Administrator & Assistant Administrators			
2	Directors & Assistant Directors			
3	Other Administrative Personnel			
4	Direct Nursing Service			
5	Nursing Supervisor			
6	Physical Therapy Service			
7	Physical Therapy Supervisor			
8	Speech Pathology Service			
9	Speech Pathology Supervisor			
10	Occupational Therapy Service			
11	Occupational Therapy Supervisor			
12	Medical Social Service			
13	Medical Social Service Supervisor			
14	Home Health Aide			
15	Home Health Aide Supervisor			
16				
17				

PART IV — MANAGEMENT SERVICES QUESTIONNAIRE

1	Does the provider receive management services from any outside supplier or organization?	☐ YES ☐ NO
2	Does the provider deem this outside supplier or organization to be related to the provider?	☐ YES ☐ NO

PART V — CERTIFICATION BY OFFICER OR DIRECTOR OF THE AGENCY

INTENTIONAL MISREPRESENTATION OR FALSIFICATION OF ANY INFORMATION CONTAINED IN THIS COST REPORT MAY BE PUNISHABLE BY FINE AND/OR IMPRISONMENT UNDER FEDERAL LAW.

I HEREBY CERTIFY that I have read the above statement and that I have examined the accompanying Home Health Agency Cost Report and the Balance Sheet and Statement of Revenue and Expense prepared by _____

_____ (Provider name(s) and number(s)) for

the cost report period beginning _____ and ending _____ and that to the best of my

knowledge and belief, it is a true, correct, and complete report prepared from the books and records of the provider in accordance with applicable instructions, except as noted.

(Signed)	Officer or Director	Title	Date

Form HCFA-1728-81 (6-81)

Form Approved
OMB No. 0638-0022

RECLASSIFICATION AND ADJUSTMENT OF TRIAL BALANCE OF EXPENSES

PROVIDER NO.:

PERIOD:
FROM
TO

WORKSHEET A

	SALARIES (Fr Wks A-1)	EMPLOYEE BENEFITS (Fr Wks A-2)	TRANS-PORTATION (See Instructions)	CONTRACTED/PURCHASED SERVICES (Fr Wks A-3)	OTHER COSTS	TOTAL AGENCY COST	RECLASSIFI-CATION (From Wks A-4)	RECLASSIFIED TRIAL BALANCE (Col 6 & 7)	ADJUSTMENTS TO EXPENSES (INCREASE/DECREASE)	FOR COST ALLOCATION (Col 8 ± 9)	
	1	2	3	4	5	6	7	8	9	10	
1 GENERAL SERVICE COST CENTER											1
2 Depreciation — Bldg. & Fixed Equipment											2
3 Depreciation — Movable Equipment											3
4 Plant Operation & Maintenance											4
5 Transportation (See Instructions)											5
6 Administrative — General											6
7 REIMBURSABLE SERVICES											7
8 Skilled Nursing Care											8
9 Physical Therapy											9
10 Speech Pathology											10
11 Occupational Therapy											11
12 Medical Social Services											12
13 Home Health Aide											13
14 Medical Appliances											14
15 Durable Medical Equipment											15
16 Supplies (SEE INSTRUCTIONS)											16
17 TITLE XVIII NONREIMBURSABLE SERVICES											17
18 Homemaker Service											18
19 Home Dialysis Aide Services											19
20 Respiratory Therapy											20
21 Private Duty Nursing											21
22 Clinic											22
23 Health Promotion Activities											23
24 Day Care Program											24
25 Home Delivered Meals Program											25
26 OTHER NONREIMBURSABLE COSTS											26
27											27
28											28
29											29
30											30
31											31
32 Insurance — Malpractice											32
33 Insurance — Other											33
34 Interest											34
35 TOTAL											35

Form HCFA-1728-81 (6-81)

Form Approved
OMB No. 0638-0022

COMPENSATION ANALYSIS
SALARIES & WAGES

PROVIDER NO.: _____

PERIOD:
FROM _____
TO _____

WORKSHEET A-1

		ADMINIS-TRATORS	DIRECTORS	CONSULTANTS	SUPERVISORS	NURSES	THERAPISTS	AIDES	ALL OTHER	TOTAL (1)	
		1	2	3	4	5	6	7	8	9	
1	GENERAL SERVICE COST CENTERS										1
2	Depreciation – Bldg. & Fixed Equipment										2
3	Depreciation – Movable Equipment										3
4	Plant Operation & Maintenance										4
5	Transportation										5
6	Administrative–General										6
7	REIMBURSABLE SERVICES										7
8	Skilled Nursing Care										8
9	Physical Therapy										9
10	Speech Pathology										10
11	Occupational Therapy										11
12	Medical Social Services										12
13	Home Health Aide										13
14	Medical Appliances										14
15	Durable Medical Equipment										15
16	Supplies										16
17	TITLE XVIII NONREIMBURSABLE SERVICES										17
18	Homemaker Service										18
19	Home Dialysis Aide Services										19
20	Respiratory Therapy										20
21	Private Duty Nursing										21
22	Clinic										22
23	Health Promotion Activities										23
24	Day Care Program										24
25	Home Delivered Meals Program										25
26	OTHER NONREIMBURSABLE COSTS										26
27											27
28											28
29											29
30											30
31											31
32	Insurance – Malpractice										32
33	Insurance – Other										33
34	Interest										34
35	TOTAL										35

(1) Transfer the amounts in column 9 to Wks. A, column I

Form HCFA-1728-81 (6-81)

Form Approved
OMB No. 0938-0022

COMPENSATION ANALYSIS EMPLOYEE BENEFITS (PAYROLL RELATED)

PROVIDER NO.: _____

PERIOD: FROM _____ TO _____

WORKSHEET A-2

	ADMINIS-TRATORS	DIRECTORS	CONSULTANTS	SUPERVISORS	NURSES	THERAPISTS	AIDES	ALL OTHER	TOTAL (1)
	1	2	3	4	5	6	7	8	9
1 GENERAL SERVICE COST CENTERS									
2 Depreciation – Bldg. & Fixed Equipment									
3 Depreciation – Movable Equipment									
4 Plant Operation & Maintenance									
5 Transportation									
6 Administrative—General									
7 REIMBURSABLE SERVICES									
8 Skilled Nursing Care									
9 Physical Therapy									
10 Speech Pathology									
11 Occupational Therapy									
12 Medical Social Services									
13 Home Health Aide									
14 Medical Appliances									
15 Durable Medical Equipment									
16 Supplies									
17 TITLE XVIII NONREIMBURSABLE SERVICES									
18 Homemaker Service									
19 Home Dialysis Aide Services									
20 Respiratory Therapy									
21 Private Duty Nursing									
22 Clinic									
23 Health Promotion Activities									
24 Day Care Program									
25 Home Delivered Meals Program									
26 OTHER NONREIMBURSABLE COSTS									
27									
28									
29									
30									
31									
32 Insurance – Malpractice									
33 Insurance – Other									
34 Interest									
35 TOTAL									

(1) Transfer the amounts in column 9 to Wks. A, column 2

Form HCFA-1728-81 (8-81)

Form Approved
OMB No. 0938-0022

WORKSHEET A-3

COMPENSATION ANALYSIS CONTRACTED SERVICES/PURCHASED SERVICES	PROVIDER NO.:	PERIOD: FROM ___ TO ___

	ADMINISTRATORS 1	DIRECTORS 2	CONSULTANTS 3	SUPERVISORS 4	NURSES 5	THERAPISTS 6	AIDES 7	ALL OTHER 8	TOTAL (1) 9	
1	GENERAL SERVICE COST CENTERS									1
2	Depreciation – Bldg. & Fixed Equipment									2
3	Depreciation – Movable Equipment									3
4	Plant Operation & Maintenance									4
5	Transportation									5
6	Administrative–General									6
7	REIMBURSABLE SERVICES									7
8	Skilled Nursing Care									8
9	Physical Therapy									9
10	Speech Pathology									10
11	Occupational Therapy									11
12	Medical Social Services									12
13	Home Health Aide									13
14	Medical Appliances									14
15	Durable Medical Equipment									15
16	Supplies									16
17	TITLE XVIII NONREIMBURSABLE SERVICES									17
18	Homemaker Service									18
19	Home Dialysis Aide Services									19
20	Respiratory Therapy									20
21	Private Duty Nursing									21
22	Clinic									22
23	Health Promotion Activities									23
24	Day Care Program									24
25	Home Delivered Meals Program									25
26	OTHER NONREIMBURSABLE COSTS									26
27										27
28										28
29										29
30										30
31										31
32	Insurance – Malpractice									32
33	Insurance – Other									33
34	Interest									34
35	TOTAL									35

(1) Transfer the amounts in column 9 to Wks. A, column 4

Form HCFA-1728-81 (8-81)

Form Approved
OMB No. 0938-0022

WORKSHEET A-4

RECLASSIFICATIONS

PROVIDER NO.:

PERIOD:
FROM
TO

EXPLANATION OF RECLASSIFICATION ENTRY	CODE (1)	INCREASE			DECREASE		
		COST CENTER	LINE NO.	AMOUNT (2)	COST CENTER	LINE NO.	AMOUNT (2)
	1	2	3	4	5	6	7
1							
2							
3							
4							
5							
6							
7							
8							
9							
10							
11							
12							
13							
14							
15							
16							
17							
18							
19							
20							
21							
22							
23							
24							
25							
26							
27							
28							
29							
30							
31							
32							
33							
34							
35							
36	TOTAL RECLASSIFICATIONS (Sum of col 4 must equal sum of col 7)						

(1) A letter (A, B, etc.) must be entered on each line to identify each reclassification entry.

(2) Transfer to Worksheet A, col 7, line as appropriate.

Form HCFA-1728-81 (6-81)

Form Approved
OMB No. 0938-0022

ADJUSTMENTS TO EXPENSES		PROVIDER NO.:	PERIOD: FROM _____ TO _____	WORKSHEET A-5

	DESCRIPTION (1)	BASIS FOR ADJUSTMENT(s)	AMOUNT	EXPENSE CLASSIFICATION ON WORKSHEET A	
				COST CENTER	LINE NO.
		1	2	3	4
1.	Investment income on commingled restricted and unrestricted funds (chapter 2)	B	$		
2.	Trade, quantity, time and other discounts on purchases (chapter 8)	B			
3.	Rebates and refunds of expenses (chapter 8)	B			
4.	Home office costs (chapter 21)	A			
5.	Adjustment resulting from transactions with related organizations (chapter 10)	Fr Wks A-6			
6.	Sale of medical records and abstracts	B			
7.	Income from imposition of interest, finance or penalty charges (chapter 21)	B			
8.	Sale of medical and surgical supplies to other than patients	A			
9.	Sale of drugs to other than patients	A			
10.	Grants, gifts and income designated by donor for specific patient care expenses	B			
11.	Physical Therapy Adjustment (chapter 14)	Fr. Supp Wks A-8			
12.					
13.					
14.					
15.					
16.					
17.					
18.					
19.					
20.					
21.					
22.					
23.					
24.					
25.					
26.					
27.					
28.					
29.					
30.					
31.					
32.	TOTAL. (Sum of lines 1-31)		$		

(1) Description — All line references in this column pertain to the Provider Reimbursement Manual, Part I.

(2) Basis for adjustment (SEE INSTRUCTIONS).

    A. Costs — if cost, including applicable overhead, can be determined.

    B. Amount Received — if cost cannot be determined.

Form HCFA-1728-81 (6-81)

Form Approved
OMB No. 0938-0022

| STATEMENT OF COSTS OF SERVICES FROM RELATED ORGANIZATIONS | PROVIDER NO.: | PERIOD: FROM ___ TO ___ | WORKSHEET A-6 |

A. Are there any costs included on Worksheet A which resulted from transactions with related organizations as defined in the Provider Reimbursement Manual, Part I, chapter 10?

☐ No   ☐ Yes   (If "Yes," complete Parts B and C)

B. Costs incurred and adjustment required as result of transactions with related organizations:

LOCATION AND AMOUNT INCLUDED ON WORKSHEET A, COLUMN 8				AMOUNT ALLOWABLE IN COST	NET ADJUSTMENT (COL. 4 MINUS COL. 5)
LINE NO.	COST CENTER	EXPENSE ITEMS	AMOUNT		
1	2	3	4	5	6
1.			$	$	$
2.					
3.					
4.					
5.	TOTALS (Sum of lines 1-4) (Transfer col 6, lines 1-4 to Wkst A, col 9, lines as appropriate) (Transfer col 6, line 5 to Wkst A-5, col 2, line 5)		$	$	$

C. Interrelationship of provider to related organization(s):

The Secretary, by virtue of authority granted under Section 1814(b)(1) of the Health Insurance for the Aged and Disabled Act, requires the provider to furnish the information requested on Part C of this worksheet.
The information will be used by the Health Care Financing Administration and its intermediaries in determining the costs applicable to services, facilities and supplies furnished by organizations related to the provider by common ownership or control, represent reasonable costs as determined under Section 1861 of the Health Insurance for the Aged and Disabled Act. If the provider does not provide all or any part of the requested information, the cost report will be considered incomplete and not acceptable for purposes of claiming reimbursement under title XVIII.

SYMBOL (1)	NAME	PERCENT OWNERSHIP OF PROVIDER	RELATED ORGANIZATION(S)		
			NAME	PERCENT OF OWNERSHIP	TYPE OF BUSINESS
1	2	3	4	5	6
1.					
2.					
3.					
4.					
5.					

(1) Use the following symbols to indicate the interrelationship of the provider to related organizations:
A. Individual has financial interest (stockholder, partner, etc.) in both related organization and in provider.
B. Corporation, partnership, or other organization has financial interest in provider.
C. Provider has financial interest in corporation, partnership, or other organization.
D. Director, officer, administrator, or key person of provider or relative of such person has financial interest in related organization.
E. Individual is director, officer, administrator, or key person of provider and related organization.
F. Director, officer, administrator, or key person of related orgnization or relative of such person has financial interest in provider.
G. Other (financial or non-financial) specify.

| DEPRECIATION | PROVIDER NO.: | PERIOD: FROM ___ TO ___ | WORKSHEET A-7 |

1 Depreciation reported in cost report:

A. Straight-Line $ ___   C. Sum-of-the-Years' Digits ___

B. Declining Balance ___

D. Depreciation reported on Worksheet A, column 10 (Sum of A, B, and C) $ ___

		YES	NO
2	Is Depreciation Funded? (If Yes: Balance In Fund At End of Period $___)		
3	Were There Any Disposals of Capital Assets During Period?		
4	Was Accelerated Depreciation Claimed On Any Assets In The Current Or Any Prior Cost Reporting Period?		
	If Yes: A. Was Accelerated Depreciation Claimed On Assets Acquired On Or After August 1, 1970? (See Provider Reimbursement Manual, Part I, chapter 1)		
	B. Did Provider Cease To Participate In The Medicare Program At End Of Period To Which This Cost Report Applies? (See Provider Reimbursement Manual, Part I, chapter 1)		
	C. Was There Substantial Decrease In Health Insurance Proportion Of Allowable Costs From Prior Cost Reporting Periods? (See Provider Reimbursement Manual, Part I, chapter 1)		

Form HCFA-1728-81 (6-81)

Form Approved
OMB No. 0938-0022

WORKSHEET B

COST ALLOCATION – GENERAL SERVICE COST

PROVIDER NO.:

PERIOD: FROM ___ TO ___

COST CENTER	NET EXPENSE FOR COST ALLOCATION (Fr Wks A) 1	DEPRECIATION BLDG & FIXTURES 2	DEPRECIATION EQUIPMENT 3	PLANT OPERATION MAINTENANCE 4	TRANS-PORTATION 5	ADMINISTRA-TIVE & GENERAL 6	TOTAL 7	
1 GENERAL SERVICE COST CENTERS								1
2 Depreciation – Bldg. & Fixed Equipment	$	$						2
3 Depreciation – Movable Equipment			$					3
4 Plant Operation & Maintenance				$				4
5 Transportation					$			5
6 Administrative – General						$		6
7 REIMBURSABLE SERVICES								7
8 Skilled Nursing Care							$	8
9 Physical Therapy								9
10 Speech Pathology								10
11 Occupational Therapy								11
12 Medical Social Services								12
13 Home Health Aide								13
14 Medical Appliances								14
15 Durable Medical Equipment								15
16 Supplies								16
17 TITLE XVIII NONREIMBURSABLE SERVICES								17
18 Homemaker Service								18
19 Home Dialysis Aide Services								19
20 Respiratory Therapy								20
21 Private Duty Nursing								21
22 Clinic								22
23 Health Promotion Activities								23
24 Day Care Program								24
25 Home Delivered Meals Program								25
26 OTHER NONREIMBURSABLE COSTS								26
27								27
28								28
29								29
30								30
31								31
32 TOTAL	$	$	$	$	$	$		32

Form HCFA-1728-81 (6-81)

Form Approved
OMB No. 0938-0022

WORKSHEET B-1

COST ALLOCATION — STATISTICAL BASIS

PROVIDER NO.:

PERIOD:
FROM
TO

COST CENTER	DEPRECIATION BLDG. & FIXTURES (Sq Ft)	DEPRECIATION MOVABLE EQUIPMENT (Sq Ft or $ Value)	PLANT OPERATION & MAINTENANCE (Square Feet)	TRANSPORTATION (Mileage)	ADMINISTRATIVE & GENERAL (Net Cost Col 1, Wkst B)	
	1	2	3	4	5	6	7
1 GENERAL SERVICE COST CENTER							1
2 Depreciation – Bldg. & Fixed Equipment							2
3 Depreciation – Movable Equipment							3
4 Plant Operation & Maintenance							4
5 Transportation							5
6 Administrative – General						$	6
7 REIMBURSABLE SERVICES							7
8 Skilled Nursing Care							8
9 Physical Therapy							9
10 Speech Pathology							10
11 Occupational Therapy							11
12 Medical Social Services							12
13 Home Health Aide							13
14 Medical Appliances							14
15 Durable Medical Equipment							15
16 Supplies							16
17 TITLE XVIII NONREIMBURSABLE SERVICES							17
18 Homemaker Service							18
19 Home Dialysis Aide Services							19
20 Respiratory Therapy							20
21 Private Duty Nursing							21
22 Clinic							22
23 Health Promotion Activities							23
24 Day Care Program							24
25 Home Delivered Meals Program							25
26 OTHER NONREIMBURSABLE COST							26
27							27
28							28
29							29
30							30
31							31
32 Cost to be allocated (Per Wkst B)	$	$	$	$	$	$	32
33 Unit Cost Multiplier							33

Form HCFA-1728-81 (6-81)

Form Approved
OMB No. 0938-0022

WORKSHEET C

APPORTIONMENT OF PATIENT SERVICE COSTS — TITLE XVIII — ONLY

PROVIDER NO.: ____

PERIOD:
FROM ____
TO ____

PART I — COST PER VISIT COMPUTATION

Patient Service	Fr Wkst. B Line:	Amounts 2	Total Visits 3	Average Cost Per Visit 4	Medicare visits				Cost of Services				Total Medicare Cost Sum of cols. 8, 9, and 10 11	
					Post Hosp. Plan-Part A 5	Medical Plan — Part B			Post Hosp. Plan-Part A 8	Medical Plan — Part B				
						Part of HH Plan 6	Not Part of HH Plan 7			Part of HH Plan 9	Not Part of HH Plan 10			
1 Skilled Nursing	8	$		$					$	$	$		$	1
2 Physical Therapy	9													2
3 Speech Pathology	10													3
4 Occupational Therapy	11													4
5 Medical Social Services	12													5
6 Home Health Aide Services	13													6
7 Total (Sum of lines 1–6)		$			visits	visits	visits		$	$	$		$	7

PART II — LIMITATION COST COMPUTATION

Patient Service			Medicare Cost Limits 4	Medicare Visits				Medicare Limitation Costs				Total Limitation Cost Sum of cols. 8, 9, and 10 11	
	1	2	3	Post Hosp. Plan-Part A 5	Medical Plan — Part B			Post Hosp. Plan-Part A 8	Medical Plan — Part B				
					Part of HH Plan 6	Not Part of HH Plan 7			Part of HH Plan 9	Not Part of HH Plan 10			
1 Skilled Nursing								$	$	$		$	1
2 Physical Therapy													2
3 Speech Pathology													3
4 Occupational Therapy													4
5 Medical Social Services													5
6 Home Health Aide Services													6
7 Total (Sum of lines 1–6)				visits	visits	visits		$	$	$		$	7

PART III — SUPPLIES, APPLIANCES, AND EQUIPMENT COST COMPUTATION

Other Patient Services	Fr Wkst. B Line 1	Cost 2	Charge 3	Ratio 4	Medicare Covered Charges				Cost of Services				Total Medicare Cost Sum of cols. 8, 9, and 10 11	
					Post Hosp. Plan-Part A 5	Medical Plan — Part B			Post Hosp. Plan-Part A 8	Medical Plan — Part B				
						Part of HH Plan 6	Not Part of HH Plan 7			Part of HH Plan 9	Not Part of HH Plan 10			
1 Cost of Medical Appliances and/or Durable Medical Equipment Rented	14	$	$	%	$	$	$		$	$	$		$	1
2 Cost of Medical Equipment Sold	15			%										2
3 Cost of Medical Supplies	16			%										3
4 Total Other Patient Services Cost (Sum of lines 1, 2 and 3)		$	$		$	$	$		$	$	$		$	4
5 Total Cost of Medicare Services (Enter the sum of the lower of PART I, line 7, OR PART II, line 7, plus PART III, line 4 — columns 8, 9, and 10 respectively) (Transfer the amounts in columns 8, 9, and 10 to Worksheet D, line 2, columns 1, 2, and 3 respectively)									$	$	$		$	5

Form HCFA-1728-81 (8-81)

CALCULATION OF REIMBURSEMENT SETTLEMENT PART A AND PART B SERVICES	PROVIDER NO.:	PERIOD FROM _____ TO _____	WORKSHEET D

PART I — COMPUTATION OF THE LESSER OF REASONABLE COST OR CUSTOMARY CHARGES

		Post Hospital Plan - Part A	Medical Plan - Part B	
			Part of HH Plan	Not Part of HH Plan
		1	2	3
1	Reasonable Cost of Title XVIII - Part A and B Services			
2	Cost of Services (From Wkst. C, Part III, line 5)	$	$	$
3	Allowable return on Equity Capital (From Supp. Wkst. F-3, Part III, columns 1, 2 and 3, respectively, line 2)			
4	Total Reasonable Cost (line 2 plus line 3)	$	$	$
5	Total Charges for Title XVIII - Part A and B Services	$	$	$
6	Customary Charges			
7	Aggregate amount actually collected from patients liable for payment for services on a charge basis (From provider records)	$		
8	Amounts that would have been realized from patients liable for payment for service on a charge basis had such payment been made in accordance with Health Insurance Regulation Section 405.455(b) (From provider records)			
9	Ratio of line 7 to 8 (Not to exceed 1.00000000)			
10	Total Customary Charges - Title XVIII (Multiply line 9 x line 5 each column)	$	$	$
11	Excess of Customary Charges Over Aggregate Cost (Sum of cols 1, 2, & 3, line 10 minus the sum of cols 1, 2 & 3, line 4) (Complete line 13)			
12	Excess of Aggregate Cost Over Aggregate Charges (Sum of cols 1, 2 & 3, line 4 minus the sum of cols 1, 2 & 3, line 10) (Complete line 14)	$		
13	Excess of customary charges over reasonable cost (complete only if line 10 exceeds line 4) (Enter lesser of line 10 minus line 4 or line 11) (Transfer to Supp. Wkst. D-3, Part I, line 1)			
14	Excess of reasonable cost over customary charges (complete only if line 4 exceeds line 10) (Enter lesser of line 4 minus line 10, or line 12) (Transfer to Supp. Wkst. D-3, Part II, line 3b)	$	$	$

PART II — COMPUTATION OF REIMBURSEMENT SETTLEMENT

15	Total Reasonable Cost (From line 4)			
16	Amounts paid and payable by Workers' Compensation	( )		
17	Part B deductibles billed to Medicare patients (Exclude coinsurance amounts)		( )	( )
18	SUBTOTAL (line 15 minus lines 16 and 17)			
19	Excess reasonable cost (From line 14)			
20	SUBTOTAL (Line 18 minus line 19)			
21	80% of Part B cost (col. 3 line 20)			
22	Part B coinsurance billed to Medicare patients (From provider records)			
23	Net Cost - Part B (line 18 minus line 22)			
24	Reimbursable bad debts (SEE INSTRUCTIONS)			
25	TOTAL COST - Current cost reporting period (For cols. 1 and 2 enter amounts from line 20 plus line 24) (For col. 3 enter lesser amount from line 21 or 23, plus line 24)			
26	Recovery of unreimbursed cost under lesser of cost or charge (From Supp. Wkst. D-3, Part II, cols 1, 2, and 3, line 2e)			
27	20% of recovery of unreimbursed cost under lesser of cost or charges (col 3, line 26 x 20%)			
28	Amounts applicable to prior cost reporting periods resulting from disposition of depreciable assets			
29	Recovery of excess depreciation resulting from agencies termination or a decrease in Medicare utilization	( )	( )	( )
30	Unrefunded charges to beneficiaries for excess costs erroneously collected, based on correction of cost limit	( )	( )	( )
31	TOTAL COST - reimbursable to provider (Part A - sum of lines 25 and 26 plus/minus line 28 plus sum of lines 29 and 30) (Part B - sum of lines 25 and 26 minus line 27 plus/minus line 28, 29 and 30)	$	$	$
32	NET TOTAL COST (Part A from line 31) (Part B from line 31 sum of cols 2 and 3)			
33	Total interim payments (From Supp. Wkst. D-1, line 4)	( )	( )	
34	Balance due HHA/Medicare program (Line 32 minus line 33) (Indicate overpayments in brackets)			

Form HCFA-1728-81 (6-81)

Form Approved
OMB No. 0938-0022

| ANALYSIS OF PAYMENTS TO PROVIDERS FOR SERVICES RENDERED TO TITLE XVIII (MEDICARE) BENEFICIARIES | PROVIDER NO.: | PERIOD: FROM _____ TO _____ | WORKSHEET D-1 |

	Description			* Category 1 PART A			Category 2 PART B	
				Mo. Day, Yr.	Amount		Mo. Day, Yr.	Amount
1	Total interim payments paid to provider				$			$
2	Interim payments payable on individual bills, either submitted or to be submitted to the intermediary, for services rendered in the cost reporting period. If none, write "NONE." (1)				$			
3	List separately each retroactive lump sum adjustment amount based on subsequent revision of the interim rate for the cost reporting period. Also show date of each payment. If none, write "NONE." (1)	Program to Provider	a					
			b					
			c					
			d					
			e					
		Provider to Program	f	(	)		(	)
			g	(	)		(	)
			h	(	)		(	)
			i	(	)		(	)
			j	(	)		(	)
	SUBTOTAL (Sum of lines 3a-3e minus sum of lines 3f-3j).		k					
4	TOTAL INTERIM PAYMENTS (Sum of lines 1, 2 and 3k) (Transfer to Wkst D, Part II, column as appropriate, line 33)				$			$

TO BE COMPLETED BY INTERMEDIARY

	Description			* Category 1 PART A			Category 2 PART B	
5	List separately each tentative settlement payment after desk review. Also show date of each payment. If none, write "NONE." (1)	Program to Provider	a		$			$
			b					
			c		$			$
		Provider to Program	d	(	)		(	)
			e	(	)		(	)
			f	(	)		(	)
	SUBTOTAL (Sum of lines 5a-5c minus sum of lines 5d-5f)		g		$			$
6	Determined net settlement amount (balance due) based on the cost report (SEE INSTRUCTIONS) (1)	Program to Provider	a		$			$
			b					
			c		$			$
		Provider to Program	d	(	)		(	)
			e	(	)		(	)
			f	(	)		(	)
7	TOTAL MEDICARE PROGRAM LIABILITY (Reimbursable cost, net of deductibles and coinsurance) (line 4 plus/minus lines 5g, 6c or 6f) (Should equal amounts entered on Wkst D, Part II, column as appropriate, line 32)				$			$

Name of Intermediary | Intermediary Number

Signtaure of Authorized Person | Date   Month, Day, Year

(1) On lines 3, 5 and 6, where an amount is due "Provider to Program," show the amount and date on which the provider agrees to the amount of repayment, even though total repayment is not accomplished until a later date.

Form HCFA-1728-81 (6-81)

Form Approved
OMB No. 0938-0022

CALCULATION OF REIMBURSABLE BAD DEBTS TITLE XVIII — PART B	PROVIDER NO.: _____	PERIOD: FROM _____ TO _____	WORKSHEET D-2

PART I — CALCULATION OF REIMBURSABLE BAD DEBTS FOR MEDICARE PATIENTS — PART B — MEDICAL PLAN SERVICE NOT PART OF A HOME HEALTH PLAN

1	Total cost applicable to Medicare (From Wkst. D, Part I, line 2, column 3	$
2	Allowable return on equity capital (Line 1 x ratio _____ from Supplemental Wkst. F-3, Part II, line 22)	
3	SUBTOTAL (Sum of lines 1 and 2	
4	Reimbursable Expense (See Instructions)	
5	Balance to be recovered from Medicare (Part B Medical Plan — Service not part of a home health plan) patients (line 3 minus line 4)	$
6	Deductibles and coinsurance billed to Medicare (Part B Medical Plan — Service not part of a home health plan) patients	$
7	Bad debts for deductibles and coinsurance, net of bad debt recoveries	( )
8	Net deductibles and coinsurance billed to Medicare (Part B Medical Plan — Service not part of a home health plan) patients (line 6 minus line 7)	$
9	Unrecovered from Medicare (Part B Medical Plan — Service not part of a home health plan) patients (line 5 minus line 8) (If line 8 exceeds line 5, enter zero on lines 9 and 11, and enter the excess amount on line 10)	$
10	Excess recovered from Medicare Part B Medical Plan (Service not part of a home health plan) patients	
11	Gross bad debts — current period (lesser of line 7 or line 9) (Enter on Wkst. D, Part II, column 3, line 24)	$

PART II — CALCULATION OF REIMBURSABLE BAD DEBTS FOR MEDICARE PATIENTS — PART B — MEDICARE PLAN SERVICE PART OF A HOME HEALTH PLAN

1	Bad debts for Medicare Net of Bad Debts Recoveries (Part B — Medical Plan — Service part of a home health plan) (From agency's records)	$
2	Excess recovered from Medicare (Part B — Medical Plan — Service not part of a home health plan) patients (From Part I, line 10)	
3	Reimbursable bad debts (Subtract the amount on line 1 from the amount on line 2) (If the amount on line 2 exceeds the amount on line 1, enter zero on line 3) (Enter on Wkst, D, Part II, col. 2, line 24)	$

BALANCE SHEET

Form Approved
OMB No. 0938-0022

WORKSHEET F

PROVIDER NO.: _____

PERIOD: FROM _____ TO _____

(To be completed by all providers maintaining fund type accounting records. Nonproprietary providers not maintaining fund type accounting records, should complete the "General Fund" column only.)

ASSETS (omit cents)	GENERAL FUND	SPECIFIC PURPOSE FUND	ENDOWMENT FUND	PLANT FUND
Current Assets				
1. Cash on hand and in banks				
2. Temporary Investments				
3. Notes receivable				
4. Accounts receivable				
5. Other receivables				
6. Less: Allowance for uncollectible notes & accounts receivable	( )	( )	( )	( )
7. Inventory				
8. Prepaid expenses				
9. Other current assets				
10. Due From Other Funds				
11. TOTAL CURRENT ASSETS (Sum of lines 1-10)				
Fixed Assets				
12. Land				
13. Land improvements				
14. Less: Accumulated Depreciation	( )	( )	( )	( )
15. Buildings				
16. Less: Accumulated Depreciation	( )	( )	( )	( )
17. Leasehold improvements				
18. Less: Accumulated Amortization	( )	( )	( )	( )
19. Fixed Equipment				
20. Less: Accumulated Depreciation	( )	( )	( )	( )
21. Automobiles and Trucks				
22. Less: Accumulated Depreciation	( )	( )	( )	( )
23. Major Movable Equipment				
24. Less: Accumulated Depreciation	( )	( )	( )	( )
25. Minor Equipment Nondepreciable				
26. Other Fixed Assets				
27. TOTAL FIXED ASSETS (Sum of lines 12-26)				
Other Assets				
28. Investments				
29. Deposits on leases				
30. Due from owners/officers				
31.				
32. TOTAL OTHER ASSETS (Sum of lines 28-31)				
33. TOTAL ASSETS (Sum of lines 11, 27, & 32)				

LIABILITIES AND FUND BALANCES (omit cents)	GENERAL FUND	SPECIFIC PURPOSE FUND	ENDOWMENT FUND	PLANT FUND
Current Liabilities				
34. Accounts Payable				
35. Salaries, Wages & Fees Payable				
36. Payroll Taxes Payable				
37. Notes & Loans Payable (Short term)				
38. Deferred Income				
39. Accelerated Payments				
40. Due to Other Funds				
41.				
42. TOTAL CURRENT LIABILITIES (Sum of lines 34-41)				
Long-Term Liabilities				
43. Mortage Payable				
44. Notes Payable				
45. Unsecured loans				
46. Loans from Owners: a. Prior to 7/1/66 b. On or after 7/1/66				
47.				
48.				
49. TOTAL LONG-TERM LIABILITIES (Sum of lines 43-48)				
50. TOTAL LIABILITIES (Sum of lines 42 & 49)				
Capital Accounts				
51. General Fund Balance				
52. Specific Purpose Fund Balance				
53. Donor created - Endowment Fund Balance - Restricted				
54. Donor created - Endowment Fund Balance - Unrestricted				
55. Governing Board created - Endowment Fund Balance				
56. Plant Fund Balance - Invested in Plant				
57. Plant Fund Balance - Reserve for Plant Improvement, replacement and expansion				
58. TOTAL FUND BALANCES (Sum of lines 51 thru 57)				
59. TOTAL LIABILITIES AND FUND BALANCES (Sum of lines 50 & 58)				

( ) = contra amount

Form HCFA-1728-81 (6-81)

Form Approved
OMB No. 0938-0022

	STATEMENT OF REVENUE AND EXPENSES	PROVIDER NO.:	PERIOD: FROM_____ TO_____	WORKSHEET F-1

1	Total Patient Revenues	$	
2	Less: Allowances and Discounts on Patients' Accounts		
3	Net Patient Revenues (line 1 minus line 2)		
4	Operating Expenses (From Worksheet A, column 6, line 35)	$	
5	Additions to Operating Expenses (Specify)	$	
6			
7			
8			
9			
10			
11	Subtractions from Operating Expenses (Specify)	(	)
12		(	)
13		(	)
14		(	)
15		(	)
16		(	)
17	Less Total Operating Expenses (Net of lines 4 thru 16)		$
18	Net Income from Service to Patients (line 3 minus line 17)		
19	Other Income:	$	
20	Contributions, Donations, Bequests, etc.		
21	Income from Investments		
22	Purchase Discounts		
23	Rebates and Refunds of Expenses		
24	Sale of Medical & Nursing Supplies to Other Than Patients		
25	Sale of Durable Medical Equipment to Other Than Patients		
26	Sale of Drugs to Other Than Patients		
27	Sale of Medical Records and Abstracts		
28	Other Revenue (Specify)		
29			
30			
31			
32			
33			
34	Total Other Income (Sum of lines 19 through 33)		$
35	Net Income or Loss for the Period (line 18 plus 34)		$

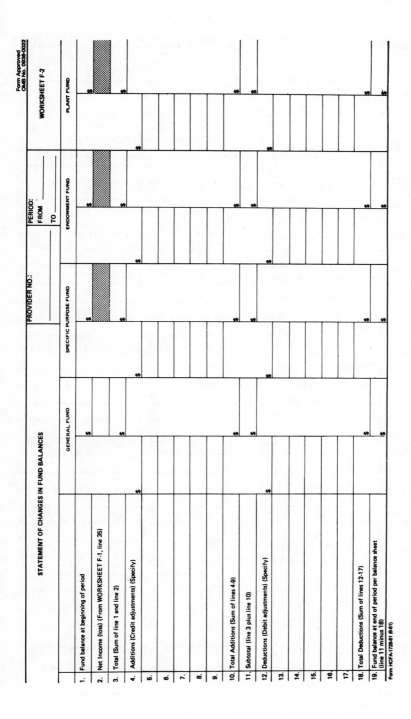

This report is required by law (42 USC 1395g; 42 CFR 405.406(b)). Failure to report can result in all interim payments made since the beginning of the cost report period being deemed as overpayments (42 USC 1395g).

Form Approved.
OMB No. 0938-0022

RECOVERY OF UNREIMBURSED COST

PROVIDER NO. :
_____

PERIOD :
FROM _____
TO _____

SUPPLEMENTAL
WORKSHEET
D-3

AGENCY STATUS
☐ New Provider
☐ Other Than New Provider

	Post Hospital Plan — Part A	Medical Plan — Part B	
		Part of HH Plan	Not Part of HH Plan
	1	2	3

PART I — COMPUTATION OF RECOVERY OF UNREIMBURSED COST UNDER LESSER OF COST OR CHARGES

		1	2	3
1	Excess of customary charges over reasonable cost (From Worksheet D, Part I, line 13)	$	$	$
2	Carryover of unreimbursed cost (Must equal Part II, columns 1, 2, and 3, line 1e)			
3	Recovery of unreimbursed cost (lesser of line 1 or line 2)			

PART II — COMPUTATION OF CARRYOVER OF UNREIMBURSED COST UNDER LESSER OF COST OR CHARGES

		1	2	3
1	Carryover—Beginning of current period (From prior years cost report Supp. Wkst. D-3, Part II, line 4a, 4b, 4c, 4d, 4f)			
a	Base Period 19 __			
b	Prior Cost Reporting Period Ended 19 __ (1)			
c	Prior Cost Reporting Period Ended 19 __			
d	Prior Cost Reporting Period Ended 19 __			
e	TOTAL (Sum of lines 1a thru 1d)	$	$	$
2	Recovery of unreimbursed cost (SEE INSTRUCTIONS) (2)			
a	Base Period 19 __	( )	( )	( )
b	Prior Cost Reporting Period Ended 19 __ (1)	( )	( )	( )
c	Prior Cost Reporting Period Ended 19 __	( )	( )	( )
d	Prior Cost Reporting Period Ended 19 __	( )	( )	( )
e	TOTAL (Sum of lines 2a thru 2d)	( )	( )	( )
3	Unreimbursed costs current period (From Worksheet D, Part I, line 14)			
a	Base Period 19 __			
b	Current Cost Reporting Period			
c	TOTAL (Sum of lines 3a and 3b)	$	$	$
4	Carryover — End of current period			
a	Base Period (Net of lines 1a, 2a, and 3a)			
b	Prior Cost Reporting Period Ended 19 __ (line 1b minus line 2b) (1)			
c	Prior Cost Reporting Period Ended 19 __ (line 1c minus line 2c)			
d	Prior Cost Reporting Period Ended 19 __ (line 1d minus line 2d)			
e	Current Cost Reporting Period (From line 3b)			
f	TOTAL (line 1e minus line 2e plus line 3c)	$	$	$

(1) Complete Part II, lines 1b, 2b, and 4b, only with respect to a cost reporting period in which the two succeeding cost reporting periods include fewer than 24 calendar months.

(2) Transfer the amounts in Part II, columns 1, 2, and 3, line 2e to Worksheet D, Part II, columns 1, 2 and 3 respectively, line 26

This report is required by law (42 USC 1395g; 42 CFR 405.406(b)). Failure to report can result in all interim payments made since the beginning of the cost report period being deemed as overpayments (42 USC 1395g).

Form Approved.
OMB No. 0938-0022

REASONABLE COST DETERMINATION FOR PHYSICAL THERAPY SERVICES FURNISHED BY OUTSIDE SUPPLIERS	PROVIDER NO. :	PERIOD : FROM ——— TO ———	SUPPLEMENTAL WORKSHEET A-8 PARTS I, II, & III

PART I — GENERAL INFORMATION

1	Total Number of Hours Worked By: (If HHA time records are not available, 1 visit equals 1 hour)	
	a. Supervisors	
	b. Therapists	
	c. Assistants	
	d. Aides	
2	Total Number of Weeks Worked (During which outside supplier (excluding aides) worked) times 15 hours per week	
3	Total Cost of Outside Supplier Services	$
4	Total Number of Treatments or Visits	

PART II — TRAVEL ALLOWANCE/EXPENSE COMPUTATION

5	Standard Travel Allowance/Expense (Services performed at provider site)	1 Number of Days	2 ½ Hourly Rate Allowance Plus Standard Expense Rate	3 Standard Allowance Expense (column 1 x column 2)	4
	For Period From ——— To ———				
	a. Therapists		$	$	
	b. Assistants		$	$	
	For Period From ——— To ———				
	c. Therapists		$	$	
	d. Assistants		$	$	
	e. Total Standard Travel Allowance/Expense at Provider Site (Sum of 5a-5d, column 3)				$
6	Standard Travel Allowance/Expense (Services performed outside provider site)	Number of Visits	½ Hourly Rate Allowance Plus Standard Expense Rate	Standard Allowance Expense (column 1 x column 2)	
	For Period From ——— To ———				
	a. Therapists		$	$	
	b. Assistants		$	$	
	For Period From ——— To ———				
	c. Therapists		$	$	
	d. Assistants		$	$	
	e. Total Standard Travel Allowance/Expense Outside Provider Site (HHA only) (Sum of 6a-6d, column 3)				$
7	Optional Travel Allowance/Expense (Only used for HHA services if time records available)				
	TRAVEL ALLOWANCE	Number of Hours	Hourly Rate Allowance	Optional Travel Allowance (column 1 x column 2)	
	For Period From ——— To ———				
	a. Therapists		$	$	
	b. Assistants		$	$	
	For Period From ——— To ———				
	c. Therapists		$	$	
	d. Assistants		$	$	
	e. Total Optional Travel Allowance (Sum of 7a-7d, column 3)				$
	TRAVEL EXPENSE	Number of Visits or Miles Driven	Expense Rate or Mileage Rate	Optional Travel Expense (column 1 x column 2)	
	For Period From ——— To ———				
	f. Therapists		$	$	
	g. Assistants		$	$	
	For Period From ——— To ———				
	h. Therapists		$	$	
	i. Assistants		$	$	
	j. Total Optional Travel Expense (Sum of 7f-7i, column 3)				$
	k. Total Optional Travel Allowance/Expense (Sum of 7e and 7j)				$
8	Total Travel Allowance/Expense (Sum of lines 5e and 6e or 7k)				$

PART III — SALARY EQUIVALENCY COMPUTATION

9	Salary Equivalency Computation When Part I, Line 2 Is Greater Than Part I, Sum of Lines 1a-1c	Hours	Hourly Rate Allowance	Salary Equivalence Amount (column 1 x column 2)	
	For Period From ——— To ———				
	a. Therapists and Assistants		$	$	
	b. Aides		$	$	
	For Period From ——— To ———				
	c. Therapists and Assistants		$	$	
	d. Aides		$	$	
	e. Total Salary Equivalency (Sum of lines 9a-9d, column 3)				$
10	Salary Equivalency Computation When Part I, Line 2 Is Less Than Part I, Sum of Lines 1a-1c	Hours	Hourly Rate Allowance	Salary Equivalence Amount (column 1 x column 2)	
	For Period From ——— To ———				
	a. Supervisor		$	$	
	b. Therapists		$	$	
	c. Assistants		$	$	
	d. Aides		$	$	
	For Period From ——— To ———				
	e. Supervisor		$	$	
	f. Therapists		$	$	
	g. Assistants		$	$	
	h. Aides		$	$	
	i. Total Salary Equivalency (Sum of lines 10a-10h, column 3)				$

Form HCFA-1728B (10/80)

Form Approved.
OMB No. 0838-0022

REASONABLE COST DETERMINATION FOR PHYSICAL THERAPY SERVICES FURNISHED BY OUTSIDE SUPPLIERS	PROVIDER NO. : _____	PERIOD : FROM _____ TO _____	SUPPLEMENTAL WORKSHEET A-8 PARTS IV & V

PART IV — OVERTIME COMPUTATION

	For Period From _____ To _____	Therapists	Assistants	Aides	Total (Sum of columns 1-3)
		1	2	3	4
11	Overtime Hours Worked During Period				
12	Overtime Rate (Multiply appropriate hourly rate allowance amount times 1.5)	$	$	$	
13	Total Overtime (Including base and overtime allowance (line 11 x line 12))	$	$	$	
14	Limitation				
15	Percentage of Overtime Hours by Class (Divide the hours in each column, line 11 by the total hours in column 4, line 23)	%	%	%	
16	Allocation of Provider's Standard Workyear for One Full Time Employee (See Instructions) (Multiply by percentage on line 15)				
17	Determination of Overtime Allowance:				
18	Base Hourly Rate Allowance	$	$	$	
19	Overtime Cost Limitation (line 16 times line 18)	$	$	$	
20	Maximum Overtime Cost (Enter less of line 13 or line 19)	$	$	$	
21	Portion of Overtime Already Included in Hourly Computation at the Base Hourly Rate (Multiply line 11 by line 18)	$	$	$	
22	Overtime Allowance (line 20 minus line 21) (If negative, enter zero)	$	$	$	$
	For Period From _____ To _____				
23	Overtime Hours Worked During Period				
24	Overtime Rate (Multiply appropriate hourly rate allowance amount times 1.5)	$	$	$	
25	Total Overtime (Including base and overtime allowance (line 23 x 24))	$	$	$	
26	Limitation:				
27	Percentage of Overtime Hours by Class (Divide the hours in each column, line 23, by the total hours in column 4, line 23)	%	%	%	100%
28	Allocation of Provider's Standard Workyear for One Full Time Employee (See Instructions) (Multiply by percentage on line 27)				
29	Determination of Overtime Allowance:				
30	Base Hourly Rate Allowance	$	$	$	
31	Overtime Cost Limitation (line 28 times line 30)	$	$	$	
32	Maximum Overtime Cost (Enter lesser of line 25 or line 31)	$	$	$	
33	Portion of Overtime Already Included in Hourly Computation at the Base Hourly Rate (Multiply line 23 by line 30)	$	$	$	
34	Overtime Allowance (line 32 minus line 33) (If negative, enter zero)	$	$	$	$
35	Total Overtime Allowance (Sum of line 22 and line 34)				$

PART V — LIMITATION COMPUTATION

36	Travel Allowance/Expense (from Part II, line 8)	$
37	Salary Equivalency Amount (from Part III, line 9e or 10i)	$
38	Overtime Allowance (from Part IV, line 35)	$
39	Equipment Cost (Owned or Leased) (See instructions)	$
40	Supplies (See instructions)	$
41	Total Allowance (Sum of lines 36-40)	$
42	Excess Over Limitation (Line 3 minus line 41) (If negative, enter zero) (Transfer to Worksheet A-5, line 11)	$

Form HCFA-1728B (10/80)

This report is required by law (42 USC 1395g, 42 CFR 405.406(b)). Failure to report can result in all interim payments made since the beginning of the cost report period being deemed as overpayments (42 USC 1395g).

RETURN ON EQUITY CAPITAL OF PROPRIETARY PROVIDERS
(To be completed by proprietary providers only)

PROVIDER NO.: _____

PERIOD:
FROM _____
TO _____

SUPPLEMENTAL
WORKSHEET F-3
PART I

PART I — BALANCE SHEET FOR COMPUTATION OF EQUITY CAPITAL

ASSETS (OMIT CENTS)	BALANCE SHEET PER BOOKS	ADJUSTMENTS INCREASE (DECREASE)	ADJUSTED BALANCE SHEET FOR COMPUTATION OF EQUITY CAPITAL	LIABILITIES AND CAPITAL (OMIT CENTS)	BALANCE SHEET PER BOOKS	ADJUSTMENTS INCREASE (DECREASE)	ADJUSTED BALANCE SHEET FOR COMPUTATION OF EQUITY CAPITAL
1	2	3	4	5	6	7	8
CURRENT ASSETS				**CURRENT LIABILITIES**			
1. Cash on hand and in banks	$	$	$	34. Accounts Payable	$	$	$
2. Temporary Investments				35. Salaries, Wages & Fees Payable			
3. Notes Receivable				36. Payroll Taxes Payable			
4. Accounts Receivable				37. Notes & Loans Payable (Short Term)			
5. Other Receivables							
6. Less: Allowance for uncollectible notes and accounts receivable	( )	( )	( )	38. Deferred Income			
7. Inventory				39. Accelerated Payments			
8. Prepaid Expenses				40.			
9. Other Current Assets	$	$	$	41. Total Current Liabilities (Sum of lines 34-40)	$	$	$
10. Total Current Assets (Sum of lines 1-9)	$	$	$	**LONG-TERM LIABILITIES**			
				42. Mortgage Payable	$	$	$
FIXED ASSETS				43. Notes Payable			
11. Land	$	$	$	44. Unsecured Loans			
12. Land Improvements				45. Loans from Owners prior to 7/1/66			
13. Less: Accumulated Depreciation	( )	( )	( )	46. On or after 7/1/66			
14. Building	( )	( )	( )	47.			
15. Less: Accumulated Depreciation	( )	( )	( )	48.			
16. Leasehold Improvements				49. Total Long-term Liabilities (Sum of lines 42-48)	$		
17. Less: Accumulated Amortization	( )	( )	( )				
18. Fixed Equipment				50. TOTAL LIABILITIES (Sum of lines 41 & 49)	$	$	$
19. Less: Accumulated Depreciation	( )	( )	( )	51. Capital	$	$	$
20. Automobiles & Trucks							
21. Less: Accumulated Depreciation	( )	( )	( )				
22. Major Movable Equipment							
23. Less: Accumulated Depreciation	( )	( )	( )				
24. Minor Equipment Non-depreciable							
25. Other Fixed Assets				52. TOTAL CAPITAL	$	$	$
26. Total Fixed Assets (Sum of lines 11-25)	$	$	$	53. TOTAL LIABILITIES & CAPITAL (Sum of lines 50 & 52)	$	$	$
OTHER ASSETS				54. Equity in assets leased from related organizations			
27. Investments	$	$	$	55. Difference between total interim payments and net cost of covered services (SEE INSTRUCTIONS)			
28. Deposits on leases				56. TOTAL EQUITY CAPITAL (Line 52 plus/minus lines 54 and 55) (1)			
29. Due from owners/officers				57. Return on equity capital			
30. Special Funds				58. Adjustments to health care program costs			
31.				59. Federal, state and local income taxes			
32. Total Other Assets (Sum of lines 27-31)	$	$	$	60. Total Equity Capital Beginning of Following Cost Reporting Period (Sum of lines 56 and 57) plus or minus lines 58 and 59)	$		
33. TOTAL ASSETS (Sum of lines 10, 26 & 32)	$	$	$				

(1) If computed as of end of cost reporting period, transfer the amount to Part II, column 8 for the last month or period in the cost reporting period. If computed as of beginning of cost reporting period (first reporting period under the health care programs only), transfer this amount to Part II, column 2, all lines and column 8, line 1.   ( ) = contra amounts

Form HCFA-1728 D (10/80)

Form Approved.
OMB No. 0938-0022

SUPPLEMENTAL
WORKSHEET F-3
PARTS II & III

RETURN ON EQUITY CAPITAL OF PROPRIETARY PROVIDERS

PROVIDER NO.: _____

PERIOD:
FROM _____
TO _____

PART II — COMPUTATION OF EQUITY CAPITAL OF PROPRIETARY PROVIDERS

MONTHS OR PERIODS WITHIN THE COST REPORTING PERIOD	EQUITY CAPITAL BEGINNING OF PERIOD (1)	CAPITAL INVESTMENTS DURING PERIOD (1)	GAIN OR (LOSS) ON SALE OF ASSETS (1)	WITHDRAWALS OR DIVIDEND DISTRIBUTIONS (1)	OTHER INCREASES OR (DECREASES) (1)	INCREASES OR (DECREASES) DUE TO OPERATIONS	EQUITY CAPITAL END OF PERIOD (NET TOTAL OF COLS 2 THRU 7)	EQUITY CAPITAL ALLOCATED FROM RELATED ORGANIZATIONS	NET EQUITY CAPITAL AT END OF PERIOD (COLUMNS 8 & 9)	
1	2	3	4	5	6	7	8	9	10	
										1
										2
										3
										4
										5
										6
										7
										8
										9
										10
										11
										12
										13
										14
15 TOTAL										15
16 Number of months or periods in cost reporting period Plus one =										16
17 Average equity capital during the period (line 15, column 10 divided by line 16, column 10)										17
18 Annual rate of return										% 18
19 Amount of return for full year (line 17 times line 18, column 10)										19
20 Amount allowable for current period (Do not use this line if reporting period is full year)										20
21 Total allowable costs subject to allocation of return on equity capital (Worksheet B, column 7, sum of lines 8 through 26)										21
22 Ratio of allowable return on equity capital to total allowable cost (line 19 or 20 ÷ line 21)										22

(1) Do not include any amounts in columns 3 through 6 applicable to amounts eliminated on Part I, columns 3 and 7 (except for intercompany accounts)

PART III — APPORTIONMENT OF ALLOWABLE RETURN ON EQUITY CAPITAL OF PROPRIETARY AGENCIES

		MEDICAL PLAN — PART B	
	POST HOSPITAL PLAN PART A	Service Part of a Home Health Plan	Service Not Part of a Home Health Plan
	1	2	3
1 Reimbursable Cost (For Column 1, enter the amount from Worksheet D, Part I, column 1, line 2 less line 3. For Columns 2 and 3, enter the amount from Worksheet D, Part I, line 2, columns 2 and 3 respectively.)			
2 Apportionment of allowable return on equity capital (Part II, line 22 times the amount in each column, Part III, line 1)			
3 Title XVIII, Reimbursable Return on Equity Capital (Multiply the amount on line 2 by the percentage in each column, line 3, respectively) (SEE INSTRUCTIONS)	x 100%	x 100%	x 80%

Form HCFA-1728D (10/80)

FORM HCFA-339 (2-84)
FORM APPROVED
OMB NO. 0938-0301

This questionnaire is required under the authority of sections 1815(a) and 1833(e) of the Social Security Act. Failure to submit this questionnaire will result in suspension of Medicare payments.

PROVIDER COST REPORT REIMBURSEMENT QUESTIONNAIRE
(Please Read Instructions Before Completing Questionnaire)

Provider Name:	Provider Number:
Filed with Form HCFA– ☐ 1728 ☐ 2552 ☐ 2088 ☐ _____ (Other Specify)	Period: From _____ To _____

INTENTIONAL MISREPRESENTATION OR FALSIFICATION OF ANY INFORMATION CONTAINED IN THIS QUESTIONNAIRE MAY BE PUNISHABLE BY FINE AND/OR IMPRISONMENT UNDER FEDERAL LAW

CERTIFICATION BY OFFICER OR ADMINISTRATOR OF PROVIDER(S)

I HEREBY CERTIFY that I have read the above statement and that I have examined the accompanying information prepared by _____ (Provider name(s) and number(s)) for the cost report period beginning _____ and ending _____, and that to the best of my knowledge and belief, it is a true, correct and complete statement prepared from the books and records of the provider(s) in accordance with applicable instructions, except as noted.

(Signed) _____

Officer or Administrator of Provider(s)

_____   _____
Date   Title

Name and Telephone Number of Person to Contact for More Information

_____

_____

	Yes	No	N/A

A. Financial Data and Reports

   1. During this cost reporting period, the financial statements are:

      a. Audited

      b. Compiled

	Yes	No	N/A

c. Reviewed

by certified public accountants or public accountants (submit complete copy). Where there is no affirmative response to the above described financial statements, attach a description of changes in accounting policies and practices adopted.)

2. The cost report was prepared by the provider's independent accountant. If "yes," attach a copy of the accountant's compilation report.

B. Provider Organization and Operation

1. The provider has

a. Changed ownership
If "yes," submit name of new owner and date of change.
b. Terminated participation
If "yes," list date of termination.

2. There have been significant changes in management personnel during the cost reporting period.
If "yes," attach list of names and positions.

3. The provider's organizational chart has changed.
If "yes," submit copy and date of change.

4. The provider, members of the board of directors, officers, medical staff or key employees are associated in the following business transactions.

a. Involved with related organizations, management contracts and services under arrangements as owners (stockholders), management, by family relationship, or any other similar type relationship.

b. Employees of major suppliers of the provider (drug, medical supply companies, etc.)

C. Capital Related Cost

1. Assets have been relifed for Medicare purposes.
If "yes," attach list showing classes of assets.

2. Due to appraisals made during this cost reporting period, changes have occurred to depreciation expense.
If "yes," attach copy of Appraisal Report and Appraisal Summary by class of asset.

3. New leases and/or amendments to existing leases for equipment or facilities costing in excess of $150,000 and/or land has been entered into during this cost reporting period.
If "yes," submit copies.

4. There have been additions to fixed assets used to provide covered services during this cost reporting period for capitalized leases.
If "yes," attach list showing classes of assets.

5. Significant assets were sold during the period.
If "yes," submit copies of the sales agreements.

	Yes	No	N/A

6. Capital related expenses have been directly assigned to cost centers in addition to those cost indicated on Worksheet A, column 2, lines 2 and 3 of Form HCFA-2552. (See HCFA Pub. 15-2, chapter 3, section A.306 for a definition of those costs normally classified as capital related costs.)

D. Interest Expense

New loan or mortgage agreements were entered into during the cost reporting period.
If "yes," submit copies of loan documents for significant borrowing.

E. Insurance

Changes in insurance arrangements have occurred for the following types of coverage:

1. Malpractice
2. Comprehensive General Liability
3. Unemployment Compensation
4. Workmen's Compensation

If "yes," submit policies, agreements or contracts which reflect these arrangements and subsequent addendums.

F. Deferred Compensation and Pension

1. A new plan has been instituted.
   If "yes," submit plan.

2. There has been a change to the existing plan.
   If "yes," attach description or submit addendums.

3. The liability for payments to the Pension Plan was liquidated within the time frame established in HCFA Pub. 15-1, section 2142.6.

   If "no," attach explanation including date liquidated and amount involved.

G. Educational Activities

1. Costs were claimed for educational activities.
   If "yes," attach list.

2. Approvals and/or renewals were obtained during this cost reporting period.
   If "yes," submit copies.

3. Educational cost has been directly assigned to cost centers in addition to those costs indicated in Intern-Resident services in an approved and/or nonapproved teaching program on Worksheet A, Form HCFA-2552.
   If "yes," submit appropriate workpapers indicating to which cost centers assigned and the amounts.

H. Nonpaid Workers

Current agreements with the organization of nonpaid workers and/or changes to those agreements have been submitted.
If "no," submit copies.

	Yes	No	N/A

I. Cost to Related Organizations

All amounts in the cost report for services rendered by related organizations have been reduced to cost to that related organization. If "no," attach explanation as to why the services were not reduced to cost.

J. Purchased Services

1. Management, administrative and/or patient care services are furnished through contractual arrangements with suppliers of services. If "yes," attach a list of services purchased.

2. There have been changes in purchased services, contracts or new contracts entered into during the period. If "yes," submit copies of changes or contracts, or where there are not written agreements, attach description.

3. The requirements of HCFA Pub. 15-1, section 2135.2 were applied pertaining to competitive bidding. If "no," attach explanation.

4. All nonphysician services provided to inpatients are paid as hospital services (see "Note" to instructions for further clarification). If "no," submit copy of the waiver excluding this requirement.

K. Provider-Based Physicians

1. Services are furnished at the provider facility under an arrangement with provider-based physicians. If "yes," submit completed provider-based physician questionnaire.

2. The provider has entered into new agreements or amended existing agreements with provider-based physicians during this cost reporting period. If "yes," submit copies of new agreements or amendments to existing agreements and assignment authorizations.

3. The provider employees certified registered nurse anesthetists (CRNAs). If "yes," (a) number of FTEs employed 1st day of FY_____, (b) number of FTEs employed last day of FY_____.

L. Intensive Care Type Inpatient Hospital Unit

1. An intensive care type inpatient hospital unit has been established or changed during the period. If "yes," submit copy of floor plan that identifies the unit and a copy of the written policies for the unit.

2. The new or changed intensive care type inpatient hospital unit shares nursing staff with

   a. Other intensive care type inpatient hospital unit(s)

   b. Other unit(s) or area(s) furnishing different levels or types of care. If "yes," attach description.

	Yes	No	N/A

3. The new or changed intensive care type inpatient hospital unit utilizes float nurses during the same 8 hour shift.
If "yes," attach description of basis for allocating costs to the appropriate units.

M. Home Office Costs

The home office cost statement has been submitted in accordance with HCFA Pub. 15-1, section 2153.
If "no," all home office cost and equity capital should be removed from the cost report.

DEPARTMENTAL ALLOCATION OF PHYSICIAN COMPENSATION	SCHEDULE 1

PROVIDER NAME: _____

PERIOD:
FROM _____

PROVIDER NUMBER: _____

TO _____

DEPARTMENT: _____ TOTAL HOURS PER WEEK (AVERAGE) _____

Basis of Allocation: ☐ Estimate ☐ Time Study ☐ Other (describe): _____

Description   Amounts

1. Gross Salary or Other Payments .... $_____

2. Fringe Benefits .... _____

3. Deferred Compensation .... _____

4. Other Forms of Compensation (excluding office space or billing and collection services) .... _____

5. Total Compensation (lines 1 thru 4) .... $_____

6. Portion of Total Compensation Applicable to Services Furnished before October 1, 1983 .... _____

7. Portion of Total Compensation Applicable to Services Furnished after September 30, 1983 .... _____

8. Total physician hours worked during the year for the department .... _____

_____   _____
Signature-Provider Representative   Date

| PROVIDER SUMMARY PROVIDER-BASED PHYSICIANS | PROVIDER NAME_____ PROVIDER NUMBER_____ | PERIOD: FROM_____ TO_____ | | | | | SCHEDULE 2 |

DEPARTMENT	Services Furnished		Provider-Based Arrangement		Billing Methodology				Professional Component Total
					Physician, Group or Provider Bills on Form 1500 (Note)		Combined Billing on Forms HCFA 1453/1483		
	Yes	No	Yes	No	I/P	O/P	I/P	O/P	
1	2a	2b	3a	3b	4a	4b	5a	5b	6
1. General Routine Services									$
2. Anesthesiology									
3. Radiology									
4. Pathology									
5. Cardiology (EKG)									
6. Neurology (EEG)									
7. Surgery									
8. Physical Therapy									
9. Pulmonary Functions									
10. Routine O/P Services									
11. Occupational Therapy									
12. Emergency Room Services									
13. Renal Dialysis									
14. Other (Describe)									
15.									
16.									
17.									

Note: Indicate Letter Code: F = Physician; G = Group; and P = Provider for those who bill on Form HCFA 1500 and include the name and address of those designated as "group" billing on Form HCFA 1500.

| ALLOCATION OF PHYSICIAN COMPENSATION | PROVIDER NAME _____ PROVIDER NUMBER _____ | PERIOD: FROM _____ TO _____ | SCHEDULE 3 |

DEPARTMENT _____

TOTAL HOURS PER WEEK (AVERAGE) _____

NAME OF PHYSICIAN OR GROUP OF PHYSICIANS _____

BASIS OF ALLOCATION: ☐ Estimate
☐ Time Study ☐ Other (Describe) _____

PROVIDER SERVICES	Hours
	1
1. Supervision of technicians, nurses, etc.	
2. Utilization review, other committee work	
3. Administration	
4. Supervision of Interns/Residents	
5. Teaching	
6. Quality Control	
7. Autopsies	
8. Other	
9. Total (lines 1 thru 8)	
10. Medical and surgical services to individual patients	
11. Nonreimbursable activities, e.g., research (see HCFA Pub. 15-1, section 500ff)	
12. Total hours – All Activities (lines 9, 10 and 11)	
13. Professional Component Percentage (line 10, col. 3 ÷ line 12, col. 3)	%

Signature — Provider Representative _____ Date _____

Signature — Physician _____ Date _____

SCHEDULE 4

PERCENTAGE OF CHARGES   PROVIDER NAME _____   PERIOD:
PROVIDER-BASED PHYSICIANS   PROVIDER NUMBER _____   FROM _____
   TO _____

DEPARTMENT _____

Physician Name	Compensation Arrangement		Gross Department Charges for this Fiscal Period	Percentage of Charge Per Physician Agreement	Physician Remuneration (Cols. 3 x 4) (See Note)	Actual Remuneration (See Note)	Professional Component (See Schedule 3, col. 1, line 13)	Amount of Professional Component (Cols. 6 x 7)
	Fixed Variable							
1	2a	2b	3	4	5	6	7	8
			$	%	$	$	%	$

9. Do physicians have an established schedule of charges. ☐ yes ☐ no
   If "yes," and you have a separate identifiable schedule of charges, attach a copy to this schedule.
10. If there is a negative response to question 9, check which method you elect to determine the schedule of charges.
    ☐ Item by Item, or   ☐ Uniform optional percentage

Note: If the amount in column 5 differs from column 6, attach supporting schedules which reconcile the difference.

HCFA considers the compensation information to be confidential and, therefore, qualifying for exemption from disclosure under the Freedom of Information Act, and specifically under 5 U.S.C. section 552(b)(4). The compensation information also qualifies for exemption from disclosure under 5 U.S.C. section 552(b)(6) which covers "personnel and medical files and similar files, the disclosure of which would constitute a clearly unwarranted invasion of personal privacy." An individual's compensation is a personal matter, and its release would be an invasion of privacy. Accordingly, HCFA will not release or make available to the public compensation information collected on this form.

VARIABLE COMPENSATION ARRANGEMENT PROVIDER-BASED PHYSICIANS	PROVIDER NAME _____ PROVIDER NUMBER _____	PERIOD: FROM _____ TO _____	SCHEDULE 5

DEPARTMENT _____

NAME OF PHYSICIAN _____

Description of Service or Procedure	Number of Services or Procedures	Charges for each Service or Procedure	Gross Departmental Charges (Cols. 2 x 3)	Percentage of Charge Per Physician Agreement	Physician Remuneration (Cols. 4 x 5)
1	2	3	4	5	6
		$	$	%	$
TOTAL			$	%	$

*See Instructions for Calculation

HCFA considers the compensation information to be confidential and, therefore, qualifying for exemption from disclosure under the Freedom of Information Act, and specifically under 5 U.S.C. section 552(b)(4). The compensation information also qualifies for exemption from disclosure under 5 U.S.C. section 552(b)(6) which covers "personnel and medical files and similar files, the disclosure of which would constitute a clearly unwarranted invasion of personal privacy." An individual's compensation is a personal matter, and its release would be an invasion of privacy. Accordingly, HCFA will not release or make available to the public compensation information collected on this form.

EMERGENCY ROOM SERVICES — GUARANTEED STANDBY FEES PROVIDER-BASED PHYSICIANS	PROVIDER NAME _____ PROVIDER NUMBER _____	PERIOD: FROM _____ TO _____	SCHEDULE 6						

Physician Name	Gross Charges Billable by or on Behalf of Emergency Room Physicians			Contract Guarantee (See Note)		Unmet Guaranteed Amount (Cols. 3a-2c)	Distribution of Unmet Guarantee (See Instructions)	
	Inpatient Services	Emergency Room	Total (Cols. 2a + 2b)	Amount	Hours		I/P Part A (Cols. 2a ÷ 2c x 4)	O/P Part B (Cols. 2a ÷ 2c x 4)
1	2a	2b	2c	3a	3b	4	5a	5b
	$	$	$	$		$	$	$

Total of Columns 5a and 5b must agree with adjustments reported on Schedule or Worksheet A-8 of Medicare cost report.

Indicate which lines are used to report the adjustment on Schedule or Worksheet A-8 of Medicare cost report.

Note: If inpatient in 2a is imputed amount, indicate.

HCFA considers the compensation information to be confidential and, therefore, qualifying for exemption from disclosure under the Freedom of Information Act, and specifically under 5 U.S.C. section 552(b)(4). The compensation information also qualifies for exemption from disclosure under 5 U.S.C. section 552(b)(6) which covers "personnel and medical files and similar files, the disclosure of which would constitute a clearly unwarranted invasion of personal privacy." An individual's compensation is a personal matter, and its release would be an invasion of privacy. Accordingly, HCFA will not release or make available to the public compensation information collected on this form.

COST OF SERVICES FURNISHED UNDER ARRANGEMENT PROVIDER-BASED PHYSICIAN	PROVIDER NAME _____ PROVIDER NUMBER _____	PERIOD: FROM _____ TO _____			SCHEDULE 7	
Service	Name and Address of Facility Furnishing Service (Physician Name)	Indicate if the Provider Pays Facility Furnishing the Service		Total Cost Incurred	Amount Applicable to Physician Professional Component	HCFA Billing Form Used for Physician Professional Component
		Yes	No			
1	2	3	4	5	6	7
Radiology				$	$	
Pathology						
Cardiology (EKG)						
Neurology (EEG)						
Other						
TOTAL					$	

HCFA considers the compensation information to be confidential and, therefore, qualifying for exemption from disclosure under the Freedom of Information Act, and specifically under 5 U.S.C. section 552(b)(4). The compensation information also qualifies for exemption from disclosure under 5 U.S.C. section 552(b)(6) which covers "personnel and medical files and similar files, the disclosure of which would constitute a clearly unwarranted invasion of personal privacy." An individual's compensation is a personal matter, and its release would be an invasion of privacy. Accordingly, HCFA will not release or make available to the public compensation information collected on this form.

TEACHING AMENDMENTS —
HOSPITALS ONLY
PROVIDER-BASED PHYSICIANS

PROVIDER NAME
PROVIDER NUMBER

PERIOD:
FROM
TO

SCHEDULE 8

DEPARTMENT

Type of Payment:
☐ Rendered by Medical School or ☐ Paid by Hospital ☐ Related Organization

Physician Name 1	Basic Compensation 2	Fringe Benefits 3	Gross Remuneration (Cols. 2 & 3) 4	Professional Compon. (See Note 1) 5	Total Amount of Professional Component (Cols. 4 x 5) 6
	$	$	$	%	$ $
TOTAL	$	$	$		$

NOTE 1: Add hours in Schedule 3, line 10, column 1, and line 4, column 1. Divide total hours on Schedule 3, line 12, column 1.

HCFA considers the compensation information to be confidential and, therefore, qualifying for exemption from disclosure under the Freedom of Information Act, and specifically under 5 U.S.C. section 552(b)(4). The compensation information also qualifies for exemption from disclosure under 5 U.S.C. section 552(b)(6) which covers "personnel and medical files and similar files, the disclosure of which would constitute a clearly unwarranted invasion of personal privacy." An individual's compensation is a personal matter, and its release would be an invasion of privacy. Accordingly, HCFA will not release or make available to the public compensation information collected on this form.

Chapter 3

Legal Concerns in Community-Based Nursing Practice

Virginia C. Haggerty

Everything you ever learned about legal problems as they affect nurses and nursing is appropriate in a discussion of community-based nursing practice. Because of the special circumstances in which home health nurses work, some of those basic concepts take on new importance.

SCOPE OF PRACTICE

Whether a nurse, prepared at the basic entry level, can provide specific nursing services in the home is a matter of statutory definition in each state. Look to the practice act in your state, and become familiar with your state's definition of nursing and any specific requirements or limitations.

In general, the practice acts of most states provide that registered nurses may perform acts of care, comfort, and counseling to the sick, injured, or infirm.[1] Or, in the more modern statutes, they may perform acts requiring substantial skill and judgment, based on principles of applied physiological, psychological, and behaviorial sciences.[2]

In almost all statutes some reference is made to the educational base that establishes the foundation for the practice of nursing. Typical phrases include "based upon educational preparation and experience, the nurse may . . . "[3] or, on other statutes, the registered nurse is accountable for making decisions based upon his or her educational preparation and experience.[4] Clearly, therefore, the practice of nursing includes the performance of acts taught in the basic educational preparation of the nurse and other acts that are derived from principles learned through that educational preparation. If it were otherwise, nurses would all be frozen in time, competent only to practice at the level of expertise they attained when they graduated from their nursing programs. As the educational base for the practice of nursing expands, so also does the actual performance of nursing activities.

83

No statutory restrictions are placed on where the nurse may practice his or her profession. If an activity is lawfully within the scope of practice, the nurse may perform that activity in any location within the state jurisdiction. If a nurse can lawfully perform the activity in the hospital, a nurse can perform the same activity in the home. Because the decision whether to perform or not to perform a nursing activity is within the professional discretion of the nurse, such activities are commonly referred to as independent nursing functions.

INDEPENDENT VS. INTERDEPENDENT ROLES

In addition to the independent performance of nursing activities, most statutes also recognize a dependent role of the registered nurse and the licensed practical nurse. This is most clearly seen in the provisions that enable nurses to administer medications and treatments as ordered by someone authorized, under the laws of the state, to prescribe. Since the performance of the act of administration is contingent on the prescription or order of another, this role has historically been viewed as being dependent. The individual with prescriptive authority observes and assesses the status of the client and then makes a judgment on the medication of choice for the particular condition, taking into account the condition of the client.

In home health nursing, however, even this traditionally dependent role is modified. Here the assessment and evaluation of the client's condition is done in the field, by the nurse. Information regarding the client's condition is transmitted to the individual with prescriptive authority, and the prescriber, relying on the accuracy and completeness of the evaluation, issues prescriptions. Clearly the role of the nurse in this situation takes on a different character. No longer a passive receiver of orders, the nurse becomes an active participant in the process, supplying crucial information to the decision maker. In this "interdependent" role the responsibilities and potential liabilities of the nurse increase.

In many community nursing settings nurses are expanding their role to include functions previously held to be the exclusive province of physicians. In some states the expanded practice of nurses is sanctioned by specific statutory language and regulation of "nurse practitioners." In other states a broad interpretation of the definition of nursing has given legal sanction to the expanded role.

While the controversy continues to rage within the nursing profession as to the preferred mechanism for recognizing advanced practice, it is important that every nurse in home health nursing practice be aware of the state practice act and the interpretations of the individual Board of Nursing.

In Missouri, registered nurses who were taking histories, performing breast and pelvic examinations, conducting laboratory testing of Pap smears and gonococcus (GC) cultures and serologies, and providing and informing patients about oral contraceptives, condoms, and intrauterine devices were cited by the State Board of Registration for the Healing Arts (Medical Board) for the unauthorized practice of medicine. The Supreme Court of Missouri, finding for the nurses, stated that, under the broad definition of nursing in the law, "a nurse may be permitted to assume responsibilities heretofore not considered to be within the field of professional nursing so long as those responsibilities are consistent with her or his 'specialized education, judgment and skill based on knowledge and application of principles derived from the biological, physical, social and nursing sciences.'" The result of the *Sermchief v. Gonzales, et al.*[5] case would appear to give support for maintaining broad all-inclusive language in the statutory definition of nursing rather than the more narrow identification of specific functions. Home health care nurses in states with similar broad statutory language in the definition of nursing can feel comfortable in performing such activities within the scope of their practice. In states that separately identify advanced level nursing practice and identify advanced level functioning as including some activities routinely performed by home health care nurses, the nurse must determine whether the activities so identified are exclusive to advanced level nursing practice or are merely permissive.

LIABILITY OF HOME CARE PROVIDERS

One of the questions most frequently asked by nurses is whether they will be liable under certain circumstances. "If I teach the wife how to administer the insulin and she gives the wrong dose, am I liable?" "If the patient refuses to change the dressing using sterile technique and gets an infection, can I be sued?" "Can I lose my license?"

Such questions reveal a basic lack of understanding of the differences between liability to administrative agencies for deviations from the legal parameters governing nursing practice and civil liability to individuals injured as a result of the professional's negligence. Under the first concept a nurse may lose his or her license to practice nursing after a finding by a administrative agency, usually the Board of Nursing, that the nurse is practicing in violation of the statutory grounds for discipline in the nurse practice act. Grounds commonly found in most practice acts include fraud or deceit in obtaining a license, the habitual use of alcohol or drugs so as to render the practitioner incompetent, or conviction of a felony relating to the practice of nursing. In most states disciplinary violations of the practice act can result in suspension, probation, or revocation of the nurse's license.

Civil liability, on the other hand, occurs when an individual or his or her family has been damaged by the negligent action of the health professional. In such a case the individual initiates a malpractice action or suit against the nurse and the employer.

In any action for negligence the burden of proof lies with the injured party. The four essential elements to any action for negligence are duty, standard, breech, and injury. To be successful in a suit, the client must show

- that a particular relationship existed between the agency or nurse and the client that gave rise to obligations being owed between the parties;
- that the obligations included the responsibility of the agency or nurse to perform according to an established standard of care;
- that the agency or nurse did not perform according to that established standard of care;
- that as a result of the failure to perform according to the standard of care, an injury resulted to the client; and
- that the injury was reasonably foreseeable.

Let's examine the essential elements in more detail.

Duty

It must be shown that a duty exists between the parties, that an obligation is owed from one to the other. Duties classically arise from the operation of law or from the existence of legally recognized relationships. Clearly, when a home health agency accepts a client on its case rolls and is seeing that patient on a regular basis, there is an obligation owed from the agency to the client. It is less clear when an individual actually becomes a client of the agency. Is it when the referral is received? When the agency agrees to send a nurse to the home? When the admitting nurse develops the plan of care, or when the attending physician actually signs the plan of care?

In most instances it is a question of fact as to whether an obligation has arisen between the parties. Determining elements may include length of contact, what was said or not said at the time, and the mutual understanding of the parties. For these reasons it is advisable that a home health agency adopt policy and procedure that would allow the agency to make provisional visits before accepting the patient. The referring physician, the patient, and the family should be advised that the agency will be glad to evaluate the patient's condition, the environment, and the family situation in order to determine whether the agency will be able to provide the services requested. Once the agency has accepted the patient as a client, it has exposed itself to liability.

Standard

The standard of performance required is universally the same: what a reasonably prudent similar health care provider would do under the same or similar circumstances. So deceptively simple, yet so difficult to understand. The standard does not require that the performance of the nurse be "correct" or "right," rather that the nursing actions be ones that similarly educated individuals in similar circumstances would be likely to do. It is not what the best of us would do, but what we would expect of ourselves or our colleagues. A reasonably prudent individual, in making decisions and taking actions, assesses the circumstances, understands the consequences that are likely to flow from different courses of action, and embarks on a specific course of action. A reasonably prudent nurse does not make impulsive decisions, but rather rational ones. It may happen that the patient sustains injury as a result of the rational course of action that has been identified. This is not, in itself, a deviation from the standard of care.

Breech

A breech of the standard of care occurs when the nurse deviates from what a reasonably prudent nurse would do in the same circumstances. He or she may act impulsively or carelessly, without thought as to the consequences of the action. Or thoughtful of the consequences, the nurse may still do what others reasonably would not do. It is not necessary that the nurse perform an affirmative action to breech the standard of care. Frequently it is the *failure* of the nurse to do what others would do that establishes the breech in care. Typical situations that give rise to liability include the failure of the nurse to observe the patient's condition adequately, failure of the nurse to report changes in the patient's condition to the physician promptly, and failure of the nurse to supervise ancillary personnel adequately.

Injury

Injury is the most crucial of the elements, but the one most overlooked by nurses. The patient must suffer some injury, some damage, as a result of the nurse's breech of the standard of performance. It is not enough that the patient is injured; the injury must result from the nurse's action or lack of action.

In many common situations the actions of the nurse may fall below the accepted standard of care. Short staffing and excessive case loads may cause the nurse to take shortcuts that are not consistent with good practice. Although these situations create a *potential* liability for the nurse, no liability will attach unless the patient sustains an actual injury because of the nurse's action or lack of action.

RESPONDEAT SUPERIOR

In the majority of home health care situations, when the actions of the nurse or other health care professional give rise to a cause of action for malpractice, the patient will initiate a suit against the employing agency rather than solely against the individual nurse. It is common in most jurisdictions to also include the nurse and all others who are potentially involved in the incident as named defendants. The legal theory involved is that the employing agency as "master" is responsible at law for the wrongful actions of its agents. Any negligent act committed by the employee in the course of his or her duties is imputed to the employer as if it were committed by the employer. For this reason many agencies inform their employees that they are covered by the agency insurance for malpractice claims.

Generally, this is true. The agency's policy will insure against claims arising out of the negligent actions of an agency employee as long as the employee is acting within the scope of his or her duties as an employee. Other restrictions may apply. For this reason it is important for home health care providers to determine the scope of the agency's insurance protection. Nurses should determine whether the agency policy covers them for acts performed outside of scheduled working hours and for incidental acts or "favors" done for members of the patient's family.

CORPORATE RESPONSIBILITY

In some instances agencies do not employ health professionals, but rather contract with them as independent contractors in order to limit the extent of the agency's liability for the actions of the health professional. Even so, the agency may still be found to be responsible to exert a sufficient amount of judgment in the selection of the independent contractor and supervision of the care provided to ensure that the agency is fulfilling its responsibility to provide safe and competent services.

DELEGATION OF NURSING FUNCTIONS: LIABILITY FOR THE ACTIONS OF OTHERS

The nurse, in providing home health nursing services, frequently makes use of others in the actual performance of tasks. A clear distinction should be drawn between the nurse's liability for the supervision of ancillary workers and the liability that may occur from the actions of family members whom the nurse has taught to perform nursing procedures. First let us consider ancillary workers. Many agencies make use of nursing assistants and licensed practical nurses (LPNs). Both of these types of worker are intended to assist the nurse in the provision of care. The registered nurse directing the care is responsible for the safety and competency of the care provided by LPNs and nursing assistants. Home health care nurses ask how they can adequately supervise and be liable for the actions of others when they are not in the home at the time the services are provided. This is a real problem. Nursing assistants, as unlicensed personnel, are authorized to *assist the nurse* in the performance of nursing functions. It seems clear that they can assist the nurse only when they are both physically present in the same home at the same time. Certainly this does not mean that the nurse must be present when the aide is assisting the patient with bathing or other hygenic measures; the direct supervision of the nurse is required only when the activity being performed is one that requires the skill and judgment of a registered nurse.

The same holds true for LPNs. Even though they are licensed health care workers, they are required by state statute to perform nursing activities under the direction of a registered nurse. The LPN is not educated or licensed to make patient assessments and clinical judgments of a patient's condition; rather, the role of the LPN is to report specific observations to the nurse. If an agency chooses to employ LPNs for these specific tasks, it should also be aware of the registered nurse's responsibility for direct supervision in the field.

Family members present an entirely different question. All state nurse practice acts allow an exception for family members providing nursing care for the sick. In most cases the goal of home health nursing is to transfer the responsibility for care to the patient, the family, or another individual. The nurse's role becomes one of teacher. Several unique problems arise in this context. Can the nurse be held liable if the family member performs the task incorrectly? If the patient's wound becomes infected because the wife did not use sterile technique, is the nurse, and ultimately the agency, liable?

The responsibility of the nurse as teacher is

- to make certain the learner has the mental and physical ability to understand and perform the procedure correctly.
- to present the information required clearly until the learner shows evidence of understanding and accepting.
- to inform the learner of the consequences of improper performance of the procedure.
- to supervise the learner in the performance of the procedure until the learner demonstrates competency in technique.

If a family member who was taught to perform a nursing activity performs the activity incorrectly and injures the patient, the nurse will not automatically be liable unless it can be shown that the nurse did not teach or supervise the individual adequately. There will continue to be instances in which family members who were taught to administer medications by injection do so incorrectly and the patient sustains nerve injury. The nurse and agency can limit their liability in such cases by having a clearly defined teaching plan, by making sure that the patient and family have a written procedure that includes the consequences of using improper techniques, and by testing the individual who will be responsible for the procedure after the training is complete. Copies of these documents should be incorporated into the patient's record.

EXPANDING TECHNOLOGY

Recent changes in reimbursement policies have increased the move toward early discharge of patients who require high-intensity nursing care. Rarely does a week go by that a home health agency is not confronted with deciding whether a new procedure can be performed safely in the home. Cancer chemotherapy, platelet infusions, morphine drips, all once exclusively inpatient care, have now moved into the home or community-based clinic. To date, most of the decisions as to the appropriateness of the procedure to home care have been made on a case-by-case basis, more often than not in consideration of the fiscal intermediaries' payment policies and a superficial evaluation by the corporation's counsel as to the agency's liability "in case something goes wrong." There is a more rational approach to making these decisions, one that will provide the agency much more protection from liability.

The initial evaluation as to whether a specific procedure can be performed appropriately in the home should be made by a committee of the medical and nursing staff set up for the purpose of reviewing new procedures. This joint committee should evaluate the procedure by asking specific questions, such as:

- What is the nature of the procedure?
- What are the expected results of the procedure?
- What untoward results are reasonably foreseeable?
- What are the known risks or hazards inherent in the procedure?
- What equipment or supplies are available in the home to counteract the potential injury?

- Will the known risks lead to irreversible injury to the client?

- If the potential injury is irreversible, is it life threatening?

The critical element in this initial review is the evaluation of the risk of harm to the client as a result of the procedure. A realistic appraisal should be done. Certainly, every procedure done in the home has a potential for harm to the client. A routine injection may precipitate an anaphylactic reaction or, given incorrectly, may cause paralysis. The committee should brainstorm to identify each possible harm that could befall the client if the procedure were performed first correctly and then, in the alternative, incorrectly.

After having identified all the possible problems, the committee should attempt to identify the *probability* of such results. Again, the committee should consider all possible circumstances that would affect the probability of the event occurring. Balancing these factors—the nature of the risk and the possibility and probability of it occurring—the committee can make reasoned decisions as to whether it is appropriate to perform certain procedures in the home.

An example having to do with the intravenous infusion of fluid and medication may help to clarify the process. Here the nature of the procedure is fairly routine. Intravenous therapy has been part of home care for some time. Recognized risks include infiltration, tissue damage, blood clot formation, and irregular rate of flow, causing congestive failure. All of these risks are irreversible, but only two (blood clot formation and congestive failure) have a potential for being life threatening. In both instances well-accepted methods may be instituted to limit the probability or likelihood of the event occurring. With proper equipment, instruction of the family, and monitoring by health care professionals, the risks can be reduced to minimal. Because the benefits of intravenous therapy in the home substantially outweigh the minimal risks, the procedure may be determined to be safe to be performed in the home.

In summary, a procedure may be considered safe to be performed in the home unless there is a reasonable risk of irreversible injury to the patient as a consequence of the action.

Having decided that the procedure itself is safe to be done in the home, the home health agency must now decide whether it wants to include that procedure in the services it renders. Here the administration of the agency needs to look at the cost of providing the service versus the recoverable billing.

To determine the cost of providing the service, the administrator should ask:

- Are the current personnel competent to perform this procedure?
- Will additional training be required to assure that personnel can perform the procedure safely?
- Will additional personnel be required to perform the procedure?
- Will additional safety equipment be required to be present when the procedure is performed?
- Will the existing insurance protection cover incidents resulting from the performance of the procedure?
- What would be the negative impact of *not* providing the service?

It is important to stress that the decision to include a procedure previously not performed by the agency in the list of services provided is twofold: whether the procedure is safe to be performed in the home and whether the agency chooses to provide that service. Just because a procedure is safe to be performed in the home, does not necessitate an agency agreeing to provide that service.

In these times when patients are increasingly likely to initiate malpractice actions, it would appear to be advisable for an agency to specialize in providing specific types of services for patients, rather than attempting to provide any and all services. In this way the agency can be better ensured of the competence level of all personnel. The more diversified the services the agency seeks to provide, the more exposure to liability it accepts. This is particularly true in regard to unusual procedures that are done infrequently.

The purpose of this chapter has been to highlight the manner in which the special circumstances in which home health care nursing is practiced can alter or modify the basic principles of nursing law.

REFERENCES

1. *See, for example,* Arizona Nurse Practice Act: Arizona Rev. Stat., Ch. 32-16.

2. Arizona Rev. Stat., Ch. 32-16, California Business and Professional Code Sec. 2725, Florida Stat., Ch. 464., etc.

3. Missouri Rev. Stat., Ch. 335.

4. Florida Stat., Ch. 464.

5. Sermchief v. Gonzales, 660 SW 2nd 683.

Chapter 4

Competition in Home Health Care

William H. Boothe

In order to understand home health care today and the competitive environment in which we find it we must first understand its history. As with many, if not most, health or social services organizations, home health care evolved out of the concerns of a few individuals who took it on themselves to do something about a problem they saw in their community. Industrialization, increased mobility, and the rise of large urban centers contributed to the development of significant public health problems that demanded the attention of local citizens.

One result of these developments was a response to the problems of the poor, particularly their health problems. The Visiting Nurse Service of New York City, established in 1893 by Lillian Wald, was the first organized home health nursing service in the United States.[1] Thus the first home health care service was established as a voluntary, not-for-profit agency. By 1900, 20 such agencies had been established. With the development and use of automobiles, physicians limiting their practices to hospitals and offices, and the acceptance of home health care by the general public, visiting nurse associations grew rapidly to meet the growing need for home health care. The most significant event in the history of home health care in the United States was the passage of P.L. 89-97, Title XVII of the Social Security Act, in 1965. Known as Medicare, this legislation and the regulations that were written to implement it changed home health care in a revolutionary way.

Before Medicare the primary service offered was nursing, and the emphasis was on providing care to the chronically ill elderly, with payment coming from welfare organizations, the patient in some cases, or charitable entities, such as Community Chests. Most care was rendered by visiting nurse associations.

Medicare changed all this. It changed the payment source obviously, but in addition and for a number of reasons, Medicare changed the reason home care was provided, the means with which it was provided, and the eligibility of the patients for home care. Medicare was developed using the medical model. Its purpose was to take the place of hospitalization, and eligibility was based on the acute condition of the patient. And therefore today we know that Medicare means skilled care in which the patient is homebound, acutely ill, and under the direction of a physician.

With the entry of the federal government and its requirement that the medical model be the sole approach to home care, the stage was set for the next step in the evolution of home health care. Over the next decade and a half Medicare would contribute to the inflation in health care costs to such a degree that those costs would be placed near the top of the national political agenda. Through a series of Congressional acts the federal government tried in vain to control the costs of health care. With few exceptions all of these efforts failed.

The most recent effort directed at health care cost containment was the passage of Public Law 98-21, amendments to the Social Security Act, in 1983. This act required the federal government to change the method by which it paid hospitals for inpatient care from a cost-based, retrospective reimbursement system to a diagnostic-specific prospective payment system. The stage was set again for significant change in home health care; only this time it would involve competition for scarce resources—federal, Blue Cross and Blue Shield, commercial insurance, and private payment for services. For the first time since 1965 health care providers, especially hospitals, would be placed at financial risk, and the result would appear to be the most revolutionary change in the health care system since Medicare's establishment.

BACKGROUND

Between 1893 and 1965 the home health care market consisted almost exclusively of providing nursing visits in the home to chronically ill elderly people. And in most cases these people were poor. In 1965, with the passage of Medicare, the market changed to those over 65 who had recently been discharged from the hospital. Many agencies providing home care before 1965 chose to participate in the Medicare home health care program and became certified. These agencies were, generally speaking, visiting nurse associations or local health departments. Because Medicare was a cost-based reimbursement source, there seemed to be no incentive for proprietary or other entities to get into the Medicare home health care business. At that time there was little, if any, incentive for organizations other than those then involved to become home health providers. Market forces had not yet come into play that would provide the necessary incentives to encourage involvement in the home care market. Most organizations providing home health care of that day were more interested in the "need" for home health care than the demand for it and in providing a service whether or not it would be paid for. In 1966, the first year after the Medicare program went into effect, there were just over 1,000 certified home health agencies. Approximately 90 percent of these agencies were either visiting nurse associations (VNAs) or local health departments (see Figure 4–1).

In the next ten years the number of certified home health agencies doubled and the proportion of VNAs and health department-sponsored agencies dropped to 75 percent. Before 1982 Medicare regulations would not allow a proprietary entity to participate in the home health care program unless it was in a state that allowed it through the licensure process. As a result, an entity known as a private not-for-profit home health agency came into existence.

Figure 4–1 Certified Home Health Agencies—1968-1983

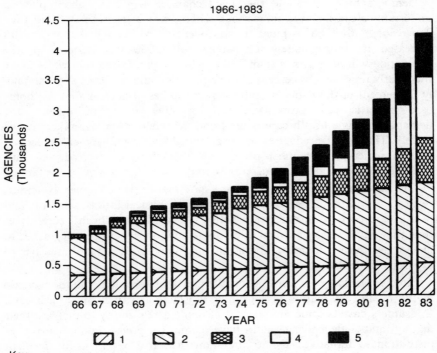

Key:
1–Visiting Nurse Associations
2–Combination and Official
3–Hospital, Rehabilitation, and Skilled
   Nursing Facilities
4–Proprietary
5–Private and Nonprofit and Others

Source: National Association for Home Care, 1983.

Today market forces exist that were not considered several years ago, or at least are more clearly recognized now. These include cost containment, demographic considerations, consumer awareness, patient satisfaction, and technological developments. These factors are combining together now in such a way as to force the health care community to respond to changes in the way it has operated for the past one hundred years.

Perhaps the most significant factor affecting development of the home care market is the current focus on health care cost containment. With the inception of prospective reimbursement for inpatient care for hospitals, a number of significant changes have been brought about. As a result, hospitals are facing declining revenue from inpatient stays and are looking for ways to maintain the revenue they currently have as well as to generate new sources of revenue. With this incentive, hospitals are diversifying into previously unexplored services, including home health care.

Demographic factors and the social changes they bring about play an important role in the development of the home care market. In 1900 less than 2 percent of the U.S. population was over age 65. Today that figure has increased to approximately 12 percent. By 2030 this segment of the population will have grown to more than 20 percent. Given that while today the elderly represent 12 percent of the population and consume approximately 30 percent of the nation's health care resources, it is clear that the home care market is due to grow significantly. Another factor that influences the demand for home health care is the trend for reduction in caretakers in the society. Through the reduction in the extended family and women's changing role in society, the number of caretakers is likely to be reduced, thus increasing the demand for someone else to perform these tasks for the family.

The third factor affecting the home care market is consumer awareness regarding such things as preventive medicine, physical fitness, self-care, and health care costs. Consumers are better informed about health care issues than they have ever been. In addition, more and more they are being asked to pay for health care directly and thus are more concerned about alternatives to expensive inpatient care.

Closely related to the third factor, the fourth factor impacting the increase in the home care market is consumer satisfaction with home health care. Consumers have become more aware of home care's ability to increase their dignity and independence and have come to prefer home care over institutional alternatives. Home care allows a degree of patient involvement in personal care that is not found in institutions, and consumers prefer this approach to more traditional health care.

Technological advances have greatly influenced the development of home care and will continue to do so. Health problems that yesterday could only be treated in the hospital can now be dealt with effectively in the home. This technology allows cost-saving, effective, safe, and easily provided care of a sophisticated nature. These advances, as well as advances in communications, will allow the elderly and others to remain at home by themselves. Such advancements have also introduced the "high-tech" provider, who specializes in those services requiring sophisticated technology. Many high-tech providers have been developed by durable medical equipment companies, pharmaceutical firms, and consumer health product companies.

When these factors and others of lesser significance are combined, the result is a dramatically expanding market for home care services and products, many of which did not exist even a few years ago. It is clear that these developments have encouraged the private sector, including proprietary interests, to enter the home care market in large numbers. It is also clear that, with a few exceptions, home care is moving from a cottage industry with a few suppliers to a sophisticated market involving large diversified businesses made up of manufacturers, distributors, and providers.

THE MARKET

In the past the home health care market was seen as the acutely ill person over age 65 needing skilled nursing care. In other words the market was defined as the Medicare patient. Today the market is much broader in terms of targets, products, services, and competitors. At best the market for home care can be characterized as highly fragmented and dynamic. It can also be characterized as one with tremendous opportunity for those who are willing and in a position to take advantage of the market.

The home health care market can no longer be considered limited to Medicare patients. In fact, because the market has expanded to the degree that it has, the term for the market is now "home care" rather than "home health care."

The home care market can now be divided into two major branches. The branch most familiar to home health nurses is the medical home care market, which can be further divided into a services segment and a supplies and equipment segment. Included in the services segment are

- the traditional medical home health services, including Medicare intermittent skilled nursing

- support services, such as companion, sitter, respite, and reassurance services. The latter are now more frequently provided on a private-pay basis and are affiliated with another home care entity.

- high-tech services, such as total parenteral nutrition and related services

- nonmedical services, such as claims processing, data processing, equipment repair, and other business-oriented services that many organizations are using in an attempt to diversify both services and revenue.

The equipment segment includes such areas as home oxygen, respiratory therapy, intravenous nutrition solutions, durable medical equipment, and home dialysis. A number of home health agencies have expanded their business ventures to provide the supplies and equipment that are associated with the services they deliver or have entered into joint ventures with existing suppliers that will generate revenue for the home health agency.

The other major branch of the home care market has to do with self-care, diagnosis, and prevention. This branch is also broken down further into the services segment and the equipment segment. The services side of this market is characterized by such things as health promotion, including exercises and stop-smoking clinics; self-improvement efforts; assistance with daily living, including homemaking and home maintenance; and personnel counseling.

The equipment portion includes self-diagnosis and screening products, self-treatment products, preventive products (such as vitamin supplements), exercise equipment, and supportive and security-oriented communication equipment.

Louden & Company estimates the size of the current home care market to be between $2.5 and $5.7 billion. By 1990 it estimates that the market will have grown to between $8 and $19 billion. This represents a growth of between 13 and 17 percent. With this amount of money involved it is not difficult to understand why the large number and variety of organizations have decided to enter the home care market. As the home care market has become more attractive, more suppliers have entered the market and more competition has taken place among those suppliers.[2]

The variety of competitors in the home care market matches the variety of products and services that make up the market. Much of the efforts of these competitors are directed toward capturing one segment of the market in order to provide it with another product that that particular customer would use. In some cases this is the only reason the provider becomes involved in home care at all. Thus, through diversification into home care, the hospital can attempt to ensure that the patient returns to that hospital for other services, including inpatient care. Other providers choose to offer home care in an effort to promote the use of some other products or services they currently sell.

THE COMPETITORS

The competitors in the home care market can be viewed in the same format as the products they sell. Within the medical home care market there are providers that compete for services and products. Those competing for services include hospitals, visiting nurse associations, public agencies, nursing homes, private agencies, private not-for-profit agencies, and major health care corporations (chains). Those competing in the product segment include durable medical equipment manufacturers and suppliers, home care retail centers (both independent and chain), pharmacies, major consumer product companies, and mail order houses. This segment also includes such major American corporations as Sears and J. C. Penney.

The wellness side of the market is represented by such groups as hospitals, physicians, public agencies, physical fitness centers, and the same groups involved in the medical home care market.

Perhaps the most interesting aspect of the new competition is that those groups who, in the past, have cooperated in providing home care and other health services are now competing with one another. This may be misleading, however. The "new" competition, like politics, is creating some rather strange bedfellows. In addition, a number of groups that have previously not provided home care services are now entering the market in aggressive ways. In 1965 it was difficult to find organizations that were interested in providing home health care services; now it is difficult to find a major American or international corporation that is not interested in the home care market.

Since its inception in 1965, Medicare has spawned a large number and variety of home health care providers. As Figure 4–1 shows, the volume and variety of certified home health care providers have changed significantly since the 1960s. These changes have been brought about by changes in the regulations governing the Medicare program and, more important, by changes occurring in the marketplace of home care.

The two major agencies involved in home care in 1966 were the visiting nurse associations and local health departments. Between 1966 and 1983 these two certified provider groups, while growing, diminished in proportion to the growth in other agencies. As shown in Figure 4–1, the fastest-growing certified home health care agency, at least in terms of the number of agencies certified, are proprietary, hospital-based, and private not-for-profit, respectively. Again, these changes are occurring because of fundamental changes that are taking place in the health care environment based on the factors discussed earlier.

THE RESPONSE

A major restructuring of the health care industry is taking place because of the factors now operating in the health care environment. This restructuring, as it affects the major providers of health care—hospitals and physicians—is affecting, in turn, home care providers.[3] What this means is that those providers that have been around since 1893, or even 1966, must develop successful strategic responses to the current environment or perish. Providers that wish to survive must be in a position to compete with those they cooperated with in years past as well as those that came to the community last week. Providers wishing to survive must also be willing and in a position to develop alliances, ventures, agreements, and other formalized efforts with other providers and organizations in ways that are unfamiliar and untested.

The basic issue that has brought about this restructuring is the fact that hospitals and, to some degree, physicians are becoming more and more at financial risk. Before prospective payment, hospitals and physicians faced no significant risk of economic failure. With prospective payment, every provider faces economic risk for the decisions it makes and the manner in which its organization operates.

The new health care industry will be characterized by the entry of large numbers of new providers, including the entry of nontraditional providers in nontraditional settings; further diversification of products and services will mean further fragmentation of the market. At the same time more alliances and systems will be built among existing providers in an effort to develop effective competitive positions. Physician practice patterns will change as the result of reimbursement incentives and the predicted oversupply of physicians. Alternative delivery systems, such as health maintenance organizations and preferred-provider organizations, will continue to expand and compete with traditional providers. The pressure for price competition and efficiency will see the continued growth in investor-owned health care companies.

Traditional home health care agencies in general are ill prepared to compete in the marketplace and must develop strategic responses to the threats that exist in the environment. Most agencies are ill prepared because they have never had to compete before and because the current management is not trained to compete.

If a home health agency is to compete successfully, it must develop a set of strategic responses similar to those adopted by other providers in the health industry. These responses fall into one of five general areas.

1. The most important response is to develop or acquire the management talent capable of carrying out the competitive strategy. This includes management talent in operations, marketing, finance, and other areas. Most important, this involves an open acceptance of the change in philosophy that

such management would bring to the organization. It is one thing to give lip service to wanting an organization run like a business and quite another to accept to the degree required the full reality of this decision. Such a level of change may be unacceptable to some organizations. The alternative, however, may be extinction. Because of their size and revenue base, many home health agencies are not in a position financially to acquire the necessary management talent.

2. Clearly a part of the first strategy is in fact a redefinition of the organization's business. If the home health agency is a voluntary not-for-profit agency, it is likely to define its business in terms of the provision of service to the poor or those with low income. Such a focused definition of one's business is inappropriate to meet the challenges of the competitive marketplace. However, if the organization comes to the realization that this mission will have to be abandoned because of the inability to compete, it is likely to develop a helpful definition of its business. These organizations must develop an understanding that in order to do good they must do well. It is no longer sufficient to hope that because what you do is a community service, you do not have to deal with the reality of the environment.

3. The third strategy is to develop an organization that is responsive to the marketplace. Although most home health agencies have had no competition until recently, they also have not had a market or consumer orientation. Many agencies have operated under the professional assumption that they know what is best for the patient (customer). Such an approach is not likely to work in the future. In addition, the organization must develop and use a marketing orientation and marketing technology. It must define its products, market segments, and market strategies. And it must devote significant resources to this function.

4. The organization must develop new relationships and new partnerships. It must be in a position to take advantage of joint ventures with a wide variety of other organizations in an effort to develop or stabilize new and existing markets. Such joint ventures would address the goal of increasing the agency's market share and acquiring the necessary capital for expansion. Such ventures can be carried out with physicians, hospitals, medical suppliers, payors, other home health agencies, and other organizations.

5. Another strategy is to diversify into other services and products. This can be done either in a joint venture, as noted earlier, or alone. Most home health agencies provide a limited product line, which, in most cases, is reimbursed at cost. Home health agencies must become as creative as other health care organizations in the development of new ways to generate revenue and capture markets. Most home health agencies have a number of strengths and resources that can be developed into revenue-producing ventures.

However, it does require management talent, capital, and an entrepreneurial approach.

When taken together, what these five factors mean is that the home health agency must develop a strategic plan that addresses the individual situation of the particular home health agency. Such a plan addresses the threats and opportunities in the environment and evaluates the strengths and weaknesses of the organization relative to that environment. The end product is a plan that presents realistic alternatives to pursue toward the survival and growth of that home health agency.

SUMMARY

Agencies that provided home health care before 1980 are not in an enviable position. The changing environment that the health care industry currently finds itself in and for the foreseeable future has caused home health care to be a market that many providers desire to enter. Since the early 1980s home care has attracted providers that just a few years before would not have dreamed of becoming home care providers. And those traditional providers of home care, such as visiting nurse associations, local health departments, and other free-standing not-for-profits, now face the challenge of their lives in order to survive.

Most of these agencies are not asking themselves whether or not they should survive, but rather what steps can they take to ensure survival. In some cases agencies must answer the question, Are we prepared to do those things that are necessary in order to survive, or will we become so changed in the process of surviving that our mission is overcompromised? In other cases the agency will not have the resources to compete because of size or location or market circumstance. In still others the organization will merge with its competitor and, in the process, lose its identity and perhaps the thrust of its mission. And finally, some home care agencies will go out of business.

The theory of the survival of the fittest may operate in nature and in the "real" business world, but a question remains about the value of those agencies, as well as the services they provide, that have provided home care long before it became profitable. Although change is clearly inevitable, judgment about the value of that change in this case may have to wait for a long time.

Those who have been involved in home health care since the 1970s are likely to judge what is happening in terms of good or bad. Although this is perhaps a natural response, if they do not move beyond this reaction and go on to a clearer understanding that they must adapt to the new environment, what they have worked for during that time will truly go out of existence.

NOTES

1. Mary O'Neil Mundinger, *Home Care Controversy: Too Little Too Late, Too Costly* (Rockville, Md.: Aspen Systems Corporation, 1983).

2. Teri Louden, "Opportunities on the Rise in Home Health Care," *Caring*, Vol. III, No. 7, July 1984, pp 12-14.

3. David J. Tanner, "Assessing Hospital Entry into Home Care," *Caring*, Vol. III, No. 7, July 1984, pp 41-48.

Chapter 5

Employee Issues

Nancy Wickens

There are an estimated 15,000[1] home health care organizations in the United States. These providers bring to the client's home a variety of services: skilled nursing, medical/social services, personal care, and companion services. The thousands of persons providing these services to the client represent a broad spectrum of employees and volunteers, from the well-educated and highly skilled to the unskilled with minimal education. Many are employed on a part-time basis to provide services to the ill or disabled at home; others are working on a full-time basis within a well-defined structure, such as a certified home health agency.[2]

The home setting as a place of employment is the choice of many health care workers, both skilled and unskilled. They like the challenge of working in the client's home. Care can be individualized and given within a holistic framework. There is satisfaction in seeing a client return to health and resume full function within the family or life style structure. Caregivers enjoy their independence; there is the freedom in the home to adjust work schedules to meet client and employee needs. There is opportunity to apply one's skills in creative and adaptive ways. Many skilled professionals, aides, companions, and ancillary health care staff regard their work in the client's home as a privilege and an opportunity.

ROLE OF THE HOME CARE SUPERVISOR

The key to the proper functioning of the home health care delivery system is the first-line supervisor. The home care supervisor, or clinical supervisor, is responsible for assessing client needs, coordinating services with the physician and other community resources, determining that caregivers complete their assigned tasks, and communicating as a member of management the organization's policies and procedures to the caregivers (Figure 5–1).

Figure 5–1 Supervisor: A Critical Link

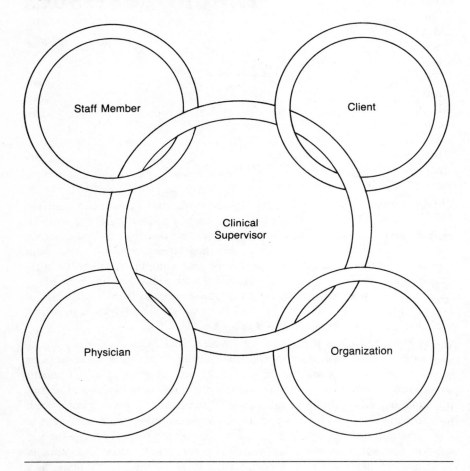

As a link to the client, the supervisor assesses client needs, determines the level of care required, develops the plan of care, delegates the tasks to the appropriate caregiver, and evaluates the quality of care given.

With the physician, the supervisor coordinates the skilled nursing care that is prescribed for the client at home. As needed, the supervisor relates with other community resources to provide total case management.

The supervisor is an active member of management. In this role the supervisor is often the only contact that caregivers have with their employer. The supervisor is the role model for the organization's philosophy of managing staff and providing client services. The supervisor functions to ensure that services are provided and documented within the framework established by the source of reimbursement. The supervisor links employees to employer, bringing to management the workers' concerns and problems and their input on forms and procedural changes. By building a fully functional home care team, the supervisor strengthens the home care organization and, subsequently, the home care industry.

The relationship of supervisor to caregiver is the focus of this chapter. How can the supervisor begin to build a strong home care team? What activities will strengthen the skills and loyalties of home care workers? What steps can the supervisor take to promote and measure the quality of services?

The home care industry will continue to grow in the United States. Whether or not tighter regulations are imposed on home care providers, the supervisor, within management's framework, can take many steps to ensure that services will be delivered to clients in the home safely and cost effectively and that they will be of high quality.

EMPLOYEE SELECTION

The success of a home care service or home health agency depends, to a large extent, on the organization's ability to employ qualified, dependable health care workers who provide quality services to their assigned clients.

In a home care organization that provides part-time or temporary assignments to a large number of employees, the clinical supervisor may be responsible for employee selection as well as for ongoing employee management. The home health agency, on the other hand, employs a full-time staff. In the latter situation, the administrator or personnel director completes employment procedures, assigning new staff to a clinical supervisor, as needed. The supervisor then accepts responsibility for orienting and supervising the new employee.

Employee selection begins before a prospective applicant contacts the home care organization. The process continues to the time of the hire decision and the worker's orientation. This process consists of recruitment and initial screening, completion of application and preemployment tests, the interview, reference checks, and evaluation of the candidate.

The hire decision is the beginning of ongoing employee management: orientation, work assignment, evaluation of performance, and staff development.

Recruitment

An organization's marketing plan will include the recruitment of prospective staff. Home care is a people business. In today's competitive milieu not only must an agency look to how client visits or services can be increased, but it must also know how to maintain a staff of qualified home care personnel to provide those services.

As determined by the administrator, nurse recruiter, or personnel director, the home care organization will advertise openings in local newspapers and industry journals, as well as develop community recruiting efforts. These efforts may include speaking in churches and to other groups that are composed of potential workers, working with the state or local employment office, and attending job fairs at colleges and nursing schools.

An important resource for recruitment is often overlooked: the organization's own employees. What do they have to say about working with a particular home care service? How visible are they within the community? Do they exhibit a high level of professionalism and enthusiasm for their work? By their behavior and words, are they reinforcing a positive public image of their employer? Active employees who enjoy their work in a home care organization are excellent resources for attracting future employees.

Initial Screen

Many people seek employment in home health care. Not all of them are qualified to provide the specific services that are involved in providing such care. The purpose of screening prospective applicants is to reduce the number of applicants to those few who meet the basic qualifications of the job for which they are applying. For example, a licensed practical nurse who wishes to supplement a full-time job by working with a home care service must be licensed to practice in the state, have the required experience to meet the organization's employment standards, and be able to work those shifts when assignments may be available. On the other hand, a home health agency position may require that the employee be a registered nurse licensed to practice in the state and a graduate of a baccalaureate degree program, with one or two years' community health experience.

Although most organizations will determine basic qualifications for each job description, federal, state, or locally funded services may have additional selection standards (see Exhibit 5–1).

By considering only those prospective applicants who meet basic job qualifications, an organization will save staff time and reduce operating expense. In addition, it will take a first step toward the assurance that services are provided by qualified staff.

Exhibit 5–1 Home Health Aide Qualifications

[¶20,101] **Regulation Sec. 405.1227.** Condition of participation: Home health aide services.—Home health aides are selected on the basis of such factors as a sympathetic attitude toward the care of the sick, ability to read, write, and carry out directions, and maturity and ability to deal effectively with the demands of the job. Aides are carefully trained in methods of assisting patients to achieve maximum self-reliance, principles of nutrition and meal preparation, the aging process and emotional problems of illness, procedures for maintaining a clean, healthful, and pleasant environment, changes in patient's condition that should be reported, work of the agency and the health team, ethics, confidentiality, and recordkeeping. They are closely supervised to assure their competence in providing care.

(See Connecticut and Oregon Addenda in the Appendix [¶20,130].)

Source: Title XVIII, Social Security Act, Section 405.1227.

10D-68.14 Home Health Aide.
(1) The home health aide shall have training in those supportive services which are required to provide and maintain bodily and emotional comfort and to assist the patient toward independent living in a safe environment. If the aide receives training through a vocational school, licensed/certified home health agency, or hospital, the curriculum shall be documented. If training is received through the agency the curriculum shall consist of at least forty-two (42) hours which include six (6) hours of introduction to the home health services program, role of the aide, and differences in families; six (6) hours of instruction relating to nutrition, food and household management; twenty-four (24) hours of instruction relating to personal care activites; and six (6) hours of instruction relating to ethics and conduct, personal hygiene, agency policies, and reports and records. Personal care activities shall be taught by a professional nurse. When prior training is not equivalent to the minimum herein described, the necessary supplementary training must be provided and documented.

Source: Minimum Standards for Home Health Agencies, Rules of the Department of Health and Rehabilitative Services, Division of Health (Florida), Chapter 10D-68.

UPJOHN HEALTHCARE SERVICES®	POSITION EVALUATION DESCRIPTION	85-399

Position Title:	Position Abbreviation	Position No.
Home Health Aide		

QUALIFICATIONS

This position requires at least six (6) months experience as a home health aide or nursing assistant, or successful completion of a home health aide course within the past three years. The incumbent must be physically capable of performing job related duties, and be able to read, write, understand and carry out directions, and keep simple records. This position also requires the ability to accurately take and record temperatures, pulse and respiration and function under minimal supervision. The incumbent must be certified where required by law, and be able to provide a reliable means of transportation. When assigned to a home health agency or a service office which is licensed by the state, this position requires the completion of a health examination prior to employment, and periodically thereafter to certify that the incumbent is free of communicable disease, and physically capable of performing assigned duties.

Source: Upjohn HealthCare Services. Reprinted with permission.

Application Review

When a prospective applicant meets basic qualifications for a job opening, an application will be completed. The application form provides a composite of the applicant's education, experience, skill level, and health status.

Those areas of the application that are incomplete provide other clues. Gaps in employment should be explained by the applicant. Not listing a recent employer as a work reference may be questioned. Frequent changing of jobs or relocating should be reviewed.

Because documentation of care given is critical to reimbursement of services, the application provides an excellent sample of the applicant's penmanship and shows how well the applicant can follow directions.

Completion of the application provides an opportunity for preemployment skills testing by those organizations that include such testing in their employment policies. Several cautions should be considered when using a preemployment skills test:

- The test must be related to required skills listed in the job description.
- The test should be validated by the agency's legal consultant.
- The test must be administered uniformly to all applicants who apply in the specific job category.

Interview

The interview augments the application's factual information by providing an insight into the applicant's motivation and aptitude for home care. Because the interview serves as an important factor in the hire decision, it must be prepared and organized; it should focus on obtaining information about the candidate's past performance, as well as on answering the applicant's questions about employment opportunity.

The interview is best conducted at a scheduled time, in an area free from distractions and telephone interruptions. Having reviewed the application for discrepancies or gaps in information, the supervisor or recruiter may start the interview by introducing herself or himself, giving her or his job title, and continuing: "The purpose of this interview is twofold, Jeannette. First, it will give me an opportunity to get to know you and assess your qualifications for the job as a home health nurse. Second, it will give you an opportunity to become acquainted with our home health agency and help you decide if you would like to work here. During the interview, Jeannette, I will be taking notes."

Questions that focus on the applicant's previous work experience will provide an indication as to how well the prospective employee will function in home care nursing.

- Tell me about a problem you encountered with one of your patients. What was the specific problem? How did you handle it?

- Tell me about a particular patient care problem you weren't able to solve. What happened?

- Give me an example of a time when you went beyond what was expected of you.

- Tell me about a situation that got you really upset. What did you do? What was the result?

- Describe a time when your work schedule was upset by an emergency or unforeseen circumstances. What did you do about it?

- Tell me about a situation when you anticipated a problem with a patient or co-worker. How did you handle it?

- Can you describe a recent patient problem that you solved in a new or creative way?

- Why do you want to work in the home care setting?

Through the interview, the employer is able to determine, to an extent, how flexible, dependable, organized, observant, and empathetic the prospective employee will be in the home care setting. How well will directions be understood and followed through? Will the employee be able to work with a minimum of supervision? Will the employee be able to cross cultural and socioeconomic lines; be self-assured and able to extend that feeling of confidence to the patient?

The employment interview is essential to the data-gathering effort of employee selection and lays the foundation for future employer-employee relationships. It also serves as a public relations tool. Applicants share with colleagues their experiences and perceptions. These shared experiences may enhance or break down the organization's stature in the health care community. A nurse, new to a southwestern city, applied to work temporarily at a home care organization. She was appalled to observe the office manager sitting casually at her desk, telling jokes to a co-worker. She did not accept temporary employment there. Later, when she became the discharge planner at a leading hospital in that city, she did not refer clients to that organization!

References

Because of legal implications, references seldom give more than verification of employment, dates of employment, and job classification. They do validate certain facts, however, and should not be omitted from the selection process. Verification of licensure from the state board of professional licensure can be accomplished as well at this time.

Hire Decision

Choosing the best qualified staff for an organization will ensure, to a degree, that services will be provided competently in the home setting. The hire decision must be made based on several sources of data: the application, skills testing (if required), the interview, and reference checks. The data are then compared with the requirements of the job description, client population, and overall staff needs.

To avoid legal problems in the event of a future employee discharge, the employer is advised[3] to make no promise of employment "for the rest of your life." Nor should an annual salary be quoted. At most, quote a weekly or biweekly rate of compensation. Home care workers who are employed on a part-time or temporary basis should have the conditions of employment reinforced so that they clearly understand them before their orientation.

EMPLOYEE MANAGEMENT

A harried clinical supervisor exclaims, "I feel like a three-armed juggler! There is so much to do! Keeping current on the clients' status, assigning caseloads to the staff, monitoring the completeness of records, getting physician cooperation, attending management meetings, and keeping current with community programs. Just when I think everything's under control, order becomes chaos! I'm juggling again!" Employee management is not easy. It is only one aspect of the supervisor's role. The supervisor relates to the clients, physicians, community, and sources of reimbursement for services. In addition, the supervisor represents management's policies and procedures to employees and brings employee concerns to the attention of management.

The challenge to the supervisor is to meet the organization's goals and at the same time reach client care goals and maintain a highly productive, motivated staff.

Supervisors who are the efficient practitioners of basic personnel management will strengthen their organization's role within its budgetary framework and enhance the quality of the services delivered in the home setting. Basic personnel management includes an organized system of orienting and training personnel, motivating and coaching them for improved performance on the job, supervising them in order to evaluate their performance, and then documenting those observations in a formal appraisal process. Dealing with problems and disciplining employees who function below established standards are responsibilities that fall on the supervisor's shoulders.

Orientation

Orientation is the process by which a new employee is introduced to the organization's philosophy, goals, policies, procedures, and standards of client care. The employee learns those tasks required for functioning in the new job. Expectations are clarified: What are the job responsibilities of the home care worker? What can the worker expect from the employer?

Perhaps in no other area is the saying, "You don't get a second chance to make a first impression" more applicable than in the area of orienting new employees. A supervisor who is prepared for the arrival of a new employee has the ability to make a long-lasting impact on that employee's attitude and productivity. If a new employee's orientation and training is done well, the foundation is laid for a long and mutually beneficial relationship.

An employee comes to his or her new job with excitement, enthusiasm, a willingness to learn, and a desire to succeed. The successful supervisor will recognize this energy and capitalize on it. Answering the new employees' questions, meeting their needs, and defining job accountabilities will ensure that new employees become productive and loyal team members. The fears and frustrations that come from undefined job expectations, unclear interpersonal relations, and lack of skill or knowledge can be eliminated by an effective orientation program.

The plan for orientation should be developed based on consultation with other supervisors and management. An assessment of learner needs may vary the content. For example, if a caregiver was previously employed in an institutional setting, she or he must be taught to function in clients' homes, using improvised equipment and dealing with the many factors that require flexibility and judgment.

A standard orientation outline for each job classification will ensure that no aspect of the organization's operations is omitted. A check-off list, signed and dated by employee and supervisor, documents topics explained or demonstrated. The check-off list is a valuable resource for the worker who complains, "I was never told!"

The dollars invested in a carefully planned orientation program will be returned in increased productivity of new employees and decreased staff turnover.

Assignment

Assignment of staff to clients may be the responsibility of a paraprofessional. One coordinator, scheduling all employees within a home care service, has the flexibility to draw from the entire pool of caregivers in order to provide service to a new client or replace a caregiver who has called in sick or is otherwise unable to report for duty. On the other hand, a clinical supervisor of a home health agency may have a staff of 15 full-time employees who will provide services to the caseload assigned to the supervisor, usually within a defined geographical area.

In such a circumstance the supervisor must distribute the workload equitably, assigning work as individual skills warrant. One worker may be exceptionally talented in caring for terminally ill clients; another may have particular ability with young children. The total group workload should be evaluated periodically, and schedules changed as needed. A nurse who is becoming too emotionally involved with a family may need to be reassigned to another case.

It is the assignment coordinators' duty to be certain that each client receives the employee who is best qualified through education, experience, or credentialing to provide that care. It is also their responsibility to safeguard the employee who has a history of physical injury so that the injury will not recur on the job.

Consider the client who is receiving round-the-clock care in the home, seven days a week. The scheduling of caregivers for that client may be as complex as those encountered by major metropolitan hospital staffing offices. But the home care organization cannot pull a nurse from the adjacent floor when an employee does not report for duty, as can the hospital! Alternate schedules are needed in case of an emergency.

It is helpful to give the client a list of all staff assigned to provide care, defining the day and shift for each nurse. This list can be posted on the refrigerator as a reminder of who the family may expect.

For the person directing the flow of staff and paperwork in a home care organization, there may be the tendency to become like a stationmaster in a railroad station: switching engines, freight cars, and passenger trains to different tracks in order to accommodate market demands. The supervisor who is responsible for scheduling must avoid this tendency. Supervisors are more than stationmasters. They are skilled communicators who direct and motivate their staffs to achieve agency goals and at the same time meet client goals of quality care.

Supervision

Contract requirements, state licensing, and Medicare regulations clearly define the type and frequency of supervision an agency must provide. However, for thousands of other organizations providing home care, there are no well-established parameters for supervision of home care workers. Is "supervision" a telephone call? A visit to the client's home? Or, a visit to the client's home when the employee is on duty? If so, how often are supervisory visits made? The nature of supervision will vary according to the standards established by an organization.

Within an institution, the supervision is a direct, on-site process. The worker's skill and attitude can be easily observed. The client's response to care is readily assessed. In the home care setting, however, supervision cannot always be by direct observation. Although regular visits to clients' homes to observe employees and clients are made, supervisory activities must be indirect as well, allowing the supervisor access to all employees assigned over a wide geographical area.

There are several components of indirect supervision. Daily telephone calls are necessary to report changing client conditions. Documentation of care provided, the client's response, and current status must be accurate and submitted each week the care is provided. The supervisor, by reviewing the documentation, has another way of keeping current on the caseload of clients and the workload of employees. Good channels of communication are essential for indirect supervision.

Motivation

The supervisor of a home care organization may be working with a large number of staff, employed in a variety of home settings on a short-term or part-time basis. The turnover of such staff may be exceedingly high. How can a supervisor motivate such a diverse, decentralized group?

Whether the caregiver is a full-time or a part-time worker, it is important to recognize that people are motivated in a variety of ways. Motivation may be from within the caregiver: pride in a job well done; satisfaction from impacting on others' lives; a sense of responsibility in providing care in an unsupervised or independent setting. By their expressions of appreciation, the client and family play an important role in motivating home care workers. Organizational recognition, such as service awards, certificates of appreciation, and birthday cards may also be important tools. These are a few of the factors that "turn on" or motivate home care workers.

The successful supervisor is the one who readily recognizes why a caregiver is choosing to work in the home setting. Assignments are made so that talents and abilities are used. The employees feel that "this is a job worth doing."

Caregivers want to assist in goal setting for client care. They want to get feedback when a job is done well and feel free to approach the supervisor with problems and concerns. By maintaining contact with employees through telephone reports and on-site visits, the supervisor demonstrates interest in the staff and fosters a climate of trust.

Staff Development

Malcolm Knowles and other proponents of androgogy (the process of adult learning) believe in the adult's lifelong capacity to learn and grow. Not only does training prepare staff to meet the changing challenges of home care services, but it also affords staff an opportunity for personal and professional growth. By meeting the learning needs of the staff, a good staff development program is a powerful tool to retain home care workers and improve the quality of client care.

As defined in the American Nurses' Association's *Guidelines for Staff Development*, staff development is "a process which includes both formal and informal learning opportunities to assist individuals to perform competently in fulfillment of role expectations within a specific agency. Resources both within and outside the agency are utilized to facilitate the process."[4] Staff development activities consist of orientation, inservice education, and continuing education.

Inservice education is an ongoing education program that includes on-the-job training, under the direction of an education specialist or inservice coordinator, designed to improve and enhance the functional capabilities of licensed and nonlicensed personnel, and volunteers. Inservice programs cover the use of new forms and policies, the introduction of new home care techniques and equipment, and the review of patient care skills. The state licensure regulations may stipulate that a home health agency conduct a specific number of inservice programs or schedule a required number of inservice hours each year. The agency itself may have established protocol concerning the delivery of inservice education.

Licensed and nonlicensed staff, new to the home care work environment, may benefit from many of the following topics:

- goal setting and prioritizing
- planning daily activities
- admitting new clients
- assessing client needs

- adapting care to the home environment
- responding to cultural differences and socioeconomic conditions
- documenting client care
- managing stress
- dealing with emergencies, such as death in the home, cardiac arrest, and accidental injury.

Whereas some inservice topics will be beneficial to both the skilled professional group and the nonlicensed group of home care workers, other topics may be better suited to groups of physical therapists, speech therapists, and licensed nurses. Some inservice subjects are best directed toward the nonlicensed worker: the home health aide, companion, or homemaker.

The inservice coordinator is accountable for maintaining a file on each education offering. This file should include:

- roster of attendees (name, signature, job title)
- curriculum outline, including teaching objectives and instructional methodologies
- name and qualifications of instructor
- bibliography
- date and place of program, as well as number of hours of instruction.

Continuing education experiences are designed to promote the enrichment of knowledge, the improvement of skills, and the development of attitudes for the enhancement of nursing practice, thus improving health care services. Continuing education may include inservice education but excludes orientation and on-the-job training.

Several states require licensed practical nurses and registered nurses to earn a prescribed number of hours of continuing education in order to be relicensed. Providers of continuing education programs become approved by the state board of nursing to grant continuing education units, or contact hours. Each state has a different approval process for its providers. Some states require American Nurses' Association accreditation.

Although a state may not mandate continuing education for registered nurses and licensed practical nurses, there may be a voluntary program administered by the state nurses' association. The Continuing Education Approval and Recognition Program in Texas and Oklahoma are two examples of such voluntary programs.

A staff development program need *not* be expensive. It *must* have consistency, i.e., be offered regularly throughout the year, and be developed as a result of a needs analysis.

Because the education coordinator may not be qualified to conduct all classes, a staff nurse or therapist with expertise in a particular area may present an inservice program. A physician, recognizing the marketing opportunity created, may agree to talk about a particular diagnosis. Durable medical equipment suppliers are excellent free sources for teaching programs. Community and military hospitals frequently open their continuing education programs to other nursing personnel. Many home care organization networks have been successful in developing joint education committees. These committees present communitywide inservice programs that are focused toward both the home care skilled professional and the nonlicensed staff.

By using a little creativity and knowledge of community resources, staff development can be a relatively low-budget item. The payoff for the energy invested is high. Nurses, unlicensed personnel, and volunteers alike want the opportunity to grow, to learn, and to work in an environment that is not only conducive to learning, but also rewards the application of new skills and attitudes to client care.

Performance Evaluation

An often-neglected activity of supervision is the maintenance of a formal performance evaluation system. Effective supervision, a staff development program, and a performance evaluation system all contribute to the professional growth of employees. It is a cornerstone of an organization's foundation in providing quality home care services.

Not only does a performance evaluation system improve the level of client care, but it also lets employees know where they stand and guides the organization in its program for staff development. A new supervisor who reviews the personnel files can learn about the home care staff's skills and abilities. Consequently, client needs can be better met through more effective scheduling.

There are several performance evaluation techniques from which to choose.

- A rating scale rates employees' abilities numerically from superior to unsatisfactory in such areas as dependability, quality of work, and accuracy of documentation. It may be quick and easy to complete but lacks the depth and insight of other techniques.
- An essay addresses aspects of employee performance in a narrative paragraph. It may be the easiest technique to implement because it requires no prior form development. The quality of this technique will vary according to the supervisor's writing skills.

- Behaviorally anchored rating scales are becoming more popular. They match actual performance against examples of expected behaviors in specific areas. The format is time-consuming to develop but a relatively objective tool to evaluate employees.
- A work standards approach compares actual performance with expected levels of performance. A work standards approach serves to clearly define performance expectations, thus avoiding subjectivity by the rater. An example of a work standard form is shown in Exhibit 5–2.

Employee performance may be evaluated by direct observation on assignment. It may also be assessed by reviewing the documentation of care or service, in case conferences, and through telephone conversations. Clients' reports of employees' dependability is another tool for performance evaluation.

Evaluating employee performance is not a once-a-year procedure. The effective supervisor communicates with employees on a daily or weekly basis, praising them when deserved and reprimanding them when needed.

Discipline

When a home care worker's performance is less than adequate, disciplinary counseling may be instituted. Examples of poor performance are chronic tardiness, inadequate client care or suspected client abuse, failure to submit records of care on a timely basis, and indications of alcohol or drug abuse by the employee.

Such behaviors cannot be ignored. Supervisors often fail to institute corrective discipline because they lack the knowledge or training in the "how-tos" of effective disciplining. Many have been promoted from the workers' ranks to their supervisory role. They fail to see that their new role demands a more formal relationship with friends and former co-workers. Disciplinary counseling is an unpleasant task; oftentimes supervisors prefer to overlook their responsibilities rather than be viewed by former co-workers as adversaries.

Supervisors cannot ignore the failure by caregivers to meet acceptable standards of performance. As a member of management, they must ensure that policies and procedures are carried out correctly. As the overseer of client services, they are accountable for ensuring that the consumer of services receives high-quality care. Finally, the supervisors' timely approach to disciplinary problems promotes the personal and professional growth of employees, eventually strengthening the home care organization.

When disciplinary counseling proves ineffectual, termination of the employee may result.

Exhibit 5–2 Work Standards: A Technique for Performance Evaluation

STANDARDS OF PERFORMANCE	Meets Standard	Below Standard	Comments
Attendance			
1. Reports to assignments on time.			
2. Follows procedure for notification of absence.			
3. Follows procedure for arranging vacation time.			
4. Completes record of time worked accurately.			
5. Obtains required approvals on record of time worked.			
Communication			
1. Keeps supervisor informed of client status.			
2. Reports client status to oncoming caregiver.			
3. Interacts with client and family appropriately.			
4. Telephones office when assistance is needed.			
Documentation			
1. Completes written record of care provided.			
2. Utilizes forms according to established procedure.			
3. Submits record of care on schedule.			
4. Writes neatly and legibly.			
Client Care			

Termination

When an employee decides to leave a home care provider, it is considered a voluntary termination or resignation. In such instances an exit interview may reveal problem areas in the supervision of personnel or overall management of the organization. Data gleaned from documented exit interviews can promote changes in policies and procedures that may result in improvement in employee selection and the quality of client services.

Involuntary terminations are instituted by the employer. Immediate discharge is recommended as a result of documented theft, physical abuse, or gross insubordination. Although the purpose of disciplinary counseling is to retain employees and improve work performance, when such counseling fails the result should be termination of the caregiver.

Because improper disciplinary counseling and termination have been the grounds for wrongful discharge suits, each organization must have procedures for such instances that have been reviewed by its legal consultant.

Problems in Home Care Supervision

The home care supervisor deals with many problems that are not encountered by the hospital supervisor. By anticipating some of these difficulties, the supervisor is able to take corrective actions to avoid their occurrence or minimize their impact.

Good *communication* between management and caregivers is essential to client care, employee satisfaction, and the reimbursement of services. All the staff must communicate effectively not only in one-on-one transactions and staff meetings, but also by telephone and in writing. Reading the records of care given is the method most used by supervisors to keep informed about what is going on in each client's home. The caregiver may have excellent nursing skills, but if these are not evident in the documentation or in telephone reports, reimbursement for services may be denied, and the supervisor will remain ill informed. In large home care organizations the logistics of keeping in-office staff and caregivers informed of procedural and other changes requires careful planning and diligent follow-through.

The caregiver often experiences a sense of *isolation* in the home. She or he is forced to adapt to the home environment of the client, which is remote from the organization, sometimes lacking telephone contact with supportive personnel. There are no co-workers; lunch is often eaten alone; paperwork is completed by oneself. Caregivers and clients, over an extended period, may become mutually dependent, developing a "me-and-my-patient-against-the-world" point of view.

Telephone contact with client and caregiver, supervisory visits, staff meetings and holiday get-togethers, a system of recognition and awards, name badges or uniforms that clearly identify the home care organization, and employee newsletters are but a few techniques for developing a cohesive home care team in which feelings of alienation are minimal.

In the home care setting, personal and nursing services are delivered to clients, many of whom are elderly and confused, without direct supervision. There is a potential for the *abuse of independence* by caregivers who wish to finish their visit schedule as quickly as possible or who otherwise lack motivation to complete the assigned tasks. Effective employee selection, careful supervision, and frequent communication may reduce the tendency for caregivers to misuse the responsibility vested in them.

Men and women frequently are attracted to the home care setting because of the opportunity to provide one-on-one care. Some leave, overwhelmed by the amount of *paperwork* that often is required. They are highly motivated to meet client needs, yet the same dedication to documentation, filing, and timeliness of paperwork is lacking. There is no hospital records department to complete the client's file; it is the home nurse who must accept that responsibility. Dictation may be one method for expediting the paperwork, if it can be done cost-effectively. When dictating systems are used, home care staff must overcome their shyness toward such a system and learn how to organize their ideas and dictate their notes effectively.

The caregiver, sometimes without the organization's prior knowledge, often enters into complex, multiproblem family situations. Workers may encounter *marked variances in cultural values or standards of living.* Problems may develop if the caregiver lacks those skills necessary to deal with such situations: maturity, good judgment, dependability, initiative, and flexibility. The value of a professional assessment of a home situation before the assignment of a worker cannot be overlooked; unfortunately, such evaluations may not be feasible because of the reimbursement structure.

Inclement conditions place added burdens on those who deliver services to homebound clients. Hurricanes, floods, and heavy snows make roads impassable and access to the client impossible. Every organization must have written procedures for dealing with a wide range of emergencies. Which clients must be transferred to institutional care? Which clients can be seen by a neighbor, another family member, or a caregiver who lives in the same neighborhood? Who is to receive calls in an emergency? What community resources may be called on? Are emergency telephone numbers posted in the client's home as well as in the office? *Other emergency situations* that require planned procedures are medical emergencies in the home, physical abuse of the client, and assault of the home care worker venturing into unsafe neighborhoods.

Union-organizing activity, staff burnout, 24-hour client coverage, and alcohol and drug abuse are problems that may be found in the institutional setting, as well as in the home care setting. They require thoughtful planning and effective actions by management to be resolved.

The Volunteer Home Care Worker

Whatever is included in this chapter, with the exception of the section on wages and fringe benefits, addresses issues associated with the volunteer home care worker as well.

Thousands of volunteers provide services to people in their homes through established programs, such as Meals on Wheels or Hospice, and through more loosely organized programs, such as those sponsored by churches and synagogues. Services range from assistance with home dialysis to visitations for supportive counseling and social contact.

The success of a volunteer program depends on the organization's ability to maximize volunteers' skills, make them an integral part of the organization's mission, and supervise them effectively.

Careful selection of volunteers is a first step. The interview of a prospective recruit should be designed to give as much information as possible about the person's skills, knowledge, and motivation. Questions that may be asked are, "What do you want to gain for yourself from this work?" "What did you like least about your last volunteer work?" "What were some of the problems you encountered?" Volunteers should be chosen as carefully as one would choose paid staff. An agency should not be afraid to tell a prospective recruit, "I'm sorry, we don't 'fit.' "

The selection interview should be professional as well as complete. Often the prospective recruit's decision whether or not to work as a volunteer is based on the first impression.

Volunteers need to be placed on assignment soon after orientation, carefully matching their knowledge, skills, and personality to the needs and personalities of their clients.

Open communication between volunteers and paid staff fosters a spirit of cooperation and shared goals. Volunteers want to feel that they represent their organization, that they belong and are valued for their contributions. Volunteers want to share their problems and concerns with the paid staff. Regularly scheduled meetings, training programs, and supervision in the home setting should be included in the routine management of volunteers.

Volunteers should be required to meet organization expectations regarding assigned schedules, record keeping, and other procedures. They should be recognized for work accomplished by providing positive reinforcement, periodic work reviews, and new and challenging assignments. Special recognition for outstanding service or longevity of service may be in the form of certificates, awards, or pins. Newspaper coverage has two purposes: recognizing volunteer accomplishments and recruiting prospective volunteers.

There are legal and business aspects of using volunteers. Are volunteers covered by the organization's professional liability insurance? What records are kept on nonpaid staff? A system should be developed to record dates of orientation and training, assignments given, hours worked, and documentation of supervisory visits. Files of inactive volunteers should be kept separate from those of active volunteers. Inactive records may be destroyed periodically.

The same management skills are used when supervising volunteers who have been carefully selected and whose personal goals are a close match to organizational goals as are used when supervising paid home care staff. Whether paid or unpaid, workers must feel that they are part of the organization or unit. They must also have a feeling of worth, of being valued and wanted by their organization. If these attitudes are lacking, an organization's ability to deliver high-quality home care services is weakened.

QUALITY OF SERVICES IN THE HOME

The services provided to clients in their homes are diverse—from the companionable visit with an isolated, elderly citizen to the high-tech nursing care for a ventilator-dependent child. The caregivers themselves represent a wide range of background experience, educational preparation, and professional credentialing. In addition, the places in which care is delivered range from an elegant apartment overlooking the Hudson River to a simple wooden shack at the end of ten miles of dirt road, lacking indoor plumbing and electricity.

Because care is decentralized, away from the organization, and because home care services have developed in a relatively unregulated environment, there is a high potential for inadequate care to go undetected. Consequently, the causes of poor nursing care or inadequate services go uncorrected. Simply saying, "Our service provides care of high quality" does not make that care meet certain standards. The presence of bedsores, unexplained weight loss, or frequent hospitalizations may signal that a client has been overlooked or disregarded by the caregiver.

Demand for Quality

It should be the focus of the home care organization to ensure that clients receive the best possible care. Care and services need to promote clients' early return to their maximum level of functioning or sustain them in the home at the highest possible quality of life. By monitoring the quality of services, the organization can anticipate problems early and begin corrective action, thus avoiding legal liabilities and costly malpractice actions.

Increasingly, payers of home care services are requiring quality assurance programs, a system of internal checks and balances designed to detect those things that would interfere with providing the best possible care for the client. The assignment of unqualified staff, lack of supervision, no documentation of care provided, overutilization of home care services, and improper care are a few of the things that signal the quality assurance team that established or regulatory standards are not being met.

Home health agency regulations have certain structural procedures to ascertain quality:

- Every 60 days the professional staff and physician must review the appropriateness of continued care for a client.
- Quarterly, the clinical record review committee, composed of professionals representing the scope of services of the agency, must conduct a clinical record review of open and closed cases.
- Periodically, an advisory committee, composed of agency and nonagency professionals and consumers, must review the agency's policies and procedures.
- The advisory committee participates in an annual review of the home health agency program, including reports from the clinical record review committee. The advisory committee evaluates the agency's achievement of its goals and recommends new programs for development.

Promoters of Quality

Quality home care service does not occur by chance. It must be *made* to happen. This requires the development of certain procedures before the delivery of care, the observation by supervisory staff that the best of care is being given, and the monitoring of the quality of care after it has been provided.

The promoters of quality that may ensure that caregivers will follow a high standard of care are:

- *Staff selection procedures.* Does the educational background of new staff prepare them adequately for home assignments? Do they have a minimum of one year's experience as caregivers? Are interviews conducted? Reference checks? Preemployment or placement testing to demonstrate competencies?

- *Functional job descriptions.* Are there written job descriptions for each classification of caregiver? Does each worker have a copy? Are they informed of the parameters of their actions, what they can and cannot do?

- *Staff development program.* Does each new caregiver attend an orientation covering the organization's policies, procedures, and protocol for emergencies? Is there a program for ongoing training? Is on-the-job instruction given by the supervisor?

- *Assignment system.* Are client needs accurately assessed? Is the most qualified caregiver assigned? Is there a written plan of care or service for each client? Are nonlicensed personnel given their assignments in writing?

- *Performance appraisal system.* Are caregivers aware of areas in which they have performed well? Areas in which they need further training in order to improve the quality of services?

When a home care organization is confident that its caregivers are well selected, trained, and assigned, it can be reasonably sure that deficiencies in delivery of service will be minimal. In addition, direct and indirect monitoring of services rendered must be implemented to measure the quality of care in the home.

Direct Measures of Quality

The most accurate assessment of quality is made by the supervisor who is actually on-site in the client's home. The supervisor can assess the client's condition and progress toward the goals of care. When the employee is present, caregiving skills may be observed, as well as the interactions among the client, family, and caregiver.

In some home health agencies and organizations a quality assurance nurse is on staff who reports directly to the administrator. The nurse not only conducts direct monitoring of quality through in-home visits and observations, but is also responsible for indirect monitoring of services.

Indirect monitoring by internal or external review does not guarantee that quality services will be provided. Rather, it is a measure of what has been provided in the hope that a check-and-balance system will reveal potential problems and inadequacies that can be remedied.

Figure 5–2 depicts the three facets of quality: before, during, and after delivery of care.

Figure 5–2 Facets of Quality: Before, During, and After Delivery of Care

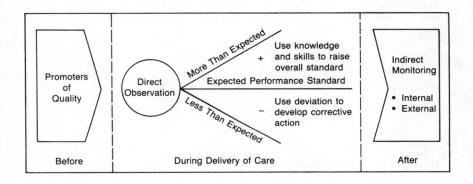

Indirect Measures of Quality

The internal quality review has several dimensions. The supervisor receives telephone and written reports from staff. Evaluation of the client status and employee skills is only as adequate as the caregiver's ability to communicate, verbally and nonverbally. How well does the caregiver communicate what has been done and the client's response?

Other dimensions of internal review are the team conference, clinical record review, and random chart audits. The client questionnaire (Exhibit 5–3) may offer insight into the degree of client satisfaction. It is sent to all new clients, at the termination of service, or periodically throughout the year.

External reviews are conducted by fiscal intermediaries to ensure that service was necessary, that it was provided, and that the quality of care was adequate. State surveyors review the agency's compliance with state and federal licensure and certification regulations or requirements.

The voluntary Accreditation Program for Home Health Agencies and Community Health Nursing Services was instituted by the National League for Nursing (NLN) in 1975. Designed to assist agencies in evaluating and improving the quality of health care, the initial accreditation is for three years. Renewals are at five-year intervals. As of October 1984, 76 home health agencies and community health nursing services in 28 states had met NLN accreditation standards.[5]

Exhibit 5–3 Client Questionnaire

Thank you for choosing to use our home care services. In order to help us to maintain the high level of service you have come to expect, please answer the following questions:

	Yes	No
Was the service provided satisfactory?	☐	☐

Comments:_____

_____

	Yes	No
Was the home care employee prompt and courteous?	☐	☐

Comments:_____

_____

	Yes	No
Was the office staff helpful to you?	☐	☐

Comments:_____

_____

	Yes	No
Would you recommend our services to a friend?	☐	☐

Comments:_____

_____

Please note below how we might improve the quality of our services. Thank you.

_____

_____

Signature_____ Date_____

Address_____

Role of the Supervisor

The professional supervision of home care workers is essential to the maintenance of quality home care services. The supervisor is accountable to the client, the source of reimbursement, the home care organization, and the supervisor's own professional standards for playing an active role in the assurance that a high standard of care is provided by the caregiver. It is the supervisor who is able to observe directly that workers are meeting set standards, that care is documented correctly, and that the content of all records is accurate. In addition, the supervisor is best able to orient and train workers, coach them to improve their work quality, and give them feedback regarding their performance.

Cost of Quality

The question is not whether a home care organization can afford to implement a quality assurance program, but rather, whether it can afford not to. As the home care industry grows, the deliverers of home care service must strengthen those factors that will promote quality of care and those systems that will testify that quality services have in fact been delivered.

WAGES

A salary administration program is the basis for the effective hiring, utilization, promotion, and retention of home care employees. Although wages may not be the primary factor in attracting, motivating, and retaining qualified caregivers, they cannot be below market average. Nor can they be administered inequitably. An equitable, competitive wage structure within an organization will promote a stable, dependable work force but will not guarantee one.

Several other factors are necessary to prevent job dissatisfaction: efficient organizational structure, agreeable working conditions, fair and personable supervision, challenging and meaningful assignments, opportunities for advancement, and pride in the organization. No matter how adequate the wage structure, other factors must be in place in order to retain and develop a health care team that will provide quality services to its clients.

Wage Determinants

A home care organization establishes wage guidelines for each job classification based on several factors:

- level of educational preparation and experience required for the job
- degree of skill needed and the amount of responsibility demanded by the job
- current rate of pay at institutions and home care services within the community. Each year the American Hospital Association publishes an Annual Nursing Personnel Survey. The NLN conducts an annual review of salaries in home health agencies and community health services. These and local Department of Labor statistics are valuable resources.

- overall cost of living within the community, which will be reflected in existing wage scales
- number of qualified recruits available for the job category. If the community's demand for home care nurses is high, this will be represented in locally higher salary levels.
- annual budget of the home care organization. A reasonable budget must be maintained while retaining a team of qualified health care workers. Recruitment and orientation costs are so high that an attractive wage package may in fact reduce overall employee costs because it reduces staff turnover.
- client population. It is the client who ultimately pays the cost of escalating wage scales through higher fees for home care, increased insurance premiums, and larger state and federal taxes. The financial health of a home care service depends on management's recognition of this factor.

If the salaries of home care workers do not now match those of workers in institutions, it is likely that this situation will change in the future. As demand for home care increases and as patient acuity in the home increases, salaries of home care workers will meet, or exceed, those of institutional employees.

Salaried Caregivers

Most home health agencies and government organizations hire full-time home care employees: skilled professionals, home health aides, companions, and homemakers who work 40 hours a week for a fixed rate of reimbursement.

In addition to the weekly salary, the organization pays for such statutory expenses as federal and state unemployment, workers' compensation, professional liability insurances, and a commercial blanket bond on all employees.

A fringe benefit package may equal in value 20 percent to 40 percent of the weekly salary. By taking advantage of group rates, additional benefits may be provided to employees at costs below those that would be charged if purchased by the employee alone. The benefit package is an important consideration when establishing a compensation structure that attracts and retains qualified personnel.

Health insurance, life insurance, dental services, a pension plan, and disability income may be included in a benefit package. Other benefits that are added costs to the total compensation program may be tuition reimbursement, paid holidays and vacation, a uniform allowance, and reimbursement of travel expenses.

If a leased car is provided to the home care nurse, the Internal Revenue Service requires written records to be kept clearly documenting the use of the car for business reasons. The record or log is to be kept daily and must indicate date, employee name, point of origin, destination, name of client visited, and beginning and ending mileage. Home health agencies are required to withhold income and Social Security taxes on the employee benefit portion of the lease car used for personal reasons.[6]

For salaried employees the organization's salary administration must include protocol for salary payment during absence, for work done on weekends and holidays, for time worked in excess of eight hours a day or 40 hours a week, and during required orientation and training.

Whether wages are paid on a salaried or unit of service basis, the salary administration must be in accordance with the Fair Labor Standards Act (FLSA), commonly known as the Federal Wage and Hour Law. The FLSA contains provisions and standards regarding minimum wages, equal pay, overtime pay, record keeping, and child labor.

Payment by Unit of Service

Most home care workers are not salaried employees. Rather, they are paid by the hour or the visit in exchange for providing care to the home care client. They may work less than eight hours a week to supplement a full-time job or provide themselves part-time employment while in school or raising a family. They may work regularly, 40 hours a week, but are still paid at an hourly rate. Their employers pay all statutory or required insurances but usually do not cover any fringe benefits. The "benefit" may in fact lay in the freedom that employees have to schedule their own hours, to work when desired, and to be free to pursue other activities without the rigidity of full-time employment. The disadvantage of such a structure may be that employees have no incentive to stay at a home care organization, moving from employer to employer, to the highest bidder.

This is the typical wage structure at a home care service that employs caregivers on a "part-time, as-needed" basis. The freedom to accept or decline an assignment is there. The guarantee of ongoing, full-time work is not.

Wages may seem higher at organizations that employ nurses, aides, and homemakers for short-term or part-time assignments in the home; however, it must be remembered that the overall wage does not include a fringe benefit package.

When caregivers are reimbursed by the hour or the visit, accurate record keeping is essential to prevent misuse of the system and, ultimately, added financial burdens on clients.

The cost of nursing services constitutes a majority of the budget of not-for-profit and proprietary home care services. It is essential that the wage issue be approached with objectivity and reason. Salary administration requires research, planning, and effort. It is not a one-time activity, as the total value of the salary and benefit package must be adjusted constantly to allow for movement in the competitive wage market. Wages must be kept within the budgeted reimbursement structure and at the same time be attractive to well-prepared, qualified home care workers.

NOTES

1. Maria Vesperi, "Looking Behind the Starched Facade," *St. Petersburg Times* (January 6, 1985), pp. 1F, 3F.

2. . . . *Home Health Line* reported that, on December 31, 1984, there were 5,247 certified home health agencies in the United States. "Changing Face of Home Health: Five Years by State," . . . *Home Health Line,* February 11, 1985, p. 45.

3. Barbara Conway Rutkowski and Arthur D. Rutkowski, "Employee Discharge: It Depends . . . ," *Nursing Management* 15 (December 1984):41.

4. American Nurses' Association, *Guidelines for Staff Development* (Kansas City, Mo.: ANA, 1976), p. 1.

5. "Home Health Agencies and Community Nursing Services Accredited by NLN/APHA," *Nursing and Health Care* 6 (January 1985):14–15.

6. Dwight Cenac, "I.R.S. Implements Stringent Auto Use Rules," *Home Health Journal* 6 (February 1985):14.

REFERENCES

American Nurses' Association. *Guidelines for Staff Development.* Kansas City, Mo.: ANA, 1978.

Arbeiter, Jean S. "The Big Shift to Home Health Nursing." *RN Magazine* 47 (November 1984):38–45.

Berg, Carol, and Diane Helgeson. "That First Home Visit." *Journal of Community Health Nursing* 1 (1984):207–215.

Brickner, Philip W. *Home Health Care for the Aged.* Norwalk, Conn.: Appleton-Century-Croft, 1978.

Bridges, Robin. "Hospitals, HCFA, Homecare." *Home Health Journal* 5 (October 1984):4.

Cenac, Dwight. "IRS Implements Stringent Auto Use Rules." *Home Health Journal* 6 (February 1985):14.

"Changing Face of Home Health: Five Years by State." . . . *Home Health Line,* February 11, 1985, p. 45.

Chapman, Elwood N. *Supervisor's Survival Kit.* 3d ed. Palo Alto, Calif.: Science Research Associates, 1982.

Elkins, Carolyn Pinion. *Community Health Nursing: Skills and Strategies.* Bowie, Md.: Robert J. Brady Co., 1984.

Harris, Marilyn D. "A Taperecording and Transcribing System to Maintain Patients' Clinical Records." *Nursing and Health Care* 5 (November 1984):503–507.

Harrison, Edward L. "Training Supervisors to Discipline Effectively." *Training and Development Journal* 36 (November 1982):111–113.

Hoffman, Frank. *The Organizational Role of Supervisors, Course 3-R*. Calabasas, Calif.: Practical Management Associates, 1979.

Holloway, Vonicha McClenny. "Documentation: One of the Ultimate Challenges in Home Health Care." *Home HealthCare Nurse* 2 (January/February 1984):19–22.

"Home Health Agencies and Community Nursing Services Accredited by NLN/APHA." *Nursing and Health Care* 6 (January 1985):14–15.

Hughes, Susan L. "Home Health Monitoring: Ensuring Quality in Home Health Services." *Hospitals* 56 (1 November 1982):74–80.

Lachman, Vicki D. "Increasing Productivity Through Performance Evaluation." *Journal of Nursing Administration* 14 (December 1984):7–14.

Lancaster, Jeannette. "Creating a Climate for Excellence." *Journal of Nursing Administration* 15 (January 1985):16–19.

Littlejohn, Carolyn E. "What New Staff Learned and Didn't Learn." *Nursing Outlook* 28 (January 1980):32–35.

McConnell, Charles R. *Managing the Health Care Professional*. Rockville, Md.: Aspen Systems Corp., 1984.

Martin, Richard G. "Five Principles for Corrective Disciplinary Action." *Supervisory Management* 23 (January 1978):24–28.

National HomeCaring Council. *Supervision in Home Care*. New York: National HomeCaring Council, 1982.

O'Donovan, Thomas R. "Performance Evaluation of Subordinates." *Supervisor Nurse* 2 (November 1971):48–57.

Partridge, Rebecca. "Evaluating Performance of Nursing Personnel." *Nursing Leadership* 2 (September 1979): 18–22.

Rutkowski, Barbara Conway, and Arthur D. Rutkowski. "Employee Discharge: It Depends . . . " *Nursing Management* 15 (December 1984):39–42.

Shinnick, Larry. "Home Care Standards Present Unique Medical and Legal Challenge." *AAR Times* 8 (April 1984):70–71.

Spiegel, Allen D. *Home Healthcare*. Owings Mills, Md.: National Health Publishing Ltd., 1983.

Stanhope, Marcia, and Jeannette Lancaster. *Community Health Nursing*. St. Louis: C.V. Mosby Co., 1984.

Stoddard, Sandol. *The Hospice Movement*. Briarcliff Manor, N.Y.: Stein and Day Publishers, 1978.

Thompson, Warren. "Everything You Ever Wanted to Know About Insurance for Home Health Agencies." *Caring* 3 (June 1984):34–45.

Tobin, H. M. et al. *The Process of Staff Development*. St. Louis: C.V. Mosby Co., 1974.

"Tom Peters' Formula for Supervisory Excellence." *Supervisory Management* 30 (February 1985):2–6.

Trager, Brahna. *Homemaker/Home Health Aide Services in the United States*. Washington, D.C.: U.S. Dept. of Health, Education, and Welfare, 1973.

Vesperi, Maria. "Looking behind the Starched Facade." *St. Petersburg Times*, 6 January 1985, pp. 1F–3F.

Wakefield, Douglas S., and Sally Mathis. "Formulating a Managerial Strategy for Part-Time Nurses." *Journal of Nursing Administration* 15 (January 1985):35–39.

Chapter 6

Marketing in Home Health Care

Joanne Meany-Handy

THE NEED FOR A MARKETING PERSPECTIVE

Competition is not new to any home health agency that has entered the field since the 1970s. Indeed, it has been around since the enactment of the Medicare home health benefit in 1966 and the subsequent explosion in the number of home care providers.

The 1980s have seen an unparalleled surge in the home care market, a trend that is expected to continue into the 1990s. The intensity of competition has been fueled by the entrance of hospitals and large health service companies into the field. The ability to function in a highly competitive market is now a necessary skill for an agency's survival.

Results of a joint study conducted by Arthur Andersen and Company and the American College of Hospital Administrators[1] predicted that competition will be redefined in the next ten years. Whereas the quality of services has traditionally been the major competitive factor, the cost of care will now become a dominant factor. Competition will be based more on financial criteria and the ability to survive in a market structured on financial factors.

This shift means that competition in home care will become more like that found in traditional business markets. Although conventional marketing wisdom applicable to selling toothpaste, soap, and other tangible products is not entirely transferable to professional services, parts of it are. Home health agencies must view themselves and their services in terms of marketing concepts and strategies.

WHAT IS MARKETING?

The term marketing usually is used by agencies to mean advertising and promotional activities only. Although such activities are part of marketing, they constitute only a piece of the marketing effort. Marketing includes all the activities an agency engages in to determine what services it will provide and to whom. It is closely aligned with strategic planning in identifying agency directions and opportunities.

Philip Kotler defines marketing as "a human activity directed at satisfying needs and wants through exchange processes."[2] The exchange process means that the consumer obtains a benefit by using the services of a provider. In health care the key task of marketing is to determine the wants, needs, and values of health care consumers, tailor services in such a manner to deliver the desired level of satisfaction, and then attract consumers to use the services.[3]

Home health agencies have historically been alert to community needs, developing programs and services in response to community demands. Marketing requires continuous responsiveness to the perceptions of an agency's constituencies and in that way keeps an agency in touch with these community needs.[4]

The major objectives of marketing in home health care include:

- generating revenues through the development and utilization of income-producing services
- assuring that services reach people who need them
- meeting the intense competition in the field
- building an image for the organization
- achieving continued growth of the services and organization.

KEY MARKETING CONCEPTS

Within the framework of an organization's specific marketing objectives are certain important concepts that are useful in approaching marketing efforts.

The Marketing Mix

The marketing mix consists of the four Ps:

- product/service
- place
- price
- promotion.

Product/Service

Product/service refers to the service that the organization offers or wants to offer. Given the market that the agency wants to serve, what should be the appropriate service mix? The tremendous expansion and resultant diversity of the home care field means that agencies are involved in multiple services: intermittent services, homemaker, private duty nursing, durable medical equipment, medical supplies, hospice, intravenous therapy. Some of these services address the needs of a specific market; others, a more general market.

To market agencywide is a difficult task. Marketing efforts are more effective if they zero in on one area or group of services. Hence the definition of service for each market segment is a crucial step.

Place

In home health care, place refers to access to the agency's services and requires finding the most effective way of making services available to the client. Such factors as hours of service, 24-hour availability, weekend coverage, intake procedures, hospital liaison services, and telephone capabilities need to be considered in developing an access strategy.

Price

Until recently, home care was not viewed as a price-sensitive market. Competition among providers was based on quality, not price. That picture is changing dramatically because of the influence of preferred-provider plans (PPOs) and health maintenance organizations (HMOs) and the approach of Medicare prospective reimbursement for home care. Although quality remains an important consideration, it now must also carry a competitive price.

The key questions in considering the price of a service are, How much will it cost? What will be charged? What incentives can be used?

Promotion

Promotion refers to communication about the services to the desired markets. It is the sales piece of marketing, encompassing selling techniques, public relations, advertising, direct mail campaigns, and brochures.

Unfortunately, many organizations jump into promotional activities without full analysis and consideration of the preceding three Ps. A successful marketing effort must pass all four tests by developing specific strategies in each area.

Market Segmentation

The consumer is the one who benefits from the provision of home health care services. This is generally the patient. Access to the patient often is controlled through referral sources: the hospital, physicians, discharge planners, and other "gatekeepers." The home health care services developed and information about their use must be specifically tailored to identified market segments.

There are multiple ways to segment the market in home care. Demographic factors, such as age, housing arrangements, health status, and income, can differentiate patient groups. Additional segments may include past patients, physicians, hospitals, and diagnosis.

One of the most important and rapidly expanding market segments is purchasers of home health care—the insurance industry, preferred-provider organizations, and the employers, who ultimately foot the bill. Because many of these payors are concerned with lowering the health care costs of a younger, working age group, they require a different mix of services than does the Medicare population traditionally served by home health agencies. For example, the idea that a postpartum nursing visit and a few days of homemaker services can dramatically decrease inpatient maternity costs would spark the interest of an HMO composed of younger enrollees.

Exchange Relationships

For each market segment identified there exists an exchange between the agency and the recipient. The key exchange relationships usually are with physicians, discharge planners, and payor groups. Each group judges a service by the benefits it provides to the group. For example, a discharge planner might want the benefit of "one-stop shopping." The agency provides this benefit by offering a complete range of services through one phone call. Certain physicians' groups place a high priority on current technical skills. An agency responds to this need by employing specialty staff in important technical areas, such as respiratory care or ostomy care.

Defining the nature of the key exchange relationships is an essential step to promoting a service. Effective communication strategies emphasize benefits to the target group rather than services. They answer the question, "What will I gain if I decide to use your services?"

THE MARKETING PLAN

Every home health agency engages in a variety of marketing activities. One could not remain in business for a week without them. The reason one organization's efforts are successful and another's are not is frequently that the marketing activities of the successful organization follow a thoughtfully designed and directed plan. Marketing efforts cannot be shotgun approaches.

A marketing plan generally includes the following six steps:

Step 1: Analyze the Market

To give a marketing strategy a solid foundation, internal and external data must be collected and analyzed. Internal data consist of demographic information on patients served, utilization patterns, sources of referrals, sources of reimbursement, and attitudes of staff.

External data include demographic information on the geographic area served, hospital discharge data, and other health planning information. To determine the agency's image with key market segments, market research in the form of image surveys or related questionnaires may be desired. Surveys should be designed professionally and use accurate sampling techniques.

Step 2: Analyze the Competition

This step starts with a list of each organization that provides home health care within the service area. Quantitative information about the number and types of services provided, number of patients and visits, payor sources, and diagnoses served often can be obtained from the state health department, at least in states in which licensing laws exist. Medicare cost reports, available from the Health Care Financing Administration under the Freedom of Information Act, contain useful cost data on certified agencies. Such quantitative data allow one to calculate percentage of market share and follow trends of changes in market share from year to year. From this list of organizations it is necessary to identify areas in which they are competitive and the degree of competition.

Next, the strengths and weaknesses of major competing organizations need to be identified. This is best approached by gathering together the staff who have any information about other companies and holding a brainstorming session on the other companies' strengths and weaknesses. A competitor's weakness may signal an opportunity for the organization.

Field, intake, and hospital liaison staffs have valuable information about competing agencies. Through their personal contacts with other agency staffs, physicians, and hospital discharge planners they learn about practices of other agencies, their unique characteristics, and reasons referral sources prefer one agency over another. Just calling a competing agency for basic information and listening to how a caller is treated conveys a certain image.

Are they friendly, polite, professional, helpful, and enthusiastic, or bored, rushed, guarded, pushy, and casual?

Competition analysis is an ongoing task. Some organizations maintain a file on each competitor and update it regularly with new information. All agency staff should be aware of this effort so that they can contribute to it as they pick up information.

Step 3: Select Target Markets

A home health agency that has traditionally had a heavy dependence on hospital referrals may determine that it wants to increase referrals from physicians. The target market thus becomes physicians, who can be delineated into certain submarkets:

- physicians who have referred to the agency
- physicians who are associated with certain hospitals
- physician members of PPOs
- physicians by specialty: internists, orthopedists, surgeons, cardiologists, oncologists

Step 4: Identify the Service Mix

As discussed earlier in this chapter, the choice of the specific services to be promoted out of the diverse range of services provided by many agencies depends on the target market selected. If physicians are targeted, a service mix that addresses the medical problems they commonly encounter may be selected. Nursing services emphasizing technological skills of intravenous therapy or respiratory care may appeal to internists and cardiologists. Chemotherapy could attract the oncologists' interests, while physical therapy meets the orthopedic surgeons' needs.

If the target market is an HMO serving a young population, the service mix could be entirely different. It might emphasize short-term ambulatory surgery follow-up care and postmaternity services.

Step 5: Select Strategies for Each Market Segment

Strategies are determined for each part of the marketing mix: product/service, place, price, and promotion.

Product/Service

Service strategies commonly include the development of new services and the emphasis on specialty services. Offering "one-stop shopping" by providing full intermittent care, continuous shift care, hospice, durable medical equipment, and other related services is a commonly seen strategy. Some organizations choose to specialize in one area, such as high-tech services or pediatrics, and become identified as leaders in that market. This often proves to be an effective strategy for smaller agencies with an appropriate target market. An agency may lead with one service, such as hospice, and allow it to open up opportunities to promote all other agency services.

An important service strategy commonly used by home health agencies is the provision of free liaison services to hospitals, physicians' groups, and community agencies. A nurse or other appropriate professional is available to these referral sources to assist with discharge planning, visit prospective patients, and provide feedback to them on patients' progress once under home care.

Additional service enhancements include free home evaluations before a patient's hospital discharge, pre-discharge teaching in the hospital, and prompt written and oral feedback to referral sources.

Place

Access strategies are at the heart of many of the referral relationships that have developed between home care providers and referral sources. A common relationship is a contractual agreement in which a hospital uses one agency for most of its home care. In such arrangements the presence of a home care coordinator or home care service team in the hospital enhances access to services by patients, physicians, and hospital staff.

The intake function of home health agencies has increasingly been handled by professional staff, primarily nurses. Although this shift began as the referral process became viewed as the first step in professional assessment, it is now an essential access strategy. Referral sources consistently express their preference to give a home care referral to a nurse, therapist, or social worker—someone who understands the clinical picture, speaks the same language, and uses professional judgment in requesting intake information.

The availability of intake services is another access issue. Agencies are extending their intake hours to accommodate late afternoon, evening, and weekend referrals. Twenty-four-hour service availability, initially provided mainly with hospice and intravenous therapy care, is becoming the norm for all types of home care services.

The ability to respond quickly to referrals is another access strategy. Although 24-hour response time is generally the norm for home health agencies, same-day service, or even four-hour response time, can be important to specialized service markets, such as phototherapy or laboratory services.

Price

Within certified home health agencies, pricing strategies are limited by the Medicare cost-reimbursement system. To compete successfully the basic strategy is to keep one's costs as low as possible and set the charge close to the cost.

Discounting is an increasingly common strategy when seeking HMO and PPO contracts. With an HMO, a capitation rate, with its attendant risks or rewards, may provide a competitive edge over a provider offering a fee for service arrangement.

In the private home care market, pricing strategies show greater variation. A fee structure that uses a declining hourly rate as hours of service increase is effective in certain markets. Charging by the service rather than by the hour, as in a bath service or a "tuck-in service," is commonly seen.

Price is not restricted to monetary values, but can include factors of convenience. For example, if a client pays a low hourly rate for service but receives that service at an inconvenient time for the family, the total price may be too high.

Promotion

Promotional activities are the most visible piece of the marketing mix. The core promotional tool of every agency usually is the brochure. Because of a variety of factors, including budgetary restrictions, agencies design and use the brochure as a universal tool for all market segments. This is difficult to do, as the information a patient wants is not necessarily the same information that a physician or discharge planner wants. Promotional materials need to be designed with the target audience in mind. Hence an agency may have a patient brochure, a physician fact sheet, and a newsletter designed for the hospital referral audience.

Differentiation of services from those of competitors is an especially difficult task when promoting professional services. One useful approach is to establish the organization as possessing certain attractive attributes and then communicate a distinctive image. For example, the need to be perceived as having experience is an important criterion for use of professional services.[5] An agency can emphasize "providing home care since 1935" or "serving the community for 25 years." Other important service features to emphasize are compassion, caring, technological innovation, caliber of staff, and dependability.

Written promotional or sales information should focus on the benefits of the service to the target market, not merely on a description of the services. Statements of benefits might include peace of mind, immediate feedback to referral source, assurance of highest quality services, ease of referral, and no paperwork. A common practice is distribution of agency information in a packet or binder that encourages retention and allows for insertion of updates.

Agencies can go to considerable effort and expense to produce promotional materials only to find that the materials are not being used appropriately by field staff or others who come in contact with target markets. Staff may not know how to use the materials or may not find them useful for their purposes. Use and distribution cannot be taken for granted—planning and training are necessary.

Sales calls to discharge planners and physicians is another common promotional technique. One-to-one personal selling is viewed as more important for promoting professional services than it is for other services or products. Referral sources and patients generally prefer to be courted by people who actually perform the services.[6] Some agencies focus this responsibility in one staff position; others distribute it among service staff and supervisors according to geographical area. As in other businesses, sales training is growing in popularity in home care.

Because physicians are such a large target market, personal selling is limited in its ability to reach every physician with a sales call. Direct mail approaches are sometimes favored when dealing with this large an individual audience. There are multiple techniques for direct mail solicitation. The use of a well-written cover letter, the size and color of the envelope, the manner of address, and the frequency of contact are important considerations.

All the community activities with which a home health agency is involved constitute promotional opportunities. Offering health education classes in senior housing, providing blood pressure screening at nutrition sites, attending corporate health fairs, speaking to church groups all provide important contacts with potential clients. These activities, although initiated for many reasons, should be woven into the marketing plan.

Step 6: Implement the Marketing Plan

Although the responsibility for the plan should rest with one person in the agency, marketing activities should be part of everyone's job. The field staff of a home health care organization constitute a built-in sales force, who, with appropriate training and marketing tools, can be an integral part of the marketing effort.

The key to agencywide marketing is the creation of a market-oriented organizational climate in which staff understand the competition in the home care field, contribute to the marketing plan, and view promoting the agency's services as part of their job responsibility. The switchboard operator, the secretaries, and the billing clerks need to realize the importance of the manner in which they deal with each client on the telephone and their contribution to the agency's image. Staff generally respond well to professional public relations. They are the people who have the majority of contact with clients and referral sources, and every effort should be made to use their contributions and marketing potential.

The activities of the marketing plan generally are plotted out over the course of the year. The responsible staff person monitors progress, assures that time frames are met, revises activities as needed, and integrates additional marketing opportunities that arise spontaneously.

Progress toward the marketing objectives determines the success of the efforts. Perhaps one goal was to increase physician referrals by 10 percent. Did it occur? Referral statistics broken down by key market segments are an essential evaluative tool. All new clients or referral sources can be asked on intake how they heard about the organization. Some service requests may stem from Yellow Pages advertising, whereas others are generated by a personal sales call. Each activity that has been implemented should be evaluated for its contribution to the marketing objectives and subsequent determination of its continuance.

CONCLUSION

In the dynamic and competitive home health care arena the organization that has a well-designed and carefully thought out marketing plan will occupy a strong position. Now more than ever home care professionals are applying the principles and practices of marketing traditionally used by commercial businesses to the home health field.

NOTES

1. American College of Hospital Administrators, *Health Care in the 1990's: Trends and Strategies*.

2. Philip Kotler, *Marketing Management, Analysis, Planning and Control 1980* (Englewood Cliffs, N.J.: Prentice-Hall, 1980), p.19

3. Philip Cooper, ed. *Health Care Marketing* (Rockville, Md.: Aspen Systems Corp., 1979), p. 7.

4. Robin MacStravic, *Marketing Health Care* (Rockville, Md.: Aspen Systems Corp., 1977), p. 16.

5. Paul Bloom, "Effective Marketing for Professional Services," *Harvard Business Review* 62 (September/October 1984): 104.

6. Ibid., p. 107

Chapter 7

Planning

Steven Rosenberg

For many years advocates of home health services for the residents of rural communities have been frustrated in their efforts to design a mechanism that delivers home health services in remote areas. The development of such a mechanism has been impeded by the vast distances that separate one beneficiary from another and that exist between the homes of the beneficiaries and the offices of the providers; the high costs in time and money that are involved in traveling such distances; the difficulties in recruiting and maintaining qualified providers; and the stress and burn-out factors of being an isolated provider to an incapacitated patient population.

The problem has been complicated by the fact that the more isolated the community, the greater the difficulty of developing a cost-effective system to provide this much-needed care. The proposed shift in Medicare reimbursement to a prospective rate for home health care has only increased the difficulty of providing care in isolated rural communities. A strategy recently developed for providing home health services to an isolated community in northeastern California may be applicable for other rural areas as well.

THE TARGET COMMUNITY

The target communities for the strategy are located in two isolated valleys in the northern California Cascade and Sierra mountain ranges, just south of Oregon. The service area encompasses approximately 5,000 persons, over 15 percent of whom are elderly. The population is located over a sprawling countryside (more than 7,500 square miles) that is plagued by severe travel problems in winter owing to hazardous road conditions and a lack of public transportation. These conditions made transportation to medical treatment at the nearest hospital, 30 miles to the north, extremely difficult, particularly for the frail elderly and postpartum mothers; the problem was compounded by the lack of physicians in the area.

The nearest home health agency, a Visiting Nurses Association (VNA), was located more than 50 miles away, over one of the mountains that surrounded the valley. The offices of the VNA were inaccessible one to two days a week during the winter because of storms. Although the VNA had, over the years, been making a sincere effort to service the valley, the distances had proved too vast for that agency to service effectively.

The problems that confronted the VNA are not much different from problems that confront providers of home health care in most remote rural communities. These include:

- Difficulty in recruiting qualified staff into these communities because they tend to feel isolated professionally.

- Without a support staff nearby, staff have to take on increased responsibilities for such patient care-related issues as negotiating the purchase and delivery of durable medical equipment, arranging for medication delivery, acting as the patient's advocate in enrolling and negotiating social support services, and often serving as the only contact to the outside world for incapacitated, isolated elderly. This level of responsibility quickly burns out professionals who often have their own heavy load of "rural life style" chores to undertake.

- Nurses on staff have difficulty arranging delivery of the full range of skilled in-home services, as it is usually impossible to access necessary ancillary services, such as skilled therapies, medical social services, and physicians.

Given the constraints of today's fiscal climate, few nonprofit corporations can afford the costs of recruiting, training, and marketing home health services in a rural community, no matter how apparent the need. And given the time it is likely to take to build a full caseload in a rural area, these difficulties will probably increase under home health prospective payment.

In the target community the pressure for home health services was increasing because of a concerted effort on the part of the local hospital to promote early discharge as its response to the prospective payment of diagnosis-related groups (DRGs). The only health provider in the area, a National Health Service Corps (NHSC) site, staffed by a nurse practitioner who gets backup from a physician located 30 miles away, was unable to respond to the hospital's pressures for early discharge.

The NHSC clinic had, over the years, received grant funds from the state through a categorical grant program targeted to isolated rural communities such as this valley. In an attempt to increase the access to a full range of health services in the community and respond to the pressures of prospective payment, the state provided the clinic with funds to procure the services of Rosenberg Associates.

An assessment of the area quickly identified home health care as a much-needed community service. The distances to the VNA had impeded its ability to serve the community effectively. In addition, DRG pressure on small rural hospitals was promoting earlier home discharge. Although the NHSC site had considered developing its own home health agency, the costs of such development and the administrative expertise required to run a home health agency were likely to tax the clinic beyond the ability of its small staff, which consisted of a family nurse practitioner, a registered nurse, and a receptionist. A feasibility study was done to determine the economic viability of home health care in the community and explore alternative strategies for development.

One potential strategy for development was a provision of Public Law 95-210, the Rural Health Clinics Act, that created a mechanism for rural clinics to receive reimbursement for home health nursing services in their communities. This law provides reimbursement for nursing services only, not for home health aides or other ancillary services. Therefore, the feasibility study needed to determine whether a strategy that provided nursing services only might be more viable than a full-service home health agency.

ASSESSING THE NEEDS AND DEMAND FOR HOME HEALTH CARE SERVICES

In trying to determine the likely level of home health need/demand in the area, it was quickly realized that most health planning formulas developed for such purposes were based on normative usage data gathered in well-served urban areas. A review of the literature failed to discover any proven methods for predicting home health need in isolated rural areas.

In addition, the urban-based formulas include formulas for predicting the need/demand for home health aide services that function as a complement to skilled nursing and therapy care. The strategy of using 95-210, however, did not allow for such nonnursing services as aides or therapies. It was felt, therefore, that the feasibility study would need to develop a mechanism for predicting the need for nursing services when those services were provided in a rural community without all the ancillaries of a traditional home health agency.

Forced to rely on experience, the actual utilization experience at the more than 15 rural Medicare- or Medicaid-certified agencies throughout the United States that the firm of Rosenberg Associates had helped to establish over the past 10 years was surveyed. Average market penetration and visit averages by service type were extracted from the actual initial experiences of

each provider. These averages were then compared with the initial penetration and visit averages experienced by a sampling of home health agencies
located in northern California counties that were primarily rural. After it was
seen that the service utilization was fairly comparable, this approach served
to establish probable normative user levels for a new rural home health
agency.

These normative values provided a basis of prediction for nurse visits in an
average rural home health agency. In our target community, however, we
needed to factor in the effect a lack of ancillaries would have on utilization of
nurses. To determine that effect, we needed to place the problem of rural
home health delivery within the context of delivery of all services in a rural
environment.

When working within a rural context the first observation professionals
make is the blurring of distinctions between roles. This is particularly true at
95-210 sites, where nurse practitioners function in the traditional role of
physician. A nurse delivering in-home nursing services in a rural area is
expected to go beyond the simple delivery of skilled care to assist patients
with many activities of daily life that, in highly compartmentalized urban
agencies, are considered home health aide tasks.

In addition, the need for home health aides is slightly alleviated in the rural
areas, where community and family volunteerism is traditionally stronger
than in urban centers. Family and friends can usually be counted on to visit
infirm   elderly on an ongoing basis and to perform many of the duties
traditionally performed by skilled aides in an urban setting. The key is to
have the clinic's home health nurse time her or his visits in order to provide
basic in-home care training and supervision for the client's informal care
network.

When family and friends are not available, the clinic can work with the
local area agencies on aging to target their limited homemaker dollars to
these particularly isolated clients. Working with the nurse, these homemakers
can be trained to provide a range of semiskilled services in the absence of
friends or relatives.

Given the combination of alternatives, it was determined that the expected
increase in nursing visits owing to lack of ancillary providers could be
predicted to range between 20 percent and 25 percent above the normative
value for rural home health agencies.

DEVELOPING A FORMULA FOR PREDICTING
FEASIBILITY

The first step in translating these need /demand assessments to predictive
formulas was to assess the need/demand for home health services by

predicting the need generated from short-stay hospital discharges and the need generated from all other sources. The formula used was:

1. .10 $\times$ number of short-stay (acute) hospital discharges to home health care, plus

2. Half the number generated by 1., representing need generated from all other referred sources.

(Therefore, total number of persons in need of home health services = 1 + 2.)

This formula could be improved if it weighed the effects of such factors as the number of people of all ages with a limiting physical or mental disability who have not been institutionalized, the people in congregate living arrangements, the people inappropriately placed in institutions, and the people under age 65 who may need home care (such as after an accident or childbirth). Imprecise as this derived method is, it can be used to establish demand ranges until more precise methods are developed and tested and until data from their use can be collected and analyzed.

The following example demonstrates how the formula was used to estimate home health need for the area studied:

Population of rural county	6,000
Assume 15 percent acute care discharges annually	900
Predict 10 percent of those people need home health services	90
Predict 5 percent from other referral sources	45
Total potential home health patients	135

Patient Projections

Using 135 as a base, it was assumed that during its first year of operation a new home health agency (even one that is sponsored by the only medical provider in the area) will only serve 25 percent of the number estimated by the formula, or 35 patients. Also assumed was a 75 percent/25 percent Medicare/Medicaid reimbursement mix.

Caution should be used in accepting a 25 percent penetration rate for every community. The special needs of a community vary and require groups to make adjustments for such factors as existence of other providers, competition, lack of community and provider education, size of the area to be served, and special linguistic considerations.

Staffing Projections

Nationally, patients of skilled home health agencies tend to average 14 to 20 skilled nursing visits per illness, depending on such factors as region, provider type, and reimbursement coverage. Given that no home health aides are allowed under the 95-210 program, and that skilled therapists were available only on a limited basis to most of the service area, it was necessary to increase these skilled nursing projections by 20 percent to 25 percent. Thus a first-year skilled nursing visit projection of 646 visits was made.

USING THE PROVISIONS OF PUBLIC LAW 95-210

Unable to develop a free-standing home health agency, a little-known provision of the Rural Health Clinics Act, Public Law 95-210, which was passed by the 95th Congress in 1977 and contained a provision that enabled the site to provide home health services, was used as an alternative strategy. This law was passed by Congress in recognition of the problems faced by many rural communities in attracting physicians. For those small communities, the services of a nurse practitioner (NP) or physician's assistant (PA) may be the only health services available. But before 95-210, NPs or PAs in rural communities were unable to receive reimbursement for their services from the Medicaid or Medicare programs.

Thus Public Law 95-210 was enacted to enable rural health clinics to further their ability to deliver services by increasing their Medicare and Medicaid revenue. In recognizing the problem of delivery in rural areas, Congress mandated that 95-210 clinics be reimbursed by the Medicare and Medicaid programs on the basis of their costs of providing services. This cost-based reimbursement was structured so that any rural delivery site, whether operated as a private practice or as a not-for-profit community clinic, could participate in the program and receive the benefits of cost-based reimbursement as long as it met two criteria:

1. The site must be located in a federally designated medically underserved area (MUA) or health-manpower-shortage area (HMSA). If a site is located in neither one of these areas but was delivering services on July 1, 1977, in an area that is determined by the secretary of the Department of Health and Human Services to have a shortage of primary care physicians, it can also participate in the program.

2. The site must have a midlevel practitioner available at least 60 percent of the time that the clinic is open.

Once a site has met these criteria, it then applies to the State Health Department for certification as a 95-210 provider. After certification, a designated fiscal intermediary works with the site to set an all-inclusive cost-based rate for Medicare and Medicaid services. If the site is in a state that offers optional Medicaid services under its state Medicaid plan, then the state has the right to determine whether it wishes to pay for those optional services on a fee-for-service basis or whether it wishes the intermediary to include those optional services in the clinic's all-inclusive rate and therefore develop a separate rate for Medicare and Medicaid.

An all-inclusive cost-based rate means that the clinic is paid the same amount from the Medicare or Medicaid program, regardless of the service delivered. For example, if a clinic's rate for Medicare is determined to be $30, the clinic will, after a beneficiary has met its deductible, receive 80 percent of $30, or $24 for every service that every practitioner provides to beneficiaries in every location—be that service an NP doing blood pressure checks or a staff physician assisting a surgical procedure. The beneficiary is responsible for the remaining 20 percent of the charge for the service, not the all-inclusive cost. As most isolated rural clinics do limited amounts of inpatient procedures, instead of referring those to practitioners in larger communities that have hospitals, Public Law 95-210 has enabled many rural sites to increase their third party income dramatically.

In addition to increasing the third party income of a provider, 95-210 has a special section that enables certified sites that provide services in an area with a shortage of home health services to receive cost-based reimbursement for home health care provided by a registered or practical nurse. The law does not provide for the reimbursement of aide services.

In the example of the target community, the clinic was located in a HMSA and thus staffed by NHSC personnel. The NP was available 100 percent of the time the clinic was open, and the clinic was thus eligible to participate in the program. Because there was a clearly perceived need for home health services in the area, an application was made to the Health Care Financing Administration (HCFA) for designation of the clinic's community as a home health shortage area. This application for designation was the first that the regional HCFA office had received, and the HCFA staff required a substantial amount of explanation as to the provisions of 95-210.

After examining the facts, the HCFA granted this designation, and the clinic became certified to provide home health services delivered by a registered or practical nurse to a homebound patient. Because almost all of the residents of the target communities are patients of the clinic and the staff is intimately familiar with both their health status and their living situations, the marketing of the home health service has happened with great ease.

In starting the program the clinic chose to use the services of its office nurse on a part-time basis to provide homebound services. As the program grows, it is planning to add a special staff person to respond to the needs of the homebound. This incremental approach has enabled the clinic to generate additional revenue from the services of the nurse without increasing its costs. It has also enabled the clinic to provide care for patients from a practitioner they are familiar with and to provide for excellent continuity in care.

APPLICABILITY OF THE STRATEGY IN OTHER LOCATIONS

Given that many rural communities have primary care sites (both clinic and private practice) that use the services of midlevel practitioners, in those rural areas that are also experiencing a shortage of home health services, the 95-210 route may be an excellent way of providing this much-needed care.

By participating in the 95-210 program, cost-effective care is more possible both because it increases a program's ability to develop its home health service incrementally and because of the all-inclusive nature of the reimbursement. Having the home health services incorporated in the primary care site mitigates many of the problems of professional isolation, the lack of support staff, and the need for ancillary services. It also creates the foundation for continuum of care by promoting continuity of providers and excellent linkages between providers.

Part II

Delivering Home Health Nursing Care

Chapter 8

The Qualities of a Home Health Care Nurse

Linda G. Cherryholmes

This chapter addresses the unique qualities one would seek in a home health nurse. Numerous home health and hospital nurses were interviewed to see how they felt about this topic. Each was asked what "special qualities" were necessary to function well in her or his chosen role. Also queried were interviewers and supervisors, who usually conduct hiring interviews, as to what they look for in an interview that would make that person be a prime candidate for either a home health or a hospital nursing position. Clients were also queried about their view of the nurses who came to visit them.

Through the history and evolution of nursing there have been few changes in the basic principles and standards of nursing. Some of the most common and accepted standards are health promotion, health maintenance, health education, and disease prevention. Also acknowledged is the need for holistic and comprehensive planning for coordination and continuity of care. The nursing profession has gone through many changes in its process of evolution, and there has been a changing scope of nursing practice, with the trend toward increased specialization. Today's nurse can be a generalist or a specialist in the hospital as well as in the community health setting.

How does a nurse prepare for home health nursing? What does this specialty require? Is this a specialty within the framework of community health nursing, or a general area of its own with subspecialties? Does there need to be additional or specialized education? Does that body of knowledge have to come with the nurse, or can it be obtained as the nurse is oriented to home health? These are philosophical questions that are often asked. This chapter seeks to portray the uniqueness of the home health nurse.

Care in the community calls for a change in the basic attitudes on the part of many home health workers. There is a need to change the traditional modes of thinking in regard to the providers and recipients of care. Community health nursing services are directed toward developing and enhancing the health capabilities of people. The recipient of care, the client, has to be seen as part of the family and community. A holistic and humanistic philosophy of home care, the question of control and decision making, the family unity theme, and the crushing problem of paying for the many services are other areas that community nurses address.

QUALITIES

The nurse in home health has to have a philosophy that is holistic, family-centered, broad, and nonjudgmental and must accept others and their value systems. The home care ethic contends that the client and the family unit come first. The nurse entering the home health field has to have the usual educational preparation, but experience in medical-surgical, rehabilitation, and gerontological nursing will greatly enhance the breadth of care delivered.

A humane approach is paramount in meeting the needs of ill people, especially in their home environment. Some factors that show that this nurse values providing quality care in a professional manner are the kind of life experiences she has had, her value system, and her awareness of self. Her knowledge also needs to encompass religious, ethnic, social, and economic influences that affect her client and family. Just within her visiting territory these can vary widely and be of such a diverse nature that her attention is required. The customs, mores, and traditions of the family have long been established, and the nurse must be aware of this and proceed cautiously, rather than responding first to her own value system. Home health care is a total involvement with the client and family. They are to be dealt with on their own terms, in their own home, following their established habits and customs.

Out in the community, the nurse is alone on the client's turf. She cannot push, and has to know when to pull back. She has to like dealing with families. The whole family has to be involved in the care planning, along with the client, so that everyone shares the commitment of progress. The individual, the client, plays a central role, around which all else revolves. The home health nurse has to be able to be comfortable in nonstructured situations and to have an ability to relate to people in varied environments. The nurse has to be extremely tolerant of others' lifestyles and habits and to be aware that one cannot change the habits of a lifetime.

"Patience with our patients," is a saying to abide by, as well as, "love and respect the elderly." Respect their dignity, privacy, need for autonomy, and even the manner in which they are addressed. Such patients may tend to reminisce; one woman recited her medical history according to where she and her husband had been stationed during his 30-year military career — gallbladder trouble in Portsmouth, URIs in Boston, broken leg in San Francisco, and so on.

Other qualities are sensitivity, flexibility, adaptability, and a large dose of common sense. Empathy should be one of the strongest qualities of a home health nurse. Working one to one and understanding the client's problem and point of view are both elements of concern. It can be wearing on the nurse, and she has to give a great deal of herself in this role. The home health nurse works autonomously but at the same time has to be able to enlist the support, gain the cooperation, and have constant communication and rapport with the client, the family, and other health care professionals. There has to be confidence building to maximize the helping potential. She is in someone else's territory, and the main purpose is to assist the client and the family to function at their best possible level for preventing dependency. A fundamental of the nurse's practice would be health promotion activities that foster the client's well-being and that are aimed at preventing recurrence of illness.

The nurse has to feel comfortable with the unknown. One never knows what is behind that front door. A nurse is not a manager, nor is he or she in control of the situation or environment. The home health nurse has to be able to go into any type of environment or home and must be able to communicate on the appropriate level. There are many environmental distractions, and the nurse has to be able to work with and withstand the elements of nature and various creatures of nature. There is an awareness of the total environment and its influences. Also, she has to be adaptable to the environment. She can go from a less than desirable neighborhood to one of the finest. She needs to be streetwise, to know the safest way to walk and drive within her area and how to handle herself in different neighborhoods. She must have a knowledge of ethnic cultures, ways, and mores, know that certain behaviors and actions that are acceptable with one culture are unacceptable with another. It is beneficial if a nurse can speak another language, especially in communities that have large populations of foreign-speaking people.

The home health nurse has to be able to accept the clients' perceptions and the reality of their environment and lifestyle. A knowledge of the overall needs of the person is very important. In the home situation, the nurse is more intimately involved. She learns the innerworkings of the family because she is in close contact over a longer time span than in a hospital. It is a more relaxed environment, and a personal relationship develops with the client and family. She deals much more with the emotions of everyday.

The nurse must be able to terminate the therapeutic relationship effectively. This can be difficult owing to the investment of energies on the part of both the nurse and the client. It can be likened to seeing one's firstborn go to the first day of school. The goal has been the client's independence, to function the best he or she can with what he or she has, but it is also a trifle sad because so much love, caring, concern, and commitment have been expended to reach this point.

ABILITIES OR STRENGTHS

More technical skills are needed today. The home health nurse is a higher-leveled generalist who has to be able to recognize problems and trust her own judgment and clinical skills. Knowledge of norms is necessary because there is no peer just down the hall with whom to corroborate.

Fine assessment skills are crucial. The nurse has to be able to assess the client's response to medications, treatment, teaching, and changes in physical status. The nurse is a teacher and has to have the ability to think on her feet as to when the prime and optimum moment for teaching is most beneficial. There can be flexibility in this because of the visit schedule. A small amount of teaching can be done at each visit, and the nurse will be able to see how much the client is learning. She can look for feedback and give reinforcement when progress has been made. The home health nurse has to plan ahead, to determine what the goals are, what will be covered this visit and the next. Then, how is she going to assist the client to achieve his or her goals? She must be independent in her nursing functions, have keen and reliable judgment, with faith in her own abilities.

She is a problem solver and seeks, first, to assist the client in identifying the problem and then work through the problem-solving process. She should be familiar with the concept of change. Being able to use the dynamic forces that influence change is a vital part of the totality of working in community health. She has to be able to assist the client to see the need for change and then help the client through the change process.

She has initiative and is a self-starter. There has to be some flexibility in being able to deal with and treat people with challenging cases and situations. The nurse needs to have the ability to organize. Often she sets up her own schedule regarding visits, the number of visits per week, and the number of clients seen per week and per day. Also necessary is the ability to schedule for the convenience of the client as well as for the individual nurse. Truly necessary in home health is the ability to read a map, to have a sense of direction, and to be able to navigate. There are many other qualities for a home health nurse, such as versatility and systems savvy, which is a knowledge of the health care bureaucracy and how to work with it and within it. The home health nurse also needs to have the ability to make decisions, to be cost-conscious, innovative, and able to improvise.

LIMITATIONS

There is less one-on-one supervision in home health. The team leader or head nurse is not just down the hall. Also, there is far less peer support. The nurse cannot go around the corner to a peer to ask a question. True, there is a supervisor available by phone, if the client happens to have a telephone. Resources are not as readily available. There is no med room, nor is there a central supply in another part of the building. Medical libraries, journals, peers, or consultants are not in the same area with the home health nurse. There is no one at that time with whom to discuss thoughts or ideas. Also the nurse does not have backup physically present. It is in the office, but it is not nearby and there is no "next shift" to carry on. She has to do her work and do it in a complete manner and then move on to the next client, but each of her clients is her responsibility. Some environmental distractions can be extremely uncomfortable, such as safety, weather, neighborhoods, and creatures. If she cannot accept the habits of others, then home health may not be the field for her. Homes can be dirty and have a number of nature's creatures roaming about freely. Another limitation is that one does establish a close and oftentimes long-term relationship with the client and family, and sometimes that empathy can lead to sympathy, which can then be an interference.

ROLES

The nurse in home health plays multiple roles. This person wears many hats. She is part social worker, financial counselor, dietitian, consumer/client advocate, teacher, case manager, and coordinator. Many of the roles overlap. The home health nurse has to be self-reliant and have the ability to pace. It is imperative that she remain the client advocate and realize that her role is as coordinator, that she does not overstep her bounds. At times there is a fine line between nursing and medical judgment. She is a friend, a spiritual comforter, a psychologist to the client and family. She is also a physical therapist, an occupational therapist, and a translator of medical information. Another role is that of facilitator, because the client is the one with the active role, and the home care nurse seeks to assist the client to achieve the goal of positive health behaviors. It is necessary to nurture and develop an interrelationship.

There are many aspects of direct care, such as assessment, treatments, teaching, a role model for positive health behaviors, and technical skill. The home health nurse needs to have a knowledge base of the regulatory mechanisms and the methods of reimbursement that determine what is a skilled service so that the agency can receive reimbursement. There are many aspects of indirect care—consultation with other health personnel, staffings, team conferences—as everyone works together to facilitate the client in achieving the highest level of wellness.

INTERACTIONS

Communication skills are prime in the role of the home health nurse. She and the other team members convey an attitude of warmth, caring, and kindness. One of the goals is to assist the client to understand the "why" of the treatments and what is necessary to achieve wellness.

The home health nurse is a relatively independent practitioner. There is a multidisciplinary team, true, but it is not a team as in a hospital. The physician remains the "coach" of the team, but the nurse is the quarterback who coordinates and uses the strengths of the other team members.

Caution is essential to avoid using the label of "noncompliance." Give the client the benefit of the doubt. He may desire to comply, but some factor is influencing his ability not to comply. Seek to unearth the elusive factor. Because someone chooses against what we believe to be right doesn't mean that they are noncompliant. Remember, you are their advocate; I may not agree with you, but I'll support your right of choice.

In working with the client and family, teaching them, and gaining their cooperation, the home health nurse has to be able to assimilate data and then communicate it concisely to the physician and other members of the health care team. The nurse must be able to develop a working relationship with others to promote coordinated and thoughtful action.

The goals must be mutually established; they should not be just the nurse's goals but should be based on the client's perception of the situation. The nurse and client should agree mutually; then, it is hoped, there will be better compliance owing to an ownership in the goals; the client will then strive to meet them with greater enthusiasm. The nurse has to be accepting of the client's right to self-determination regarding decision making, and his decision may be not to comply with the treatment. A question that may be asked is, "How much noncompliance can the team tolerate?"

NURSING PLAN

The home health nurse has a broad knowledge of community resources. She is a practiced and skilled diplomat, is able to assess and weigh alternatives and choose the best course of action for all concerned while maintaining objectivity. The nurse has the ability to assume the role of others temporarily with direction from the supervisor or administrator, especially if nursing responsibilities are unclear or seem inappropriate. The concept of case management establishes a system of appraisal, care planning, and care evaluation. There is an enhancement of the continuity of care, and all care providers should describe the client in identical terms. In the case management system there is a professional plan to meet the individual's needs. A written plan of action is imperative to ensure that tasks are carried out, that established standards are complied with, and that there is continuous reassessment and evaluation.

The nursing process is ever ongoing, with constant reassessment, reordering of priorities, and then new mutual goal setting and revision of plan. It is imperative to tailor the nursing plan to the client and the client's environment. Using the nursing process is a way to ensure the current client need while anticipating needs that may surface in the future. Case management is a coordination of the work of various disciplines in reducing health risk, and it is usually the nurse who coordinates because she is usually the person who opens the record. The nursing process is extremely valuable, especially the reassessment and reevaluation phases to modify plans as needed.

CONSUMER

New habits of self-reliance and self-care have to be learned, and the client has to incorporate wellness, preventive health, and holistic care in his or her daily life. The nurse is a role model for these positive health behaviors. The consumer is provided with data needed to make informed decisions about promoting, maintaining, and restoring health, about seeking and using appropriate health care resources.

SYSTEMS

Utilization of a systems approach is one of the primary foundations of community health. There are social systems and subsystems; all have a mutual respect for the rights and obligations of others. There are many players in this system and, one hopes, a willingness to address the major issues. There are many alliances and supportive networks to be developed. An objective of the home health nurse is to determine the power structure of all the systems—the agency, the client, the family, and the other members of the health care community. The interactions of the team are prime in order to render the finest care in an efficient and cost-effective manner.

SUMMARY

The home health nurse is a caring, autonomous, and accountable professional. This nurse values the client and the behaviors that promote the highest level of wellness for the individual. The focus of care is on disease prevention and health maintenance. The dynamics of interactions are paramount—among the client, the family, and the multidisciplinary health care team. As with nurses in other specialty areas, certain qualities are unique to the home health nurse.

REFERENCES

American Nurses' Association. *Standards of Community Health Nursing Practice.* Kansas City, Mo.: ANA, 1973.

———. *A Conceptual Model of Community Health Nursing.* Kansas City, Mo.: ANA, 1980.

———. *A Guide for Community-based Nursing Services.* A draft document. Kansas City, Mo.: ANA, 1984.

Arbeiter, Jean S. "The Big Shift to Home Health Nursing." *RN* 47 (1984): 38–45.

Cobb-McMahon, Barbara A., David D. Williams, and Joy Hastings Davis. "Changing Health Behavior of Community Health Clients." *Journal of Community Health Nursing* 1 (1984): 27–31.

De Crosta, Tony, ed. "Home Health Care: It's Red Hot and Right Now." *NursingLife* 4 (1984): 54–60.

Florida Nurses Association. *Position Statement on the Role of the Community Health Nurse.* Orlando, Fla.: Florida Nurses Association, 1984.

Grau, Lois. "What Older Adults Expect from the Nurse." *Geriatric Nursing* 5 (1984): 14–18.

Mayers, Marlene. "Home Visit-Ritual or Therapy?" *Nursing Outlook* 21 (1973): 328–331.

Spiegel, Allen D. *Home Healthcare.* Owings Mills, Md.: National Health Publishing, 1983.

Stanhope, Marcia, and Jeanette Lancaster. *Community Health Nursing: Process and Practice for Promoting Health.* St. Louis: C. V. Mosby Co., 1984.

Stewart, Jane Emmert. *Home Health Care.* St. Louis: C. V. Mosby Co., 1979.

Weinstein, Sharon M. "Specialty Teams in Home Care." *Nursing84* (1984): 342–345.

Chapter 9

Assessing the Patient in the Home Environment

Sandra M. Hillman

From its inception, home health nursing has provided personal health care to individuals in the home environment within the context of their family unit. This family-centered approach to home health care has been, and continues to be, based on the recognition of the interrelationship between the health of a family and the community of which it is a part. The home health nurse focuses on gaining information concerning the health of individual family members not only through the use of a variety of pre-assessment and assessment tools (i.e., cultural orientation, communication, the use of a conceptual framework for working with families), but also through the identification of how the data acquired through this assessment affect the health of the individual, the family, and the community.

Often the nurse in home health care is primarily interested in focusing care on a specific patient within a family who requires physician-ordered care and is insurance-reimbursable. Despite this fact, it is important that a family focus be incorporated into the practice. This chapter focuses on the nursing assessment of the patient in the home setting. Before a comprehensive assessment of the individual can be implemented, a pre-assessment phase, in which the home health nurse assimilates into the family and establishes a trusting, open relationship with its members, must be accomplished. This phase is crucial to the future success of any interventions the nurse may initiate for the purpose of patient problem resolution.

Once the nurse has established an interaction with the patient, her next major function is to perform a comprehensive family assessment. Although this approach to assessment includes the assessment of the individual family members, it is broader, wider ranging, more detailed, and somewhat different from the assessment made by nurses who practice in other areas of health care.

This chapter operationally defines pre-assessment and assessment within the home environment; compares home health care assessment of the patient

163

with patient assessment in other health care settings; and defines the relationship between the pre-assessment and the assessment phases of the nursing process. A variety of tools available to the community health nurse that serve to facilitate the implementation of the pre-assessment and assessment phases are presented and highlighted through case study presentation.

OPERATIONAL DEFINITION OF PRE-ASSESSMENT AND ASSESSMENT IN THE HOME HEALTH CARE ENVIRONMENT

Assessment can be defined as an estimate or determination of the significance, importance, or value of something. Assessment, as a continuous process, is the first step to problem identification and the initial step necessary for sound planning. Assessment contains three elements: collection of data, analysis and presentation of data, and statement of conclusions (Braden and Herban 1976). In nursing practice, assessment is the first phase of the nursing process, followed by planning intervention and evaluation.

The home health care nurse uses assessment to gain a holistic perspective of the patient's state of well-being within the family structure and community environment. Through the collection of data concerning the patient's past and present state of existence, the nurse is able to work collaboratively with the patient in planning nursing interventions that will facilitate the realization of his or her self-defined human capability and quality of life.

In the home setting the scope of assessment is broadened significantly and precluded by a pre-assessment phase. The focus of assessment includes the patient and the patient's family. This broader approach to assessment serves to provide the nurse with information that can help to determine how the patient's role is defined within that family, as well as how the interaction of the family members affects the patient's perception of real versus ideal well-being.

In addition, assessment includes a determination of the values an individual places on certain self-defined problems and his readiness to repattern his interaction with the environment as needed to improve his well-being.

Before the home health nurse ever begins to assess the patient, she must first assimilate into the patient/family environment and establish a trusting, open relationship. This period of assimilation, or pre-assessment, is crucial to the success of the assessment and intervention phases of the nursing process. In fact, if the home health care nurse is insensitive to the importance of the establishment of an open, ongoing relationship, she may not be able to affect a therapeutic change, regardless of the accuracy of her assessment and problem identification. During the pre-assessment phase the home health nurse should use a self-defined conceptual framework to assist her in gaining acceptance and working with the patient and family. This framework will serve as a tool for the facilitation of the assimilation process and serve as a guide for the assessment of the patient/family.

Once the pre-assessment phase has been successfully initiated and the nurse has gained the trust of the patient and the family as a whole, she can begin to implement the assessment phase of the nursing process.

Before pre-assessment and assessment are discussed in further detail, it is important to articulate how the assessment of the patient in the home environment differs from the assessment of the patient in the hospital, clinic, or skilled nursing facility.

HOW PATIENT ASSESSMENT IN THE HOME ENVIRONMENT DIFFERS FROM PATIENT ASSESSMENT IN OTHER HEALTH CARE SETTINGS

As stated earlier in this chapter, nursing assessment of patient and family in the home environment is more complex and broader based than the assessment of the client in other health care environments. The home environment is not the territory of the health care professional; it is the patient's "turf." Therefore, when the home health care nurse enters a patient's home to assess his needs, she finds herself in an environment that is defined and controlled by the patient and family. This is a totally different experience from that of nurses who work in various other health care areas, such as hospitals, clinics, or physician offices, where the environment is defined and controlled by health care providers. As a result, the nurse providing home health care does not have the familiarity of a supportive health care environment in which to assess the patient's problems or implement nursing interventions. Collaboration with other health care professionals is not as accessible. What is not apparent to the inexperienced eye is that the nurse in the home care environment is like a fish out of water. Not only is she outside the safe walls of the health care delivery system, where interdisciplinary support is at her fingertips, but she may also find herself in many home environments that are culturally defined in an entirely different way from what she is familiar with, based on her individual point of reference.

In contrast to the brief interaction of nurse and patient in most health care environments, the home health nurse's relationship with the patient is often long term and involves a variety of nursing activities, such as health teaching, counseling, crisis intervention, coordinating community resources, and coordinating care with family members and other members of the health care team.

Another difference is that the home health care nurse may work with multiproblem families composed of more than one generation and displaying different levels of health needs. In the hospital or clinic the patient is the focus of attention, and in most cases the family is seen only as a support system.

In summary, the role of the home health nurse is more complex and diverse than the role of nurses who work in other settings. As a result of this broader, more complex level of functioning, the nurse in the home environment must be prepared to use all available tools to assist her in the creative development of the nurse-patient relationship through the effective assimilation into a possibly alien, patient/family defined and controlled environment, before she can begin the assessment phase of the nursing process.

TOOLS FOR FACILITATING AND IMPLEMENTING PRE-ASSESSMENT AND ASSESSMENT

Before the nursing professional can hope to be effective in implementing nursing care in the home environment, she must familiarize herself with some of the tools that are available for establishing an open interaction and comprehensive assessment.

The pre-assessment, or relationship-establishing phase, requires some important preparation on the part of the home health nurse. Before the home health nurse knocks on the patient's door, she should have done some preliminary footwork. As mentioned earlier, the primary objective for offering health care in the home is to facilitate the patient's growth toward a higher state of well-being. Before this can be accomplished the home health nurse must assimilate into the patient's environment, establish a trusting relationship, and begin an ongoing mutual interaction. Although a great deal has been written about methods for acquiring entry into a patient's environment and establishing a therapeutic relationship, I believe that the key to effective assimilation lies in the nurse's ability to approach a family with a sincere openness and acceptance of a variety of human differences (i.e., ethnicity, religion, kinship, subcultures of poverty and alien sexual preferences, etc.). Acquiring this genuine approach is not easy. It generally means that the home health care nurse must assume the responsibility of getting in touch with her own perceptions by defining her self-imposed limitations to the acceptance of human differences. In addition, she must have a willingness to increase her understanding in areas in which her lack of acquired knowledge and exposure to such human differences may be the predisposing barrier to facilitating her effective acceptance of an alien home environment.

In the community it is imperative that the home health nurse increase her knowledge of other cultures in order to acquire the heightened sensitivity to human difference that is so vital to the effective implementation of the nursing process. It is essential that the home health nurse be able to say that she feels her approach to families can be defined as "ecumenical" and "international," that the trusting relationship that is established is based on a genuine acceptance of individuals and families as they are—human beings first, acquired cultural and behavioral differences second. This is by no means an easy tool to develop, nor is it static in its development. Rather, it is as continuous and ongoing as the development of the nurse herself. Once the home health nurse makes a conscious effort to start on the road to the development of this tool, then the way to ongoing communication and therapeutic nursing intervention becomes visible.

One of the most essential tools that, once developed, will enable the nurse to become a more sensitive and skillful practitioner is her personally defined, conceptual framework for working with patients and families in the home environment. Once the home health nurse has articulated the essential elements of this personal framework, she will then be able to apply and adapt it to each patient/family she works with, fine tuning it as she goes along. The conceptual framework should include a variety of components, such as an individually understood definition of health, behavior, family, illness, wellness, and nursing intervention.

It should also contain other important areas of identified information that the nurse deems necessary for effectively facilitating the pre-assessment and assessment of the family (e.g., family social roles, kinship, ethnicity, family rituals).

Once the home health nurse has developed her framework or organized approach to family assessment, she will have developed a useful tool for the beginning assimilation into the family environment through identification of mutual areas of concerns, which will in turn lead to mutually agreed on problem resolution.

As the home health nurse establishes rapport and gains the data necessary for assessment, it is essential that she determine the client's level of readiness to make changes in the identified problem areas and to make a commitment to repattern his life style in order to increase his self-defined well-being. The nurse must recognize that unless a patient perceives a problem as a real threat to his perception of well-being, he probably will not take the necessary action to change his behavior. Therefore, it is essential that the nurse determine the patient's level of readiness to change any areas identified as problem areas before she plans any intervention with him.

CONCEPTUAL FRAMEWORK AND CASE STUDY EXAMPLE

The following is an example of a conceptual framework that I have developed and applied in working with families in a community setting. A case study application of this framework is included. The framework consists of a family, a theme, health behavior, nursing intervention, illness, and wellness.

In the context of this framework I have adopted a broad definition of family. Family is a social group characterized by common residence, economic cooperation, and reproduction. It includes adults of both sexes, at least two of whom maintain a socially approved sexual relationship, and one or more children of the sexually cohabitating adults (Murdock 1966). In addition, it is a unit of interacting persons related by ties of marriage, birth, or adoption whose central purpose is to create and maintain a common culture that promotes the physical, mental, emotional, and social development of each of its members (Duvall 1967). A family is a meeting ground of the generations, a segment of an ongoing bisocial process. Any family is subject to the influence of ancestors long since dead, and family roles are played with reference to children not yet born (Kirkpatrick 1955). In view of modern society, I feel that it is necessary to add one-parent families to this definition.

Hess and Handel (1971) explain that a family theme is a pattern of feelings, motives, fantasies, and conventionalized understanding grouped about some focus of concern that has a particular form in the personalities of the individual members of families. The pattern comprises some fundamental view of reality and some ways for dealing with it.

A theme also reflects the interrelatedness of individual images and responses (Hess and Handel 1971). It is a particularly useful unit for analysis of family life, for it proves a way of characterizing the family group in terms of broad and significant psychosocial and psychocultural dimensions. At the same time it permits flexibility and does not require that a family be understood in terms of set categories. The concept of theme provides a point of reference for understanding not only the individual members and particular relationships, but also the specific versions and expressions. It also provides a way of characterizing a whole group in a fashion that is relevant to the group's individual members.

Health behavior is an aspect of the human growth and development process that is not always smooth and without conflict. It involves a holistic approach to the family including the way in which individual family members deal with the stresses of growth and development physically, emotionally, and socially while attempting to functionally conform to their inherited cultural pattern (King 1971). Health behavior, as it relates to family within this framework, is defined as any activity undertaken by an individual who believes himself or herself to be well to avoid an encounter with illness (Wu 1972).

Nursing intervention is defined as action, reaction, interaction, and transaction, whereby the nurse assists individuals of any age and socioeconomic group to meet their basic needs in performance of activities of daily living. This intervention helps the patient to cope with health and illness at some particular point in the developmental process (King 1971).

Illness is an event experienced by an individual that manifests itself through observable or felt changes, causing an impairment of capacity to meet minimum physical, physiological, and psychosocial requirements for appropriate functioning at the level designated for the individual's stages of development. Wellness is an event experienced by an individual that manifests itself through his or her behaviors (i.e., an individual experiencing wellness will exhibit a class of behavior congruent with the event). The attributes of wellness are an ability to perceive in accordance with reality, free from real distortion, an ability to adjust actively to varying situations in one's family, and an ability to display a coherent and integrated personality (Wu 1972).

Besides the main elements in this framework, there are some supportive areas. The first of these is social roles. Roles are the behavior a family displays in connection with a given social position that it holds at any given time. Every individual plays many roles, and each particular role is culturally patterned. Roles are not static, and each family member has different roles according to age, position, and family.

Kinship includes relatives, "folks," extended family who are related by blood or marriage. Universally, we as individuals are part of two nuclear families, and this gives rise to a kinship system. Kinship is a structured system of relationships in which individuals are bound to one another by complex interlocking ties. There is a common basis on which we view the continuity of characteristics reflected through kinship of a particular family. The nuclear family has a pattern of roles that has a generic significance. Kinship bonds unite individuals, and there is often a high degree of reciprocal cooperation, loyalty, solidarity, and affection. Most families come under constant supervision of their kin, who feel free to criticize, suggest, praise, or threaten so that family members will carry out their role obligation (Schneider 1968; Murdock 1966).

Ethnicity is thought to be significant in the development of family theme. Ethnicity is any group that is set off by race, religion, national origin, or some combination of these categories as they are found within the national boundaries of the United States. The ethnic background of individual families is considered to be significant in influencing the role patterns of the nuclear family. Family life style, to a large extent, is molded by its ethnicity (Bossard and Ball 1968).

Rituals are patterns of prescribed formal behaviors pertaining to some specific event, occasion, or situation that tend to be repeated over and over (e.g., religious rituals, family recreational rituals). A pattern of social behavior develops within the family that each group member is expected to observe as a part of family functioning (Bossard and Ball 1968).

In considering some of the assumptions related to this framework, the author has incorporated some assumptions used in a developmental approach for the study of the family. Both frameworks deal with the persons who make up families and have a unified scheme of compatible sections. Developmental tasks are sets of role expectations that the family confronts at a particular point in the family life process. Each family has its own role expectations. The better equipped the family is to meet these tasks and the more closely it accomplishes its group tasks, the more successful it will be as an entity. Family development is an ever-changing dynamic process that evolves through the delineation of the stages in its life process. Family developmental tasks are growth responsibilities that arise at a certain stage in the life of a family. Successful achievement of these tasks leads to satisfaction and success with later tasks, whereas failure leads to unhappiness in the family, disapproval of society, and difficulty with later family developmental tasks. The developmental tasks of a given family are many and complex. Families, as families, are seen to have responsible goals and developmental tasks that are specifically related to the development of their members. All these developmental tasks of family members and families as a whole shift as the family grows and changes and are constantly being modified by the interplay of factors both from within and without the family.

The family does not survive in isolation, but interacts with its environment. There is a symbiotic relationship between family and society. It is a nuclear unit that develops in different ways according to the living process from within and the stimulation of society from without. Family health behavior, to a great extent, is determined by a family's feelings, motives, and conventionalized understandings (i.e., its theme). A family will engage in health behavior when it believes such activity is important to its well-being. Every person and family has healthy and sick aspects simultaneously, with one or the other predominating. It is possible to observe wellness potential in sick families and illness potential in well families. On an illness-wellness continuum a family may lean toward overt or severe illness or, conversely, toward suboptimum to optimum wellness.

In summary, family theme is indigenous to every existing family unit. Each theme is composed of many complex elements of family life, the most important being ethnicity, kinship, roles, and rituals. Family theme deals with central concerns mirrored by family interactions and defined by the family itself. It encompasses the internal dynamic processes in the life of the nuclear family, as well as the influence of kinship and ethnicity, in determining its makeup. Family members have a social role that is determined by the family as a whole. These roles are influenced by internal factors, such as rituals, stages of family development and growth changes, and family self-image, as well as by external cultural factors. The nuclear family is an outgrowth of ethnicity and kinship; it reproduces its earlier family relations in its interpretation of interpersonal relations beyond the family, thus reconstructing the generic constellation and determining its worth in contributing to the development of a new family concern.

A family theme is a major determinate of a family's subjective interpretation of its health behavior. By the assessment of the family's level of health behavior, as detected through clues presented by the family theme, the nurse can proceed toward problem identification and intervention as determined by the family as well as by the patient at whatever level of the illness-wellness continuum the family and its individual members may be. This framework has been operationalized to all family groups, including one-parent families. In addition, it has proved to be instrumental in gaining a better understanding of the interior functioning of families, thus enabling the practitioner to determine an individual's family subjective health behavior by ascertaining the influence of its individual family theme, as well as by assessing its level of illness-wellness. This framework also facilitates the determination of the extent to which ethnicity and kinship influence the family's growth and development as individuals, from dependency in childhood to independence and interdependence in adulthood. Also, it has proved useful in the evaluation of inner health concerns of family members, providing focus on those areas of concern that need the most consideration. Most important, it provides a holistic approach to the family through its unique theme, facilitating the practitioner's entrance into family dynamics. The understanding of family theme enhances the pre-assessment phase, opening further the lines of communication between the patient and the nurse, thus enabling the practitioner to be more effective in the assessment and intervention phases of the nursing process.

CASE EXAMPLE

The G family reside in a small town in Connecticut. The family consists of Mr. G., a 38-year-old white male who is the head of household, working in construction; Miss F., a 28-year-old white female who is Mr. G.'s wife-to-be and who is presently unemployed; and B., the firstborn child of Mr. G. and Miss F.

The relationship of the family members is well defined. Mr. G.'s role in this family structure is defined as a husband, father, and provider. Miss F.'s role is defined as wife and mother.

Mr. G. and Miss F. have a strong emotional relationship with each other. Miss F. is very feminine and plays a somewhat submissive role to Mr. G., who is very masculine and dominating, both in stature and personality. Mr. G. has adjusted to his new role as father very nicely. He tends to B.'s physical needs when necessary and plays with him whenever possible. Miss F. has made an excellent adjustment as mother to B. She is very aware of his needs and handles the baby with a great deal of affection and care. She has had a great deal of experience with raising children, having assisted her mother in the care of her five younger sisters.

Both Mr. G.'s and Miss F.'s parents are alive and live close by.

Additional Family Characteristics

Decision Making (Role)

The following additional information concerning this family was acquired using the described conceptual framework as the basis for organizing and categorizing the data.

Major decisions are usually unequivocally made by Mr. G., with some discussion with Miss F. The final decision, however, is Mr. G.'s.

Sleeping and Eating Arrangements (Ritual) and Leisure Activities (Ritual)

Mr. G. and Miss F. sleep together. B. has his own crib.

The kitchen in the apartment is neat and clean. Miss F. is very much a homemaker and loves to bake. Miss F. is of appropriate weight for her height; however, she seems to have an overabundance of carbohydrate intake. Mr. G., on the other hand, is about 30 pounds overweight, and his eating patterns are sporadic. B. is on formula and cereal and is developing within normal weight for his age.

Mr. G. and Miss F. spend a large part of their leisure time on Mr. and Mrs. F.'s farm.

Socioeconomic and Cultural Factors

Educational, Ethnicity Background and Religious Affiliation (Ethnicity)

Mr. G. is of Lithuanian descent, has a high school education, and is of Catholic religious affiliation. Miss F. is of French descent, has a high school education, and is a Jehovah's Witness in her religious affiliation. The family does not attend formal places of worship. The family's income is limited. Mr. G. earns over 50 percent of the total money available to this family; 30 percent comes from welfare aid and the remainder, from Mr. G.'s parents. This family's expenses are greater than their income, although they do not spend money excessively.

Social Relations (Kinship)

Both Mr. G. and Miss F. have close relationships with their respective families. Mr. G.'s parents give him a great deal of emotional and financial support. Miss F.'s parents, on the other hand, have enough to do handling their own problems. However, they do visit their daughter now and then. Mr. G. has a few male friends with whom he socializes. Miss F. has no close friends.

Environmental Factors:

Housing, Neighborhood, and Transportation

The family resides in a small, three-room dwelling, neatly kept but sparsely furnished. Food is adequately refrigerated. The apartment has adequate indoor toilet facilities and municipal water supply. There are a few accident hazards, such as a large dog that is allowed to roam around the apartment freely, and poor ventilation.

The neighborhood is semiresidential, somewhat safe from crime, in an urban area. The apartment is in a two-family house that is owned by an elderly lady. The other homes in the area range from large residential homes to three-family houses. There is a large park within walking distance of the apartment. In addition, few health facilities are available in the area. Child Health Services Clinic meets twice monthly.

There is a public school within walking distance of the apartment. The residence is on the bus line and Mr. G. has a car.

Health and Medical History

Present Illness and History (Illness-Wellness)

Mr. G. has basically been healthy except for a recent head cold. He is not taking any medication at this time; however, he is a heavy drinker and sometimes takes drugs without prescription. Mr. G. has had a few car accidents, one of which necessitated his being hospitalized. He has also been injured in a few barroom brawls.

Miss F. has also been predominantly well. During her pregnancy however, she suffered from recurrent attacks of herpes simplex II. She was followed medically throughout her pregnancy and was treated for this problem and other complications of pregnancy. Miss F. is astute about obtaining medical care and has made a point of keeping her six-weeks postpartum checkup. She is presently taking birth control pills. She has had no serious illnesses in the past.

B. was born healthy, with no apparent problems. A newborn appraisal showed that he was within normal limits. He is being followed by a private pediatrician.

Medical care for the family is financed through medical aid funds. Mr. G. and Miss F. have not had dental care in a number of years; their teeth are in poor condition and in desperate need of followup care.

Family's Knowledge and Attitude Toward Health Behavior

Mr. G. is flippant about health care and has a somewhat limited knowledge about health. Miss F., on the other hand, is concerned about health status for both herself and B. She has limited knowledge but is willing to learn more about health.

This family as a unit does not make a conscious effort to assess their health problems. Miss F. has never had a home health nurse visit her before the time I made a visit. In previous situations the family has managed in crisis through the help of their extended family, especially Mr. G.'s parents.

In this case example the triad family group has well-defined social roles. Mr. G. is husband and provider, Miss F., wife and mother. There is a strong emotional relationship among all three members of the triad. Kinship and ethnicity factors come into play in many ways in this family (Miss F. has strong feelings of religion and maintains her household in much the same way her mother did). However, Miss F.'s kinship ties are weak, in that her parent's nuclear family has many internal problems and, consequently, does not interact with her. Mr. G., on the other hand, has strong kinship ties and depends on his relatives for emotional as well as economic support.

As a whole, the family exhibits sporadic and inconsistent forms of health behavior. Some reasons for this could be that, in both Mr. G.'s and Miss F.'s kinship backgrounds, their families placed little emphasis on health. On meeting both sets of parents, I observed obvious health deficiencies (i.e., poor nutritional and dental states). Miss F. is concerned about her and B.'s health status. Although she has limited health knowledge, she does make positive efforts to maintain a good level of wellness. Mr. G., however, is neglectful in his health behavior.

Overall, the conceptual approach to the assessment of this family has disclosed a number of important favorable areas, as well as certain areas of concern in the development of a plan of intervention for the G. family, including:

- A strong emotional relationship exists between Mr. G. and Miss F.
- Mr. G.'s parents provide good emotional and financial support.
- Miss F. has made the appropriate adjustment to motherhood and has the ability to maintain a neat and clean house.
- Miss F.'s awareness of the need for health care follow-up for herself and B. and her willingness to learn more
- Mr. G.'s willingness to maintain employment and support his family as best he can
- Mr. G.'s relationship with his son and his willingness to take part in his physical care
- Miss F.'s mother and father have problems that affected Miss F.'s growth and development until age 16, when she ran away from home. Her mother was unable to cope with all of her children. Both parents' frustration manifested itself in physical abuse of their daughter. They are undergoing psychiatric care.
- Mr. G., even though presently employed, could be laid off at any time. If this were to occur, the family would have a difficult time meeting its needs economically.

- Although Mr. G. and Miss F.'s relationship is emotionally intense, it appears as if Miss F. looks to Mr. G. and his family as the strength and support she never had. This could pose a problem for her if her relationship with Mr. G. were to end.

- Mr. G.'s drinking problem has definite negative implications, not only for his own health and safety, but also for the safety of Miss F. and B., as he has been known to become abusive on occasion.

- There is a need for nutritional orientation in relation to controlling carbohydrate intake.

An overall assessment of this family places them, as a whole, at a somewhat optimum level of health and Mr. G., specifically, at the overt illness level because of his heavy drinking and neglectful behavior. The nursing intervention in relation to Mr. G. should place emphasis on reducing his stress and supporting the defense that he might present in order to offer constructive help and assistance for his obvious drinking problem as well as providing necessary health education. For the family as a whole, the home health nurse should develop intervention to support the existent health behavior and provide health education to build on this behavior.

SUMMARY

The assessment of a patient in a home environment is much broader and more complex than the assessment of a patient in other health care settings. Home health nursing involves the assessment of the family and the community of which the patient is a part. In addition, because the patient's home environment is self-defined and controlling, the home health nurse must develop an effective mechanism to facilitate the initiation of the pre-assessment phase, which involves the assimilation into the patient's unique environment and the establishment of an ongoing mutual therapeutic interaction. The essence of this pre-assessment phase involves the nurse's continued willingness to direct a self-evolutionary process that will eventually enable her to develop therapeutic relationships that are based on genuine acceptance of individuals and families.

The home health nurse must also develop her personal framework for working with families. This framework serves as an ever-evolving tool to facilitate assessment of identified common areas of concern, which leads to mutually agreed on patient-problem resolutions.

Patient-family assessment can be approached from many perspectives. What is essential, however, is that the home health care nurse adapt an approach that reflects an ongoing, professional assessment of self. Simultaneously, the home health nurse should develop a comprehensive, holistic approach that focuses on family theme, as well as other psychological and social family perceptions and attitudes related to health and health care.

REFERENCES

Avila, Donald, Arthur W. Combs, and William Purkey. *The Helping Relationship Sourcebook*, Boston: Allyn & Bacon, 1971.

Biddle, Thomas. "Introduction to Role Theory." In *Role Theory*, B.J. Biddle and E.J. Thomas (eds.). New York: John Wiley & Sons, 1966.

Bossard, James, and Eleanor Ball. *A Modern Introduction to the Family*. New York: The Free Press, 1968.

Braden, Carrie, and N. Herban. *Community Health Systems Approach*. New York: Appleton Century Crofts, 1976.

Burgess, Wendy. *Community Health Nursing*. Norwalk, Conn.; Appleton-Century-Crofts, 1983.

Duvall, Evelyn. *Family Development*. Philadelphia: J. B. Lippincott Co., 1967.

Erickson, Erick. *Childhood and Society*. New York: W. W. Norton, Co., 1963.

Handel, Gerard. *The Psychosocial Interior of the Family*. Chicago: Aldice Publishing Co., 1967.

Hardy, Mary, ed. *Theoretical Foundation for Nursing*. New York: MSS Information Co., 1973.

Havighurst, Robert J. *Developmental Tasks and Education*. New York: David McKay Co., 1966.

Hess, Robert D., and Gerard Handel. *Family Worlds: A Psychosocial Approach to Family Life*. Chicago: University of Chicago Press, 1971.

Higg, S. Z., and D. Gustafson. *Community as a Client: Assessment and Diagnosis*. Philadelphia: F. A. Davis Co., 1985.

Hymovich, Debra P., and Martha Underwood Barnard, eds. *Family Health Care*. New York: McGraw-Hill, 1973.

Jahoda, Maria. *Current Concepts of Positive Mental Health*. New York: Basic Books, 1956.

King, Imogene. *Toward a Theory for Nursing*. New York: John Wiley & Sons, 1971.

Kirkpatrick, Clifford. *The Family*. New York: Ronald Press Co., 1955.

Mead, Margaret. "Understanding Cultural Patterns." In *Nursing Outlook*. New York: AJN Co., 1956.

Murdock, George. "Analysis of Kinship," In *Role Theory*, B. J. Biddle and E. J. Thomas (eds.). New York: John Wiley & Sons, 1966.

Nye, Evan, and Felix Berardo. *The Family, Its Structure and Interaction*. New York: Macmillan, 1973.

Orque, M., B. Bloch, and L. Monroy. *Ethnic Nursing Care*. St. Louis: C. V. Mosby, 1983.

Schneider, David. *American Kinship: A Cultural Account*. Englewood Cliffs, N. J.: Prentice-Hall, 1968.

Spiegal, John. *Transactions: The Interplay Between Individual, Family and Society*. New York: Science House, 1971.

Tinkim, Catherine W., and Eleanor F. Vourhies. *Community Health Nursing: Evaluation and Process*. Norwalk, Conn.: Appleton-Century-Crofts, 1972.

Winch, R. F. *The Modern Family*. New York: Henry Holt Co., 1952.

Wu, Ruth. *Behavior and Illness*. Englewood Cliffs, N.J.: Prentice-Hall, 1972

Chapter 10

Nursing the Patient and Family in Their Own Environment

Judith L. Elkins

This chapter starts out with a discussion of the types of patients and families that the home health nurse might encounter. Then, some of the considerations the nurse must make when adapting her care to the home environment are examined and a closer look is taken at the role of the home health nurse as she works with families to provide care for patients in the home.

TYPES OF HOME CARE PATIENTS

The patient who requires visits from a home health nurse is generally one who has just left the hospital or is well enough to be home, that is, he is not in an acute crisis but does require the expertise of a nurse in making the transition to home. The home health nurse, in this case, either aids the patient in his recovery from illness or surgery or helps the patient to understand and adapt to a newly diagnosed chronic illness. Another type of patient a home health nurse may visit is the terminally ill patient; in this case the nurse works closely with the patient and family.

ADAPTING CARE TO THE HOME ENVIRONMENT

There are many environments in which the home health nurse will find the patients discharged to "home." Because home health services are provided by and large to the elderly population, many home health patients live alone and have done so for years. Some patients, after hospitalization, are well enough to go home and be alone; the majority, however, go home to their families, who will assume a large part of the responsibility for the patients's care. Some home health patients, when faced with illness, will go to the home of the nearest relative or friend, but quite often the relative or friend will come to

179

their home. Generally, it is felt, if for a short period of time, the patient will do much better in a familiar environment and respond more effectively to medical treatment.

> Mrs. A., a 96-year-old German woman with congestive heart failure and asthma, never had any children of her own, her husband had been dead for 40 years, and she had no living relatives in the United States. The closest person to Mr. A. was Sally, a friend of 15 years who was half Mrs. A's age. When Mrs. A. developed a stasis ulcer on her lower leg, a home health nurse was called in. Mrs. A. continued to live alone for a couple of months while her friend Sally came over to fix her meals. Sally eventually learned to care for the leg ulceration. As time went on Mrs. A. became increasingly confused and was confined to bed. She was unable to be left alone. Her friend Sally hired someone to stay with Mrs. A. during the day, and she stayed with her at night. This situation worked quite well and continued until Mrs. A.'s death.

What are some of the consequences that might have occurred if Mrs. A. had gone to Sally's house? Mrs. A. might have become confused earlier if she were not in a familiar environment. It might have been more difficult for Mrs. A. to be compliant with her treatment if she lacked the comfort of her own home. This could also contribute to depression, which could inhibit effective treatment. Also, Mrs. A.'s presence in Sally's home might have upset the routines at Sally's home, where her husband and three teenage daughters also lived.

As mentioned earlier, the home health nurse will often find herself dealing with many combinations of families. It is important for the home care nurse to realize that she is working not only with an individual patient, but also with those concerned people surrounding the patient and the patient's care. The nurse should know from the start who she is working with and begin to establish a relationship with each member of the family, or surrogate family. Most commonly the nurse will work with the patient and his or her spouse; however, as in the example, others living in the home or nearby may be key people in the patient's life.

When a home health nurse enters a home she should remember to acknowledge all family members; "even the family's pets should be acknowledged, particularly if they seem to hold a position of esteem" (Leahy, Cobb, and Jones 1977). This will help the patient and family to develop trust in the nurse. When a person is respected for who she or he is, it is easier for that person to respect and trust another person. This is important even if family members are not directly involved in the patient's care because each person needs to feel important in her or his role in the family. If family members have a good sense of themselves, this will help to create an environment that is conducive to healing for the patient and will lessen the chance of stress for all involved.

When working with home care patients and their families, the home health nurse must realize that she is stepping into their environment and that when she leaves they will remain in the same environment with the responsibility of care. Sometimes she will be faced with family members who are afraid to get involved in caring for the patient. This is where the nurse can come in and guide the family members step by step in the care. The nurse and the family must sit down together and set goals for what they want to accomplish. The goal may be just for the comfort of the patient, but whatever it is, it is important for the nurse not to overwhelm the family and to encourage them to participate as much as possible.

Mary, a young divorced woman in her forties, works full time. When her father became ill with end-stage chronic obstructive pulmonary disease and cancer of the colon, Mary had him move in with her. She has two children, a boy and a girl, both in their twenties, who frequently move in and out of Mary's mobile home. Mary's father's condition worsened, and he had colon surgery and came home with a colostomy. He was also on continuous oxygen and received respiratory treatments four times a day. Mary was overwhelmed with all the equipment and changes in her father. It was difficult enough for her to manage her personal life, let alone all that her father required. A home health nurse was called in, who set up goals with Mary for her father's care and taught Mary the proper use of the equipment and how to set up a system to keep the equipment separate. The first lesson was for Mary to see the potential problems if the colostomy and respiratory equipment were cleansed and maintained together. Once Mary grasped the concept of care and could identify her goals (i.e., preventing complications and learning maintenance and use of each piece of equipment), the care of her father became easier. In the meantime Mary's daughter, son-in-law, and their two-year-old son moved in. Although this was somewhat hectic for Mary, she still needed to work, so the nurse taught Mary's daughter how to manage the equipment and administer the respiratory treatments while Mary was away. The son-in-law helped with the oxygen equipment and the care of the two-year-old.

This example illustrates how important it is for the home health nurse to set goals with and involve the family in the care of the patient. It was important for Mary not to be overwhelmed with her father's care. In this particular case the nurse called in a social worker, who was able to set up other services for Mary. Hospice eventually became involved to help the patient and his family with their emotional needs. Also, a homemaker aide was set up to help with household chores, and a senior worker from the local area Agency on Aging visited Mary to help her figure out her bills and finances.

THE NURSE'S ROLE IN CARING FOR PATIENTS IN THE HOME

The major role that the home health nurse has in working with patients and their families is teaching the families to care for the patient. Along with this are many variables or considerations that influence the effectiveness of this teaching.

Long-Term Patterning

The nurse must consider that the patient or family may not be receptive to her teaching at first. She must consider that the patient and the family have built in patterns of behavior or attitudes over many years that influence their relationships with one another and their approach to health care at home. The following two cases might help to illustrate how the nurse can work with patterns of behavior.

> Fred was an 84-year-old man who lived by himself in a small, cluttered trailer. He had recently been released from the hospital with an exacerbation of congestive heart failure. Because of his condition his doctor changed some of his medications and the dosage on some he had already been taking. A home health nurse was called in to help Fred set up a medication system and teach him about the medications and how they relate to his condition. The nurse came in and set up all the medications in medicine boxes and labeled them with the times of day when they should be taken. She thought that this would help Fred to organize his new medications. The next time the nurse came to visit she discovered that Fred was not taking his medications correctly. As she discussed the situation with Fred, she realized that he knew and preferred to recognize each pill by size and color; the medicine boxes only confused him. When the nurse labeled the times on the individual bottles with the

words "Heart Pill," "Water Pill," etc., Fred was more satisfied and then took his medication as ordered.

* * *

Mrs. G. was a young 70-year-old woman who had been taking care of her emphysemic husband for ten years. Mr. G.'s condition had worsened in the past two years and he was on continuous oxygen with respiratory treatments three times daily. After Mr. G.'s last hospitalization Mrs. G. was having a difficult time coping, and she stopped giving her husband his respiratory treatments. Their son, who lived out of town, was concerned about his mother's ability to cope, and so he talked it over with the family physician. The physician ordered a home health nurse to visit and assess the patient's lung status and help the wife to cope with the care of her husband at this time. A home health nurse did go to visit but found that Mrs. G. resented her being there and thought the nurse was trying to pry into her business. After all, Mrs. G. "had taken care of Mr. G. for the past ten years!" Mrs. G. thought the nurse was spying on her when she asked what medications Mrs. G. was giving her husband and how she cleaned the oxygen equipment. Mrs. G. was under so much stress with the care of her husband that she thought she "was a prisoner in [her] own home," and she could not see the nurse's intent to help her. The nurse slowly gained Mrs. G.'s confidence by first concentrating on what Mrs. G. knew already and praising her for this. Mrs. G. eventually began to trust the home health nurse, and the respiratory treatments were resumed.

Again, these illustrations point up the fact that the home health nurse is stepping into the patient's and family's environment, and they may be quite happy with care that is being given. They may think, "I've done it this way for years and don't see any reason to change now." One can see how the nurse must consider strong ingrained patterns of behavior, and therefore, she must be able to adapt some of her methods and techniques to mesh with those of the patient or family. Wilner and his associates (1978) state that "changes in behavior, to be long-lasting and practiced regularly, must be self-imposed, and the behavior must be integrated into the individual's pattern of life."

Changes in Family Dynamics

Another consideration for effective home health nursing and teaching is the aspect of possible changes in family dynamics. Many times when a person who has always been considered the "strong one" or the "leader" in the family becomes ill, this may cause role changes in the family. Often the spouse or another family member will have to assume a new role, and this can be stressful; for example, a wife who suddenly finds herself as the decision maker when for many years she has had a more passive role, or a husband who has never assumed household chores and now becomes the cook and homemaker. These new roles obviously will affect how well the family can learn what the nurse tries to teach them. Other factors include each person's ability to cope with changes, how ill the patient is, and how long this role change is expected to last. The home health nurse will find that in many cases this role change is permanent, and she must help the family work through these role changes. She can help the family by encouraging them to acknowledge and identify these changes and perhaps make it easier for them to accept.

Previous Relationships

Another consideration in effective home nursing is what type of relationships family members shared before the illness. The spouse of one patient in a home health agency stated: "I'll do what I have to out of duty, but I don't love him." Her particular relationship with her alcoholic husband had not been good. Emotions such as these will determine the course of action and goals for care that the home health nurse will set up with the family. If the wife has disdain for her husband, it will color the type of care she gives him. In a case like this the minimum of teaching and care is all that can be expected. In this particular case, when the nurse suggested alternatives of care for the patient, the wife's response was: "I've been doing this for years and will continue as long as I'm needed."

Educational and Cultural Backgrounds

If the nurse is to be effective, she must understand the patient's educational and cultural backgrounds. If her goal is for teaching, she must assess the family's or patient's ability to read, listen, and follow directions. It is often important to simplify material and instructions for the patient and family, depending on their educational level. For example, given two patients with congestive heart failure, one may be able to read a pamphlet that explains physiology, dietary measures, and how to care for this condition, whereas another may only be able to grasp the basics of learning to weigh daily, restrict salt, and observe for swelling in the feet and may be given a simple chart, as shown in Figure 10–1.

Cultural background is important also because this often shapes one's attitude regarding health maintenance or chronic and terminal illness. As

Figure 10–1 A Simple Chart

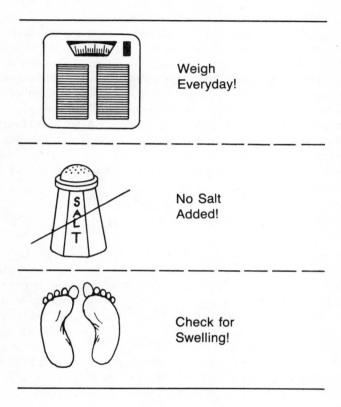

Weigh
Everyday!

No Salt
Added!

Check for
Swelling!

stated by Hall (1959), "culture is a mold in which we all are cast, and it controls our daily lives and behavior in many unsuspected ways." When a nurse plans to do teaching with patients from cultures that are different from her own, she must be sensitive to these differences and be aware of the patients' values and attitudes toward health care. Dietary teaching is one area in which this is especially important. The nurse must learn what types of foods a patient is accustomed to before she can help the patient to make dietary modifications. For example, a Mexican-American who is used to rice and beans cannot be expected to eliminate these foods from his diet. Changes in portions may be necessary if he discovers that he is a diabetic, but eliminating these foods from his diet is unrealistic.

When working within the patient and his family's own environment, it is imperative that the nurse mesh and blend with that family. Respect is a key word if the nurse wants to accomplish her goals. The nurse must respect the family for their beliefs and values and try to understand where they are coming from before a plan of care for the patient can be established and implemented. In speaking about the health education process Wilner and his co-workers (1978) state that "individuals must be involved in defining their own goals and actions and must evolve a way of achieving them within their own system of values, beliefs, and resources."

Because there are so many variables to consider when a home health nurse visits a patient and his family, it is important to realize that the home health nurse's role is all-encompassing. The home health nurse does not only assess the patient and his status; as seen from this discussion, her role is much broader than this.

THE NURSE'S ROLE IN HEALTH TEACHING

Webster's (1984) defines "teach" as "the basic inclusive word for the imparting of knowledge or skills and usually connotes some individual attention to the learner." Many families find themselves in a position of responsibility and care of a loved one without the training to meet the responsibility. This can be a frustrating situation. The home health nurse can be a tremendous help in teaching the family some of what she has learned in her training and experience. For example, a family faced with the care of a loved one who has become bedbound may need to be trained in positioning the patient and using proper body mechanics. This may be a simple task for the nurse but may be overwhelming for the family. It is important to tell the family the reasons you are teaching them a certain task. For example, change the patient's position to prevent bedsores or pneumonia; good body mechanics prevent back injuries. Understanding the rationale may be the link in determining compliance with the teaching.

For effective teaching the nurse must remember to use terms that the patient and family can understand, for instance, "bedsores" instead of "decubitus ulcers" and "opening" instead of "os." Also, the nurse must remember not to overwhelm the family with too much knowledge at one time. For example, if the home health nurse walks into a situation in which a bedbound patient is always on his back, has a new indwelling catheter, is on oxygen, and has a poor appetite, she must discuss each aspect of care with the family but should concentrate on only one or two per teaching session. In this instance it might be best if she explores with the family what they know already and then concentrate her teaching on the areas of weakness. Along these lines it is important for the nurse to praise the family for what they know and the care given already. This helps the family and patient to build trust in the nurse and be more receptive to further teaching. As mentioned earlier, it is important for the nurse to establish the plan of care with the family and patient, if he is able, so that she and the family know what the goals are and where they are heading.

OTHER ASPECTS OF THE HOME HEALTH NURSE'S ROLE

Beyond physical assessment and home health teaching, what are some of the other aspects of the home health nurse's role? One is the supportive role. The home health nurse is often an important link among the family, the hospital, and the physician. Because she is right there in the home setting, the home health nurse is often the first to see changes in the patient's condition, and she can advocate for the patient by letting the physician know of these changes. Another area of support in which the nurse may find herself is supporting decisions made by the family concerning the patient. Today many families are choosing to have their loved ones come home to be taken care of or to die. This is a difficult decision, and family members need the expertise of the nurse for support as they handle the burden of care for their loved one. The home health nurse can help the family feel positive about the decisions it has made. She might also call in others to help, like hospice or the home health social worker.

Another role for the nurse in home care is when she is called on to perform specific skills for which she was trained (e.g., insertion of indwelling Foley catheters, injections, lung assessment). When a nurse comes to a family's home to perform these specific skills on a patient, she learns fast that the conditions in performing these skills are not as ideal as in the hospital. She must learn to adapt to the patient and family's environment and involve them as much as possible in the task. For example, it may be necessary for a family member to help position a patient for better performance of the skill. Involving the family members is imperative so that they do not feel alienated by the nurse in the care of their loved one. It is important for the nurse to let the family make suggestions and help her to improvise in the performance of a task.

> Mrs. H. had a leg wound that needed the skilled assessment of a nurse and a dressing change three times a week. The lighting in the room where the patient lay was poor, and there was no space to lay a field for the dressing change. Mrs. H.'s daughter, who was involved with her mother's care, suggested a cardboard box, covered with a Chux. This made a good area for the nurse to work

on. The daughter held a flashlight for the nurse to look directly at the wound.

In this case the daughter felt good about her participation with the nurse and about the good care given to her mother.

All in all, it should be clear that the role of the home health nurse is all-encompassing. Through this discussion one can see that the home health nurse's care is not only with the patient, but also with the family, who generally provide the bulk of care in the home environment. The home health nurse must be adaptable and able to meet the challenge of this unique patient care situation. The rewards are great for the nurse who feels that she has been an effective link in teaching the family how to carry out the medical plan of treatment, so that the patient can remain at home in his own environment and with those he loves most, his family.

REFERENCES

Hall, Edward T. *The Silent Language.* New York: Doubleday, 1959, p. 31.

Leahy, Kathleen M., M. Marguerite Cobb, and Mary C. Jones. "Focusing on Families." In *Community Health Nursing,* edited by Sally J. Barhydt and Shelly Levine Langman, New York: McGraw-Hill, 1977, 129–147.

Webster's New World Dictionary. New York: World Publishing Company, 1984.

Wilner, Daniel M., Rosabelle Price Walkley, and Edward J. O'Neill, eds. "Health Education in the Community." In *Introduction To Public Health.* New York: Macmillan, 1978, pp. 487-502.

Chapter 11

Improvising and Adapting to the Home Setting in Delivering Care —Skills Needed

Joyce B. Marvan-Hyam

Home health is a challenging profession in which the nurse must use many skills and creative abilities. Improvising and adapting are essential functions for the nurse in the home setting in order to reach the anticipated goals for each patient. These ultimate objectives include stabilization or resolution of the health problems and optimal comfort measures, especially for the terminally ill patient. Home health nurses' duties do not only involve nursing care for the health problems at hand. Prevention is of utmost importance so that more problems do not develop and complicate the patient's condition.

The home health nurse is a generalist when is comes to nursing skills and evaluations. Each home care nurse usually has a broad range of assigned cases, making assessment and knowledge of a multitude of diagnoses mandatory. The nurse in the home setting must also be both trained and skilled in a variety of procedures, such as wound care, Broviac catheter care, Foley catheter insertion, and tracheostomy care. Observation, assessment, and evaluation in the home are essential nursing responsibilities and begin the moment the nurse meets the patient, family, or friends and enters the environment in which the patient is to receive the home health care. The home nursing evaluation includes observing and assessing the patient's physical, social, and psychological needs and initiating a nursing care plan that involves the patients, their caregivers, and the home health team. Health care goals must be realistic, and the nurse must be specific on what is changeable and what is not. The goals must be shared by the patient and caregivers in order for there to be successful follow through with the health care instructions and plans. This is of utmost importance, since the nurse visits the home on an intermittent basis.

Home health nurses must have excellent interviewing skills in order to obtain the information needed to plan and coordinate the care for each patient's identified parameters. Evaluation of the health care plan takes place continuously. The home health nurse must also observe each patient holistically. This means that each patient must be observed not only in relation to the identified illness, but also in regard to his or her total physical, social, psychological, and behavioral being.

Establishing a good rapport with the patient and caregivers helps the nurse to implement and organize the nursing care plan. It is also important for the nurse to listen to the patient and the caregivers in order to gain a good understanding of the problems that are significant for them.

Teaching and explaining in clear, concise language helps to accomplish the goals set for each patient. Communication skills are essential tools for the home health nurse when relaying information to the patient and transmitting the patient's health status to the physician. Because the home health nurse acts as a patient advocate and liaison between the home patient and the hospital or outpatient setting, concise descriptive language must be used in order to communicate the patient's physical, social, and psychological status accurately. The patient's needs and desires must be kept in mind when planning care. Support is also part of the nursing care plan, since the nurse in the home setting many times must act as a counselor as well as a caregiver and teacher. The home health nurse usually establishes more intimate relationships with the patients and caregivers compared with nurses working in some other settings, such as in the hospital. The nurse's sensitivity to the patient's needs and wishes may many times allow the patient to treat the nurse as a confidant. This may make for a more rewarding relationship among the nurse, the patient, and the significant others who are involved with the patient.

The home health nurse must have confidence in order to work in the home independently. He or she must be able to check the patient's condition, do procedures, give instructions, and communicate any problem or changes to the physician. Changes in the nursing care plan may need to be implemented during the patient's recovery process, so flexibility is an essential trait for a home care nurse.

Collaboration with other health care professionals is often helpful. It allows for brainstorming of patient care ideas with other nurses, therapists, social workers, physicians, and home health aides. This process can put problems and situations in perspective and allows them to be viewed more objectively. Essentially, the home health nurse establishes the trust of the patient, the caregivers, and the physician in planning and implementing the best treatment for each patient. What works for one patient may not work for another, so each patient must be viewed as a unique individual. The nurse must learn not to get discouraged if things do not go as planned initially. Persistence in attaining the patient goals will give the home health nurse many satisfying experiences. Home health nursing is a profession in which the nurse can learn from each patient and situation.

Safety is an important factor in the home. During a home health nurse's initial visit to the patient, a safety check of the home is done, and the safety information is given to the patient and caregivers. This can prevent accidents in the home. Some of the information may include the removal of loose rugs and cords, as well as instructing the patient to obtain a shower seat, nonskid mat, handheld shower, grab bars, or raised toilet seat to prevent falls in the bathroom. If a patient does not have the monetary resources for some of the equipment, such as a bath seat, sometimes safe substitutions can be made. A patient can use a sturdy stool or chair in the bathroom shower and put a towel over it to prevent sliding and make it more comfortable.

The following is a good example of how an innovative idea prevented further falls.

> Mrs. B. lived alone and had scoliosis and kyphosis, causing decreased mobility. She also had a chronic lung disease causing severe exacerbations at times. Mrs. B. had fallen out of bed one day and could not get up by herself. She stated that she slid out of bed so quickly and could not hold on to anything to lift herself back up. She informed the home care nurse and occupational therapist that she needed some safety mechanism to prevent further falls but insisted that she did not want a trapeze or side rail put on her single bed. These safety aids were suggested by the home health staff earlier. Mrs. B. complained of having difficulty turning on her sides as well. She and the occupational therapist thought of putting a grab bar onto the wall and attaching a long, sturdy, wide strap, which she holds on to in order to transfer in and out of bed. Mrs B. has not fallen since she has had this unique safety device for transfers. She ambulates with a walker and complained of nocturia but was too slow to walk to the bathroom in time. Therefore, she was instructed on the use of a female urinal, since her physical deformities prevented her from sitting on a bedside commode.

The nurse in the home setting strives to get the patient optimally mobile and mentally stimulated. The home care nurse may instruct the patient on range-of-motion exercises to increase muscle tone and strength and prevent contractures. Physical and occupational therapy may also be involved in the care of the patient. Physical therapists are important members of the home care team. Their job includes increasing bed mobility and sitting and standing balance. They strive to improve left- or right-sided function for stroke patients and instruct in independent transfers (with assistance devices if needed). Ramps may need to be installed in the home in order for patients to be more mobile. Prosthetic training, gait training, wrapping of the stumps, strengthening of muscle tissue, and evaluation of the home for safety are also part of the physical therapist's function.

The occupational therapist assists the patient in becoming more self-sufficient in activities of daily living, which include dressing, bathing, grooming, cooking, and eating. Teaching the handicapped patient ways to manage light household tasks is also part of the therapist's responsibilities. Playing cards, doing puzzles, or working on crafts are some of the modalities that the occupational therapist may use to stimulate the mind as well as increase muscle strength, dexterity, and coordination.

The home care nurse must be aware of community resources in order to further meet the patient's needs. Some of these resources may include Meals-on-Wheels, friendly visitors, or senior centers. A home care social worker, another invaluable member of the home health team, is knowledgeable about a full range of community services and can assist the patient and family in adjusting to change while encouraging independence. The social worker can also assist in making alternative living arrangements for the patient, if needed.

The home health nurse is usually the case manager, who coordinates the care for the patient and asks the other health disciplines to get involved in the home care program.

The home health aide has a necessary function in giving personal care to the patient. The aide can help all the other disciplines in following through on the patient's care by reviewing exercises, doing simple wound care treatments, and encouraging the patient during the recovery process. Any patient changes noted by the home health aide are communicated to the other home health professionals.

The home health nurse also checks for any changes in the patient's condition. Checking for signs and symptoms of infection and teaching these early warning signs are essential functions of the nurse. Medication actions, schedules, and side effects are always included in the nursing care plan. The patient and caregiver should be aware of the warning signs of toxicity or allergy to a medication. The nurse uses many improvising techniques with medication teaching. These may include using plastic medication boxes for each day of the week with the scheduled time marked on each box. Such boxes are easily obtained at a pharmacy or a medical supply store. The medication can also be placed in marked envelopes, ice trays, or muffin pans for those patients who are confused or forgetful. Medication charts, which include the action of each medicine, can be made for the patient during the initial nursing visit. Any changes can be marked on the chart. For patients with vision difficulties, the words can be printed in large letters with colored markers or pictures can be drawn to indicate each pill.

The home care nurse can draw blood in the home. A fishing tackle box is a handy, organized aid in which to keep all the needed supplies for laboratory work. If blood specimens have to be kept in the car for a period of time in warm weather, they may be stored in an insulated bag with "blue" ice.

The amount of available light in the home can be a problem. I know a nurse who wears a miner's hat with a light on it to do catheterizations in dark homes. Flashlights and tape measures are also handy devices to assist the nurse in patient assessment.

Skin care is always included in preventative teaching so that breakdown does not occur. Pillows or blankets can be used to position patients, and triangular foam wedges can be implemented to elevate the head of the bed. Cardboard boxes or wooden boards can be used as bed cradles, to prevent footdrop. Long-handled sponges and hand-held showers allow for greater independence. Hair-washing caps are available for those patients who cannot get into a shower. Otherwise, a pillow may be placed behind the patient's neck, and his or her hair may be washed in the kitchen sink.

Nutrition is an area in which adaptation can be a challenging task. The nurse must always take cultural practice into consideration when discussing dietary needs. A blender is suggested for patients who require soft diets. It is also a handy appliance for making milkshakes as high-protein supplements.

When the patient is on pain medication or is less mobile, elimination can become a problem. The patient's bowel schedule may be marked on a calendar. For urinary problems, male or female urinals can be used, or if these are not available, coffee cans or plastic dishes that don't easily tumble over may be substituted. Such devices are especially important for patients who are on diuretics or those with decreased mobility.

The home care nurse can make it easier for the patients to rise from a chair by elevating the seat with pillows. One can also organize essential kitchen utensils or lower clothes racks to facilitate access. Universal side rails can be placed on the side of the patient's bed if falling out of bed is a concern. A trapeze bar can be placed on a regular bed for those who can use this handy device.

Dressing can be a difficult task for many people with decreased mobility. The nurse can substitute a hospital gown with a robe or shirt that can be reversed in order to open and close from the back. Velcro closures make it simpler for some patients to become independent in dressing. Jogging suits or loose-fitting clothes and sneakers can also make dressing easier. Many home health nurses believe that if patients are able to get dressed rather than wear bedclothes all day, they will feel better faster.

If the nurse is concerned about safety for the patient who lives alone, a remote control safety device can be rented monthly. This device is connected to emergency switches in a nearby health facility. Telephones coded with important numbers are an easy solution for contacting health care or family members.

For wound care procedures in the home the nurse can make normal saline. The decision whether or not to use sterile or clean technique in the home must be part of the nurse's basic principles.

Medical equipment for the home can be obtained from several sources. If a patient has Medicare B (medical coverage), then 80 percent of the cost for needed equipment is covered. However, Medicare does not pay for bathroom equipment. Some health maintenance organizations or other health insurance plans cover the remaining 20 percent of the payment for the equipment. Otherwise, the patient must pay the remaining 20 percent. Medicare B can be purchased once a year by those people who already have Medicare A (hospital coverage). Medicare has restrictions on equipment rentals and purchases. For example, bedside commodes can be rented or purchased only for those patients who cannot ambulate out of their rooms or who have much difficulty getting to the bathroom. Space boots for prevention of skin breakdown will be purchased only for those patients who already have footsores.

Medicaid will pay for some equipment, but the health care professional must be specific on the required documentation. An explanation must be given stating why it is necessary that the patient obtain these health aids. Certain medications and supplies can be obtained with monthly stickers. The pharmacist is knowledgeable about the specific items that are covered.

Supplies such as dressings, catheters, and irrigation kits are provided by most home health agencies to all Medicare B and Medicaid patients. Other patients have to buy their supplies. Otherwise, the nurse can use adaptable techniques. For example, a deep dish that has been boiled can be substituted for an irrigating tray, and the patient can sterilize the syringe as well.

Health maintenance organizations supply the needed provisions to home care patients as a health plan benefit.

Most home health agencies have a storeroom for equipment that has been donated. This equipment is usually loaned to patients who cannot afford to rent the needed aids. Some organizations, such as the Multiple Sclerosis Society, the American Cancer Society, the Red Cross, and the Muscular Dystrophy Association, rent or loan equipment to patients who are experiencing financial hardship. The St. Vincent de Paul Society sometimes has used equipment that can be purchased at a cheaper rate. Some organizations may require a prescription or notification from a health professional. Also, several of the national organizations in each county have different policies, according to their available funds.

Some community home health agencies have United Way funds or special program monies allotted for medically indigent adults. These funds can be used for visits or sometimes even necessary equipment.

There are insurance and pension plans that cover medication purchased at certain pharmacies. This information should be available in the patient's insurance handbook. It is important for the patient and agency to be aware of the insurance requirements for home care. Some plans may require hospitalization immediately after or within a short time frame before home care benefits.

On discharge from the hospital some patients may require an expensive nutritional supplement or medication that they cannot afford. The situation can be brought to the attention of the directors of the hospital or the insurance plan, because it is cheaper to pay for the necessary medication than keep the person in the hospital. Such situations are usually reviewed on a case-by-case basis. The outcome depends on how the insurance plan or the hospital functions. Funding sources are researched before the hospital or insurance plan makes exceptions in coverage benefits. A cost savings must be proven before any coverage changes are instituted.

If certain supplies or equipment is considered to be helpful, but not mandatory, the health care professional can usually figure out substitute ways of dealing with the situation. Of course, these should always be safe and effective.

Home health nurses must get involved in stressful home patient situations. Many of the patients are dying at home and need the nurse to support, encourage, and instruct them and their caregivers about comfort measures as well as alleviate their anxieties. Fear of pain is a feeling that many patients express to the nurses. The patient may be concerned about family situations, and the nurse must have an understanding of how to deal with the stresses so that the patient can rest more peacefully. Through experience the home care nurse gains an understanding that each patient is unique. A caring and supporting nurse helps the patient and caregivers through the difficult times. Sincerity is an important trait for the nurse, so that the patient and caregivers feel that their needs are being met.

Some home health nurses get the motivation to continue in their home nursing endeavors from the appreciation expressed by patients and caregivers. Many caregivers feel that they could never have gone through the experience of having someone die or be ill at home if the nurse had not been there to help them through the ordeal.

Nurses must nurture themselves as well as the patients. Successful coping measures provide the nurse with the energy and stamina to continue with home care work and prevent burnout. Some of these coping mechanisms include support groups, talking with colleagues, and taking time off for vacations.

Some of these points can be illustrated with actual experiences.

Mr. K., a pleasant, retired, 65-year-old businessman, lived with his wife in a clean, neat, second-floor apartment. He had developed back pain during a vacation trip. After going through extensive testing, Mr. K. was diagnosed with bone cancer to the rib and hip areas, but the primary site was unknown. He underwent a series of radiation treatments, which helped the bone pain initially. Mr. K. became progressively weaker, and a hospital bed, commode, and wheelchair were ordered. A home health aide visited the patient several times a week to give personal care. She gave much support to the family in showing how to perform the physical care for Mr. K. The cancer spread, and after a few months the patient became paralyzed owing to spinal cord metastases. Mr. K.'s muscle tone worsened, and because of steroid treatment he became edematous and gained weight. The nurse helped the family and patient with all of the potential problems. Pain control, skin care, urinary and bowel problems, safety, and activity were of primary importance. A medication schedule was implemented. Condom catheters were used, and a bowel program was instituted, using suppositories or Fleet enemas when necessary. Because of all the sudden changes Mr. K. became worried and anxious about the situation. He was taught relaxation exercises by listening to tape recordings and by reading suggested literature. Mrs. K.'s father was approximately 92 years old and came to visit regularly during the day so that Mrs. K. could do the shopping and errands. Mr. and Mrs. K.'s daughter assisted in doing errands when she could, as she was busy with two young children. It was important for Mr. K. to stay home during his illness. Mrs. K. felt that this was a promise she needed to fulfill. They both felt that if the nurse supported, taught, and assisted in Mr. K.'s care, this goal could be accomplished. Their goals were met because the nurse, physical and occupational therapists, social worker, physician, and home health aide all worked together to keep Mr. K. at home. He died peacefully in his sleep one year later. The nurse will never forget how much it meant to know and help this family. A trusting relationship was built between all those involved. The nurse still receives letters of appreciation from Mrs. K. several years after Mr. K.'s death.

* * *

Mrs. G., who weighs 76 pounds and is in her seventies, had undergone an aortic valve replacement a few years before the nurse's involvement. The physician had informed the nurse that Mrs. G. was being sent home to die, since her valve was leaking and repairing it was too risky. The physician felt that she would develop uncontrollable congestive heart failure. Mrs. G. could no longer walk or stand and was extremely weak after being hospitalized for several months. Her medical diagnosis also included sepsis from a severe urinary tract infection. The nurse visited the patient two times initially to review the medication regimen with the attendant, check cardiopulmonary status, and instruct the safety, activity, and skin care. Mrs. G. had 24-hour attendant care in her home, since the only thing she could do was feed herself. Diuretics were given to Mrs. G. according to what the nurse's findings were during the physical check made each visit. The nurse communicated Mrs. G.'s status to the physician by telephone. Mrs. G. spent most of her time in a wheelchair and took afternoon naps as well. She preferred having a Foley catheter in place for convenience, and the physician agreed. The nurse changed the catheter once a month. The attendant and nurse checked for signs and symptoms of urinary tract infection to prevent further sepsis. Urine specimens were collected and analyzed, and the patient was placed on antibiotics as needed. After several months Mrs. G. improved, which puzzled the physician in charge. The nurse and attendant felt that the attention and care given to Mrs. G. really made a difference. As Mrs. G. stabilized, the nurse decreased her visits and instructed the attendant when to give the diuretic. This medication became a necessary treatment only for several days every three to four weeks. Ten months after first meeting Mrs. G. she only required a monthly visit to change the catheter and check her general physical status. Mrs. G. is now living in a nursing home, since 24-hour attendant care became impractical for the family. Two years later the physician is saying it is a miracle that Mrs. G. is still alive. An important incentive for living was her only granddaughter, who was born six weeks after she came home from the hospital. She continues to get much joy from her granddaughter's visits.

The home health nurse must deal with many difficult and stressful situations. There are many success stories as well. The nurse receives much appreciation from the patient's friends and family, which certainly makes the job rewarding. Something can be learned from each situation, which makes the occupation a dynamic one indeed. The nurses give of themselves but get satisfaction from within, with many thanks from others.

Chapter 12

Home Intravenous Therapy

Naomi Marco-Manelis

Diagnosis-related groups (DRGs) are forcing hospitals to scrutinize inpatient care and length of hospitalization closely. The DRG system means change, a change from convalescence in an acute care facility to early discharge and convalescence in the home. Intravenous (IV) therapy is no longer a mandatory reason to be hospitalized or require long-term hospitalization. Patients have been receiving total parenteral nutrition at home since the 1970s. Subsequently, patients have undergone IV therapies of hydration, antibiotics, amphotericin, anticoagulants, insulin, narcotics, and antineoplastics in the home setting.

In this chapter I discuss my experiences with the different IV therapies mentioned. Issues surrounding central and peripheral access lines are addressed.

CENTRAL LINE CATHETERS

Central line catheters are used for most patients receiving home IV therapy. Of the many types of central line catheters available, the Hickman and Broviac right atrial catheters are the ones most commonly used in the home setting. The jugular and subclavian line and the multilumen infusion catheter are also used with home patients.

The multilumen central venous catheter allows multiple infusions through one catheter. The catheter that I am familiar with is made by American Edwards. It has a triple lumen and three exit ports at fixed distances from the tip, referred to as proximal, middle, and distal. Injection site caps are attached to the lumen hubs, or IV tubing can be attached directly to the lumen hubs. The multilumen infusion catheter is inserted through the jugular or subclavian vein. The distal tip of the catheter can lie anywhere along the path to the right atrium, but usually it lies in the superior vena cava.

The jugular, subclavian, and multilumen catheters usually are inserted in the hospital to provide emergency access to the venous circulation for IV therapy and for measuring central venous pressure. Patients occasionally are discharged from the hospital with these catheters in place. This allows for completion of IV therapy at home, generally for only a short term.

The Broviac catheter is made of an elastic silicone rubber. A Dacron cuff encircles the catheter. The volume capacity is 0.74 ml. A modified version is available for neonates and pediatric patients. The volume capacity of the neonate catheter is 0.2 ml and the pediatric catheter, 0.3 ml.

The Hickman catheter is similar to the Broviac. It has one or two Dacron cuffs and a larger diameter lumen, which allows for easier blood drawing. The volume capacity is 1.84 ml. Available modifications include a double-lumen Hickman catheter, which can be either a combination of a Hickman/ Broviac or two Hickmans fused together.

Insertion of the Broviac or Hickman catheter is a minor surgical procedure. The catheter is first inserted at a site (exit site) away from the chosen vein, and then tunneled subcutaneously to a point near the vein, where an incision has been made (insertion site). The catheter is inserted into the vein and threaded to the right atrium. The distal tip is positioned in the lower superior vena cava at the entrance to the right atrium or just inside the right atrium. The vein insertion site is closed, and a dressing is applied here and at the catheter exit site.

The Dacron cuff is situated in the subcutaneous tunnel. Fibrous tissue infiltrates the cuff, stabilizing the catheter. The tunnel and the cuff serve as physical barriers against microorganisms.

The advantage of a central line catheter for IV therapy is that the catheter tip lies in an area of high blood flow. This allows for long-term placement and delivery of hypertonic solutions. This is ideally suited for total parenteral nutrition (TPN) because the TPN solution contains high concentrations of glucose, which cause thrombosis if they are not infused in an area of high blood flow. Peripheral access for patients requiring long-term therapy of antibiotics, amphotericin, or antineoplastic agents is often difficult. This necessitates the placement of a central line. A central line may also be indicated for patients with chronic diseases, such as cystic fibrosis and cancer. For such patients a central line would allow frequent blood drawing and infusions of intermittent fluids and drugs.

Complications include infection, venous thrombosis, air embolism (AE), and damage to the catheter. Infection of the exit site is evident by inflammation and drainage. Presence of drainage should be reported to a physician. A culture may be indicated. When drainage is present, a daily dressing change should be done with careful inspection of the site to monitor the degree of infection. Sepsis related to the catheter necessitates removal of the catheter. A culture is taken of the catheter tip and appropriate antibiotic therapy is instituted.

Clinical signs of venous thrombosis include edema and tenderness of the arm, shoulder, and neck on the same side as the catheter. Venography can confirm the diagnosis. Heparin therapy is indicated and usually the catheter is removed.

AE is a rare complication of a central line catheter. The blood pressure differential between the right atrium and peripheral veins can lead to AE if the catheter is open to the air.

> . . . blood pressure which is high in the aorta and the larger arteries, drops significantly in the capillaries and is gradually reduced until it approaches zero in the larger veins. This is due principally to the fact that when a person is standing, the blood in the lower portion of the body must rise against the force of gravity in the large veins.[1]

The suction force of the right atrium expanding helps to maintain adequate venous return to the heart. The suction force creates the blood pressure differential.

Damage to the external portion of the Hickman or Broviac catheter may occur as a result of severing, cracking, or a puncture. To prevent AE or blood loss, immediately clamp the catheter close to the exit site. Temporary measures involve inserting a cannula (14-gauge for the Hickman and 18-gauge for the Broviac) into the catheter. If the catheter is damaged more than 4 cm from the exit site, it can be repaired with a repair kit.

CATHETER MAINTENANCE PROCEDURES

Procedures for Hickman and Broviac catheter maintenance vary greatly among health professionals. These procedures have generally been adapted from central line dressing care protocols. Areas of focus are clamping, caps, heparinizing, blood drawing, and site care.

The patient usually is taught how to care for the catheter before going home from the hospital. If the patient is happy and comfortable with the procedures and there are no problems, it is probably best not to make any changes. Unfortunately, many times the procedures that have been taught are long and complex, causing some people to view the catheter as an antagonist. By reviewing the procedures and the problems perceived by the patient and significant others, catheter maintenance procedures can be simplified and adjusted to the patient's life style.

Clamping

Clamping is necessary when the adapter cap is removed or the tubing attached to the catheter is disconnected. Clamping maintains a closed system, preventing blood from backing up or air from entering the system.

Clamps with teeth damage the catheter. Therefore, heavily padded or smooth-edged stainless steel hemostats, bulldog clamps, or plastic smooth-edged clamps (similar to a hemostat) are recommended.

Continuous versus intermittent clamping is an issue. While discussing the pros and cons of these two methods with various professionals, the following views were expressed:

- Continuous clamping provides the person with ready access to the clamp. In other words, the clamp is not left in the other room or in another set of clothing.
- Continuous clamping is not necessary when using a Luer-locking cap that is securely attached.

If continuous clamping is preferred, a bulldog clamp should be used because the other types of clamps would be cumbersome if left in place on the catheter. Regardless of the type of clamp used, I recommend that a 2 × 2-inch gauze be placed between the clamp and the catheter. Use of the 2 × 2-inch gauze and alternating sites of clamping prevent possible damage to the catheter.

Patients should be able to have some choices about clamping their catheters. It may be easier for some people to use continuous clamping, whereas others may prefer intermittent clamping. Also, some people find it difficult to use the bulldog clamp, and they should be offered an alternative.

The Hickman and Broviac catheters can be clamped at all times when not infusing or at intervals when changing the cap. Most jugular, subclavian, and multilumen catheters cannot be clamped because of their construction. The inability to clamp the line makes those types of catheter less than ideal for the home setting.

Caps

Caps used for central lines include the Hickman/Broviac noninjectable Luer-locking adapter, injectable adapter plugs, and Luer-locking injectable caps. Noninjectable caps generally are used immediately after the catheter is inserted and when a patient is on TPN during specific hours of the day. These caps are discarded after removing them for an infusion, or they are soaked in various solutions between uses. The disadvantages of the noninjectable caps are having to remove them each time an infusion is necessary and the factor of noncompliance to a proper soaking procedure.

The injectable adapter plug is not Luer-locking, which increases the risk of dislodging. I prefer the Luer-locking injectable cap with a sealed rubber top that cannot be rolled off.

Changing of the injectable cap should be kept to a minimum, but to avoid the possibility of leaks developing, the cap should be changed at least once a week. Check with the manufacturer for recommendations on how many times the cap can be entered safely before it needs to be changed.

Use alcohol or povidone-iodine to clean the old cap at the junction before removing. For cleaning, either swabs or swabsticks may be used. Attach the new cap. Secure the connection with ½-inch tape, leaving a tab for easy removal.

Heparinizing

When a catheter is used for intermittent therapy, it is irrigated after completion of therapy with a heparin solution ranging from 10 U of heparin per milliliter to 1,000 U per milliliter. The volume used ranges from 1.5 to 10.0 ml. If the catheter is not being used for a daily therapy, it should be irrigated on a routine basis. The routine varies from once a week to twice a day. I feel that once a day is sufficient. The strength of the heparin used depends on the physician's preference or the institution's protocol. Since the volume capacity of the Hickman catheter is 1.84 ml and the adult Broviac is 0.74 ml, theoretically, a 2-ml flush is more than adequate. However, one physician believes that 1,000 U/ml with a 3-ml flush is necessary and that the flush should not only irrigate the catheter, but also prevent catheter-related venous thrombosis.

Heparinizing the catheter should be done with a premixed solution. Heparin comes premixed as 10 U/ml, 100 U/ml, and 1,000 U/ml solutions. These are the most common strengths used. Therefore, it is not necessary for patients to mix their own heparin solutions.

The size of the syringe should also be taken into consideration. The syringe should be larger than the final volume required in order to facilitate easier handling of the syringe. For example, for a 2-ml flush use a 3-ml syringe. Patients appreciate this change because it helps to prevent the plunger on the syringe from being accidentally pulled out. When irrigating through an injection cap, a 22-gauge needle is preferred. Patients seem to have difficulty inserting into the injection cap with anything smaller than 22 gauge. A needle larger than 22 gauge makes unnecessarily large holes in the injection cap.

Packaging of the syringe and needle is important. Many patients have difficulty removing the syringe and needle from twist-off plastic packaging (e.g., Monoject). They seem to prefer the syringe and needle in paper packaging (e.g., B-D).

Some irrigation procedures state that the catheter be clamped during the last 0.5 ml of heparin. "Simultaneously clamping and irrigating of the catheter is done to prevent backflow of blood and clot formation."[2] Another procedure states: "The syringe should not be completely empty."[3] Simultaneous clamping and irrigating are difficult for most patients or significant others to perform.

Needles should be disposed of properly. I advise that they be put in a jar or coffee can, out of the reach of children. When a sufficient amount is accumulated, they can be disposed of at a large hospital, physician's office, or pharmaceutical service.

Drawing Blood

Drawing blood is supposed to be easier with a Hickman catheter than with a Broviac. I have encountered ease and difficulty with both. The following basic procedure should be used to draw blood through these catheters. First, clean the injection cap with an alcohol or povidone-iodine swab. Then, using a 5- to 10-ml syringe with an 18- or 20-gauge needle, draw a minimum of 5 ml of blood and discard. Use another syringe (size determined by the amount of blood needed) to draw the sample. Change the injection cap and heparinize the catheter. The catheter can also be irrigated with saline before heparinizing.

Site Care

If there are sutures at the insertion site, they should be removed after ten days. If Steri-strips are used to close the insertion site, they should remain in place for about ten days, after which they begin to loosen and may be peeled off.

Clean the insertion site with hydrogen peroxide, alcohol, or povidone-iodine solution. Some people are instructed to use all three. Generally, at home, one or two are sufficient. After cleaning the insertion site, cover it with a dressing. If patients or significant others object to seeing the wound, cover it with a 2 × 2-inch gauze. The transparent dressing can be left in place for up to seven days. The gauze dressing is changed at least every other day. After the Steri-strips are removed, a dressing is no longer needed. Some professionals believe that "if steri-strips are used, this incision does not require a dressing."[4] Patient choice should be a factor. If the patient does not want a dressing at the insertion site, and if the site is clean and dry, omit the dressing.

There are many dressing procedures for care of the exit site. Alcohol, povidone-iodine solution, hydrogen peroxide, and acetone are reported for cleaning the site. Acetone is not recommended because, according to the manufacturer of the Hickman/Broviac catheters, it is absorbed through the catheter. Ointments applied to the site include povidone-iodine, Neosporin, and bacitracin. Various sizes of sterile gauze and transparent and adhesive-backed dressings are used for covering the site. Omitting the dressing has also been reported. Some procedures specify that gloves and masks must be worn during dressing care. Written techniques have been referred to as sterile, clean, or using an aseptic manner. All procedures agree that the exit site must be dressed immediately after insertion and while the site is healing. Some patients are instructed to clean the site first with six sterile cotton-tipped applicators soaked in hydrogen peroxide, followed by six alcohol swabs, followed by six povidone-iodine swabs. This is probably excessive.

Hydrogen peroxide and alcohol are equally effective as cleansing agents while the site is healing. During this time there is some oozing of blood, serous drainage, and crusting taking place. Hydrogen peroxide is the better choice for irritated skin. Use as many sterile cotton-tipped applicators as necessary to clean the site. Povidone-iodine is the preferred bactericidal agent. Again, use as many applicators as necessary. Some people are allergic or sensitive to iodines. If there is only a skin sensitivity, wipe off the povidone-iodine solution with alcohol. If an allergy exists, eliminate the povidone-iodine from the procedure and use alcohol instead.

Alcohol and povidone-iodine are available in swabs and swabsticks. The swabs are individually packaged, and the sticks generally come in packages of three. Many patients develop a preference for one or the other. Allow them the choice. Ointments come in tubes and single-use packets. Single-use packets are preferred because a tube can be misplaced or the cap can be lost or become contaminated.

The site can be covered with any convenient-size sterile gauze. Taping the dressing is done occlusively or by window framing. Paper tape, plastic tape, or silk tape can be used. Some tape sticks better than others to certain people. I prefer the silk tape because it leaves less residue and is easier to tear into the desired widths. Let the patient decide. Gauze dressing should be changed at least three times a week.

Transparent dressings are another option. Because the ability of this dressing to adhere to the skin is decreased by use of ointments, they should be omitted. It is recommended that these dressings be changed when showering or taking a tub bath. Regarding "swimming, hot tubs, etc., the patient may resume water activities after site is completely healed. Coil catheter and completely cover site and catheter with a large transparent dressing one hour before entering the water. Change dressing immediately after swimming to prevent moistness from perspiration accumulating under dressings. Change the tape on heparin cap after swimming."[5]

The purpose of site care is to evaluate the site for signs and symptoms of possible complications. The dressing is used to prevent infection. All procedures recommend using a dressing at some point. One source suggests that "when the dressing site is completely healed without redness or drainage (approximately 3 weeks) and the patient's granulocytes are greater than 200, the dressing cover may be omitted."[6] Most health professionals are uncomfortable with the omission of the dressing.

Infants and small children have especially sensitive skin and may require altered site care procedures. Rigorous site care can be detrimental.

> John, age 18 months, had a Broviac catheter in place for home antibiotic therapy. The hospital staff nurses taught his mother a daily procedure of six hydrogen peroxide-soaked applicators, followed by six alcohol swabsticks. Povidone-iodine ointment was used at the site, covered by a 2 × 2-inch gauze and secured by tape. By the end of the first week, John had red, blistered skin at the site. The skin healed after his mother used only hydrogen peroxide for cleaning and left the site open to the air as much as possible.

Using three povidone-iodine swabs, followed by three alcohol swabs and a transparent dressing works well without complications. Some transparent dressings do not adhere well to a baby's skin. Uniflex and Ensure-it seem to be the most effective. Ensure-it is available in a 3.8 × 5.1-cm size, which is especially convenient.

Dressing care of the Hickman/Broviac catheters has been adapted from experience in central venous line care. The dressing procedures discussed here can apply to jugular and subclavian lines as well. The omission of the dressing does *not* apply to the jugular and subclavian lines.

Catheter Maintenance Summary

Catheter maintenance at home needs to be simple, easy, and accomplished in a minimum amount of time. There is poor compliance with long, complex procedures. Discuss with your patients their ideas and attitudes about catheter maintenance. The change from daily gauze dressing care to once a week transparent dressing care was a big relief for many patients.

> Joan didn't want to see the catheter so she chose a 2 × 2-inch gauze dressing with the catheter coiled under a 4 × 4-inch gauze dressing.

* * *

John, a 7-year-old, hated his Broviac catheter and was depressed
because he was told he could no longer take tub baths. Letting him
bathe with a transparent dressing helped him to accept his catheter.

Most physicians are aware of the many procedures for catheter maintenance. They have certain preferences but are generally willing to make
changes to accommodate the patient's needs.

SUPPLIES

Obtaining supplies needed for central line care can pose a problem for the
patient. Many patients are discharged from a hospital with no reliable source
of supplies. Many were going to several places to obtain items.

Dan, an 18-year-old with cystic fibrosis, was discharged from the
hospital with a Broviac catheter. A few weeks later his mother
called the doctor and demanded that the catheter be removed, since
obtaining supplies was difficult and a major source of stress.

There are reliable pharmaceutical services that specialize in home IV
therapy and stock all necessary supplies. They bill Medicare, state programs,
and private insurance companies. Many times they will deliver to the
patient's home.

TPN

TPN is a method of providing nutritional needs for patients with digestive
problems through the IV route. TPN solutions contain proteins, calories,
electrolytes, vitamins, trace elements, and drugs. The formulation varies
according to individual need. The end solution will normally be in a 2- or 3-
liter bag. Lipids are used in conjunction with TPN solutions. They provide
the essential fatty acids as well as concentrated calories. Some patients are
taught how to mix their own solutions, while others have them premixed by a
pharmacist. The TPN solution should be premixed by a pharmacist using a
laminar flow hood. Mixing in a home setting, consistently maintaining an
aseptic technique, is not possible.

Karen has been on TPN at home for ten years. The first eight
years she mixed her own solution. She had multiple catheter-related

infections, requiring the insertion of 27 Hickman catheters over the eight years. For the past two years the solution has been premixed by a pharmaceutical nutrition service, and Karen has had no catheter-related infections.

Home total parenteral nutrition (HTPN) is generally infused on an intermittent basis during sleeping hours. An infusion pump or controller is used to monitor the infusion. A controller uses the force of gravity to infuse the solution. The pump infuses by exerting positive pressure. Controllers and pumps have alarms to alert the patient to possible problems.

HTPN allows mobility and independence, but in some situations this is not realistic. Involve significant others if possible. Many times others are needed for support, assistance, and to take over in the event of illness or an emergency.

Training for HTPN focuses on catheter maintenance, use of the infusion device, mixing of the solution (unless premixed), and signs and symptoms of potential problems. Teaching generally begins in the hospital, but occasionally a patient is discharged with no formal training or HTPN is begun at home. Patients need to be assured that HTPN is not impossible to learn. Each aspect of the program needs to be presented at a comfortable pace for patients and significant others.

HTPN requires a team approach. The team consists of the patient, physician, pharmacist, dietitian, and home health nurse. The team must coordinate with members of the hospital's inservice, discharge planning, and floor nursing personnel. Many hospitals have home health agencies, and pharmaceutical home nutrition services have manuals that cover all aspects of care needed for the program. If the manuals are too long and too complex for the patient to understand, use tape recorders or cue sheets for step-by-step instructions. This is especially useful for connecting and disconnecting the tubing and setting up the infusion device.

Patients can become confused when presented with different written instructions from the hospital, the home health agency, and the pharmaceutical home nutrition service. Remember the team approach, and decide at the beginning who is responsible for home teaching, and then coordinate changes in procedure with the responsible party.

Evaluation of the HTPN patient includes body weight, measuring intake and output (I and O), and blood and urine tests. These measurements and tests give an accurate indication of the patient's cardiovascular, renal, and hepatic functions. Stable and problem-free patients often do not comply with daily monitoring. Adjustments should be made on an individual basis.

Hypoglycemia may result if any infusion of TPN solution is ended abruptly. A tapered infusion period will prevent the problem. An example of a tapered infusion over 12 hours is a rate of 150 ml/hour for 11.5 hours, followed by 50 ml/hr for 30 minutes. More complex tapering rates are usually not necessary.

Sharing the HTPN experience with other HTPN patients can be beneficial. "A foundation called Lifeline, formed specifically for people on HTPN, publishes a newsletter that includes individual experiences, practical suggestions, and information on new research, equipment, and legislative efforts."[7] Lifeline is a nonprofit foundation offering free membership and benefits to patients on nontraditional nutrition. For further information write Lifeline Foundation, 30 East Chestnut St., Sharon, MA 02067.

AMPHOTERICIN B

IV amphotericin B is generally considered unsuitable for home therapy, probably because of the serious adverse reactions associated with its use.

On occasion, personal, financial, and geographical concerns override the negative attitude regarding home therapy.

Daniel received daily amphotericin B in 250 ml of 5% dextrose in water with hydrocortisone 35 mg added to each bag. The dose of amphotericin B was increased by 50 mg daily until a maintenance dose of 3 gm was reached. A pharmaceutical nutrition service mixed the solution daily. A home health nurse delivered the solution to the patient and stayed with him during the entire infusion. He was premedicated with Benadryl 50 mg and Tylenol 650 mg by mouth. The solution was infused through an infusion pump over one to two hours by way of a Hickman catheter. If severe chills developed, the infusion was to be slowed by one half and Demerol 25 mg IV push was ordered. The Demerol was ordered to be repeated every hour as needed. No severe chills were noted, and the six weeks' therapy was completed without complications.

FLUIDS AND NARCOTICS

Fluids and narcotic analgesics are often administered to patients with end-stage cancer. Such patients prefer to die at home. This can be the most stressful and challenging of the home IV therapies. Keeping the patient comfortable is the primary goal. Whatever amount of narcotic is needed to keep the patient pain-free should be used without hesitation. As the end approaches, significant others have a real need to do something for the patient. They need constant reassurance that they are doing what the patient prefers by letting death occur at home. Significant others seem to feel better if they can participate in caring for the patient. Allow them to do as much as possible.

The sound of labored, moist respirations can become difficult to tolerate. Belladona and opium suppositories often alleviate this problem by reducing secretions.

If the patient requires fluids as well as the narcotic, an infusion pump or controller is used. When just the narcotic is needed, a syringe pump can be used. "Syringe pumps have a motor that pushes in the plunger. This type of pump is used to administer only small volumes of fluid, because the syringe must be refilled manually."[8]

Flexibility and support are the key factors for success in this type of therapy.

ANTINEOPLASTICS

Antineoplastic drugs can be administered with infusion pumps, controllers, or syringe pumps. Because of their toxic potential, they should be prepared by properly trained personnel using proper protective equipment. Likewise, appropriate storage and disposal of supplies are important.

The nausea and vomiting, with associated dehydration and weight loss, commonly observed with antineoplastic agents often requires additional therapeutic measures.

ANTIBIOTICS

Home IV antibiotic therapy has gained momentum from the impact of the DRGs. Many serious infections requiring either long- (greater than ten days) or short-term antibiotic therapy can be treated in the home.

Long-term treatment of osteomylitis, acute pulmonary exacerbations of cystic fibrosis, or endocarditis is usually begun in the hospital. The patient usually is discharged with a central line in place. Some patients on long-term antibiotics can be maintained on peripheral sites. If peripheral venous access becomes a problem, then an evaluation is made whether to discontinue IV therapy or continue with a central line.

Peripheral Lines

Short-term therapy can be instituted in the home with peripheral venous access.

Jay had an infected finger from a cat bite that did not respond to oral antibiotics. His doctor prescribed a four-day course of an IV antibiotic at home. It was not necessary for Jay to be hospitalized.

Peripheral venous access is either by a plastic cannula (catheter) or by a winged, steel needle infusion set. A catheter can be maintained for a longer time in the vein. The size of catheters for home use varies from 18 to 24 gauge. The smaller sizes cause less vein irritation. The catheter is heparin-locked with a Luer-locking injection cap or injectable adapter plug. The advantage to the Luer-locking cap is that it cannot become accidentally dislodged. A Luer-locking T connector with the injection cap attached to the end allows easier access to the cap away from the vein. This decreases movement of the catheter in the vein and, consequently, decreases vein irritation.

Frequency of site changes is controversial and varies from every 48 hours to every four days. In practice, however, the frequency can be *as necessary* when peripheral access is limited.

Lisa, a 13-year-old paraplegic, was receiving a home antibiotic by way of a peripheral site. She had poor peripheral access, and an anesthesiologist had to insert the catheter before discharge. She was adamant about not wanting it changed unless it quit functioning. The site was observed Monday, Wednesday, and Friday. Site care included swabbing with povidone-iodine, applying povidone-iodine ointment at the site, and covering it with a sterile 2 × 2-inch gauze square secured with plastic tape. The T connector and injection cap were changed twice a week. A small armboard was used to secure the site on the hand. The site lasted the three weeks of therapy with no phlebitis noted.

Frequency of site changes should be dictated by the condition of the vein. Many patients who had site changes on a regular basis ended up with a central line to complete their therapy. I have been called to start an IV after a nurse discontinued a good access site and failed to gain another access after three to four venipunctures. Change the venipuncture site when the vein shows signs of irritation. Any burning sensation is a sign of irritation. Stress to patients that it is their responsibility to let someone know when the vein becomes irritated.

Sterile gauze or transparent dressings are applied to the peripheral site. Gauze dressings should be changed daily. Transparent dressings can remain for as long as a week, allowing for ready observation of the site.

Heparin is used to flush the catheter after each infusion. Heparin 10 U/ml and 100 U/ml in amounts of 0.5 ml to 1.0 ml can be used.

Tubing is used for a 24-hour period and then discarded. Needles of 22 gauge are best suited for insertion into the injection cap. They do not bend easily or make an overly large hole.

Patients or significant others are taught to change the dressing, prepare the heparin syringe, connect the tubing, infuse the solution, and flush the catheter with heparin. They are also taught to observe for signs and symptoms of phlebitis and allergic reactions.

The use of lidocaine to anesthetize the peripheral venipuncture site before catheter insertion is controversial. Opponents claim that it is unnecessary, requires an additional needle puncture, and may cause allergic reactions. Advocates point out that the lidocaine decreases the patient's anxiety, resulting in a more positive attitude for IV therapy.

Lidocaine 1% or 2% is usually used intradermally to form a wheal at the venipuncture site. An amount less than 0.1 ml is sufficient. After having a venipuncture with lidocaine, patients frequently demand that it be used for subsequent venipunctures.

ANTICOAGULANTS/INSULIN

Anticoagulant therapy has been performed in the home setting. This type of therapy can normally be accomplished using peripheral access. Blood sampling for partial thromboplastin time (PTT) is done on a routine basis, and the anticoagulant is adjusted accordingly.

Leah, a 7½-month pregnant diabetic with toxemia, had been hospitalized for two weeks. She was depressed and emotionally upset with the prospect of continued hospitalization. Her physician consented to her going home for a weekend with continuous IV therapy. The insulin and heparin were infused peripherally by way of an infusion pump. She had frequent blood tests for PTT. Her husband monitored her blood glucose with a Dextrameter, and he also monitored her blood pressure. The doctor hoped that a short leave of absence from the hospital would improve her mental state. She did so well at home that he allowed her to remain there for ten days. She was then readmitted to the hospital for a cesarean section. Baby and mother did fine.

CONCLUSION

Regardless of the type of home IV therapy ordered, written instructions need to be available in the home. Twenty-four-hour access to health care professionals is a necessity. Patients and significant others need to be encouraged to call anytime if they have questions or concerns about their home IV therapy. Identify who will be available for 24-hour access: the pharmaceutical service, the home health agency, or the emergency department of the local hospital. Documentation is as important in the home setting as in the hospital.

The most important factors for successful home IV therapy are flexibility and simplicity. IV therapy has been and continues to be managed successfully in the home setting. Home therapies, pioneering with TPN, have proceeded to more complex therapies.

There is an increased awareness on the part of insurance companies, health maintenance organizations, and government programs of the potential dollar savings. This makes home IV therapy a reality for the future.

NOTES

1. Edwin B. Steen and Ashley Montagu, *Anatomy and Physiology* (New York: Barnes & Noble, 1959), 1:292.

2. Seattle Area Hickman Catheter Committee, "Irrigation of Hickman Catheter," 2 March 1984.

3. Marianne F. Ivey et al., *Hickman Right Atrial Catheter: Description and Home Care* (Seattle: University of Washington Hospitals, 1983), pp. 16–17.

4. Katherine Perez, "Nursing Management of the Hickman-Broviac Catheter," *Nita* 5 (1982):211.

5. Seattle Area Hickman Catheter Committee, "Special Points/Precautions," 2 March 1984.

6. Ibid.

7. Dorothy Jacobson Baker, "10 Years of TPN at Home," *American Journal of Nursing*, October 1984, 1248–1249.

8. Laurie Einstein Koszuta, "Choosing the Right Infusion Control Device for Your Patient," *Nursing 84*, 14(*3*), March 1984, p. 56.

REFERENCES

Anderson, Marjorie A., Saundra N. Aker, and Robert O. Hickman. "The Double Lumen Hickman Catheter." *American Journal of Nursing* 82(*2*) (February 1982):273–277.

Bertino, Joseph S., Jr. "Home Antibiotic Therapy." *U.S. Pharmacist* 9 (*9*) (September 1984):H-13–H-15.

Bjeletich, Joan, and Robert O. Hickman. "The Hickman Indwelling Catheter." *American Journal of Nursing* 80(*1*) (January 1980):62–65.

Brendel, Vicki. "Catheters Utilized in Delivering Total Parenteral Nutrition." *Nita* 7 (1984):488–490.

Brown, Susan J. "Implantation, Care and Common Complications of the Hickman Catheter."
   Parenterals (September/October 1984):1, 5.

Carelli, Regina M., and Eleanor Herink. "Hickman/Broviac Catheters Results of Survey and
   Patient Care Considerations." *Nita* 7 (1984):287–289.

Chrystal, Cynthia. "Making Nita Standards Work for You." *Nita* 6 (1983):87–92.

Coppa, Gene F., Thomas H. Gouge, and Steven R. Hofstetter. "Air Embolism: A Lethal but
   Preventable Complication of Subclavian Vein Catheterization." *Journal of Parenteral and
   Enteral Nutrition* 5 (1980):166–168.

Gaffron, Robert E., et al. "Organization and Operation of a Home Parenteral Nutrition Program
   with Emphasis on the Pharmacist's Role." *Mayo Clin Proc* 55 (1980):95–98.

Gray, Gregory E., et al. "Multiple Use of TPN Catheter Is Not Heresy: Retrospective Review
   and Initial Report of Prospective Study." *Nutritional Support Services* 2 (1982):18–21.

Haessler, Regina M. "Transparent I.V. Dressings vs. Traditional Dressings in Inservice
   Education." *Nita* 6 (1983):169–170.

Heimbach, David M., and Tom D. Ivey. "Technique for Placement of a Permanent Home
   Hyperalimentation Catheter." *Surgery* 143 (1976):634–636.

Hickman, Robert O., et al. "A Modified Right Atrial Catheter for Access to the Venous System
   in Marrow Transplant Recipients." *Surgery* 148 (1979):871–875.

Knutsen, Carl V., et al. "A Service-Oriented Program Providing Continuity of High-Quality
   Care to the Home Hyperalimentation Patient Hospital Without Walls." *Nita* 7
   (1984):369–373.

Larkin, Mary. "The National Intravenous Therapy Association's Intravenous Nursing Standards
   of Practice Home I.V. Therapy." *Nita* 7 (1984):93.

Peralta, Gretchen. "Workbook Home Hyperalimentation and Intravenous Therapy." *Coordinator,* 2(7) (August 1983)—2(12) (January 1984).

Perez, Katherine. "Nursing Management of the Hickman-Broviac Catheter." *Nita* 5
   (1982):210–212.

Pituk, Thomas L., Joyce L. DeYoung, and Howard J. Levin. "Volumes of Selected Central
   Venous Catheters." *Nita* 6 (1983):98–100.

Poretz, Donald M., et al. "Intravenous Antibiotic Therapy in an Outpatient Setting." *JAMA* 248
   (1982):336–339.

Riella, Miguel C., and Belding H. Scribner. "Five Years' Experience with a Right Atrial
   Catheter for Prolonged Parenteral Nutrition at Home." *Surgery* 143 (1976):205–208.

Schmidt, Ann M., and Diane Williams. "The Hickman Catheter Sending Your Patient Home
   Safely." *RN* 45(2) (February 1982):57–61.

Schwartz-Fulton, Janet, and Mari Messner Tischenko. "Hickman Catheter Exit Site Skin
   Sensitivities in an Oncology Patient Population." *Nita* 8 (1985):63–68.

Vogel, Therese Cartier, and Sylvia A. McSkimming. "Teaching Parents to Give Indwelling C.V.
   Catheter Care." *Nursing83* 13(1) (January 1983):55–56.

Williams, David N. et al. "Outpatient Intravenous Antibiotic Experience with 65 Patients."
   American Journal of Intravenous Therapy and Clinical Nutrition 9(3) (March 1982):33–39.

Wilson, Jeanne M. "Right Atrial Catheters (Broviac and Hickman), Indications, Insertion,
   Maintenance and Protocol for Home Care." *Nita* 6 (1983):23–27.

Chapter 13

Hospice Nursing

Patricia S. Watters

The idea of hospice, a concept of care that is popular today, was actually conceived long ago, in medieval Europe. Shelters, maintained primarily by religious orders, were available to travelers on their way to and from the Holy Land. These early hospices offered protection, nourishment, and fellowship to the sick, dying, and poor. In the early 1950s St. Christopher's Hospice in England, noted as being the first modern hospice, began delivering a special type of care for the terminally ill. Emphasis was placed on the management of pain and other physical symptoms, as well as on caring for the emotional and spiritual needs of those served. The basis of hospice care remains the same today, but its need, its place in the health care industry, its method of delivery, and its care providers continue to evolve. The purpose of this chapter is to relate current hospice philosophy and practice and to discuss the nurse's vital role in the delivery of hospice care.

HOSPICE TODAY

Illness and disease are often viewed by modern medicine as a challenge to be met with all of the treatment modalities that medical technology can provide. Technological advances do provide early detection, prompt diagnosis, and comprehensive treatment for the sick. But for the individual who is incurably ill, continued aggressive medical care can compound the overwhelming problems already presented by the illness. It is a time of great loss and crisis for the patient and family. They face exorbitant medical expenses, loss of work and recreation, deterioration of body appearance and function, and the threat of loss of life. The prolonged disability and discomfort experienced can shatter the sick individual's self-image and damage family relationships. At a time when the easiest tasks or activities of daily living present frustrating obstacles, the patient feels that he or she is expected to "perform" through a series of physician appointments, laboratory tests, x-rays and scans, medical treatments and procedures, and complex drug regimens. An individual can easily be lost as a person to self, family, and society—for what purpose and to what end? Fear, despair, and a sense of failure and isolation can predominate.

Hospice care offers respite for the patient and family living with a terminal illness. "The philosophy of hospice affirms life. It exists to provide support and care for a person in the last months of an incurable illness, so that life can be lived as fully and comfortably as possible."[1] The goal of hospice care is to promote optimal quality of life, rather than prolongation of life, for the dying person. Although this can be viewed as a broad goal, it can be readily defined by each patient and family served. Also basic to hospice care is the reduction of outside influence and interference for the ill person. This is based on the idea that the love and care needed by a dying person is best supplied by those who are closest and most significant in that person's life. "The family understands the needs of an individual beyond the realm of what the professional can offer."[2] Therefore, the patient and family members themselves are viewed as their own caregivers. Hospice works to assist a family in functioning as independently and normally as possible, and in reducing the number of outside influences.

Although individual home care hospice programs vary in structure and staffing, they all promote the giving of palliative and supportive service to the patient and family who are living with a terminal illness. The control of pain and other physical symptoms is central to successful care. Assistance with the psychological work of grieving, support through emotional suffering, and acknowledgment of the spiritual influences as a part of the dying process are also focal points in the delivery of hospice care. All efforts are aimed at assisting the patient and family to reach physical, mental, emotional, and spiritual preparation for death. But hospice care does not end with the patient's death. Supportive follow-up with the family during their period of bereavement is an important component of any hospice program. "Services are provided by a medically supervised interdisciplinary team of professionals and volunteers."[3] Patients are accepted on the basis of need rather than the ability to pay. Programs often are financed through a combination of income sources, such as grants, foundations, community organizations, memorial contributions, and government reimbursement.

As stated, the care administered to the patient and family is a result of the hospice team's efforts. The patient and family are viewed not only as the unit of care, but also as a central part of the hospice care team. Other team members most often include physicians, nurses, therapists, social workers, and volunteers, with access to representatives from other specialty areas, such as dietitians and legal representatives. The services of professional and nonprofessional providers are blended and balanced to provide the best possible care. The amount and type of care provided by each member should be directly related to patient and family needs.

THE NURSING ROLE

The skillful, dedicated nurse can do much to promote the hospice philosophy and facilitate the achievement of what is referred to as a good or appropriate death. "An individual and family can experience a good death when a relatively high level of comfort is achieved, continuity of an individual's and family's life is maintained, communication remains open, significant relationships are reaffirmed and reach peaceful closure at the time of death."[4] The care administered by the hospice nurse is designed to assist the patient and family in caring for themselves in the place of their choice, in the manner they wish, giving them the support needed to live and die in their own way.

Just as the hospice concept is holistic in nature, so is the nursing role in administering care to the patient and family unit. The hospice nurse offers support and services that are physical, psychosocial, emotional, and spiritual. This is accomplished through the functional roles of direct caregiver, teacher, support person, counselor, and patient advocate. The nurse assumes a primary care role in offering comprehensive, continuous, coordinated, and individualized services to the hospice family. Autonomous nursing assessments and interventions are made regularly. High-level accountability to the entire hospice team is integral to hospice nursing.

PHYSICAL CARE

Palliation, the reduction of the physical distress associated with the dying process, is central to the nursing role. The nurse acts as direct caregiver and as teacher in attending to the physical needs of the hospice patient. Two nursing goals in this area of care are (1) to promote an optimal level of physical comfort for the patient and (2) to promote independent, caring behavior and activities of the patient and family.

The physical needs of the patient change often and generally become more involved as the decline toward death continues. The hospice nurse must be skillful in the assessment of what is needed and desired by patient and family. A base line nursing history and physical examination should precede the initiation of physical care. Pertinent information includes vital statistics, past medical problems, past and current treatments, medications taken, and any allergies the patient may have. Ascertaining the patient's and family's understanding of the illness, as well as their expectations for the near future, is helpful. Assessment of body systems and the functional abilities of the patient will help in identifying where to begin with interventions. An accurate pain assessment is necessary and often the first place to begin in promoting the patient's comfort. Although the gathering of information is necessary in the delivery of care, the timing in obtaining it can be of greater significance. Often the data base is built up informally, over several visits. Long questioning sessions and repetition of patient and family difficulties can alienate the hospice family from the nurse. The purpose of the first few visits is to establish a sense of trust and rapport as well as the promotion of physical comfort.

Although the nurse uses basic nursing skills to give direct care to the patient, the manner in which care is delivered requires a high degree of nursing proficiency and discernment. The nurse must be knowledgeable about the disease process and the appropriate interventions for specific problems as they arise. Timing is important in the delivery of care; it must be offered promptly, addressing current problems with immediate action for relief. Perseverance in the consideration and application of alternative care methods in the face of persistent symptoms is crucial to the promotion of supportive physical care. The administration of care must also be flexible. The nurse uses the patient's overall condition to gauge the appropriateness of specific interventions. For example, frequent turning and massaging of the back and buttocks of a bedbound patient are considered necessary measures for the prevention of decubitus ulcers. But if a patient seems close to death and expresses much discomfort with turning, the nurse may forgo aggressive treatment to the back and allow the family to do the same. Attention to detail in every aspect of the physical care promotes thoroughness and an optimal level of comfort for the patient.

The hospice nurse accomplishes several things by acting as a direct caregiver. First, the nurse gains knowledge of the patient's overall condition, including his or her strengths and weaknesses, the possibilities and limitations, identification of immediate needs and potential problems, and current level of comfort with movement and at rest. Second, the nurse provides a model for continued care for the patient and family by conveying concern, compassion, and acceptance through therapeutic touch. Promoting acceptance and self-worth for the patient in the face of a deteriorating physical state is an integral component of symptom relief.

By acting as a model for care, the nurse functions in the role of teacher, showing the patient and family how to give hospice care. Repetition of primary aspects of care and reinforcement of family efforts in administering care give positive feedback, providing impetus for further care. The nurse supervises and assesses regularly the care administered and the need for further instruction. The patient and family must be given information about body care and hygiene, the use of assistive devices and equipment, safety and transfer techniques, wound care, and any other aspect of care that is necessary in caring for the dying person. The nurse also provides information related to the disease process as requested and necessitated by changes as they occur, including the anticipated changes close to and at the time of death.

The nurse enters the patient's world as a knowledgeable and skillful ally in the struggle against pain and suffering. This perception is positive in promoting a hopeful outlook for the hospice family. A person's physical needs must first be met to a reasonable degree before psychological and emotional comfort can be achieved. Uncontrolled pain, physical deterioration, and the associated loss of independence demoralize the patient. Feelings of isolation and of being a burden can predominate. By applying continuous and comprehensive effort in alleviating distressing symptoms, the nurse can assist the patient and family in regaining a sense of control and security that their needs will be met. The patient can feel useful and purposeful even in the face of death. Through this level of involvement trust is developed, rapport is established, and the therapeutic relationship evolves. It is then that a whole new realm of needs and desires are revealed as the hospice family shares their life concerns and gestures for guidance as they cope with their grief.

PSYCHOSOCIAL AND EMOTIONAL CARE

Equally significant to the physical care given in hospice is the psychosocial and emotional care administered by the nurse. The attention in this area is highly individualized and undeniably linked to the nurse's ability to understand the patient's and family's perceptions and understanding of their plight. Although death can be viewed as a natural occurrence, the dying process must be understood as a major life crisis confronting both patient and family.

In working with hospice families the nurse acts as a primary support person, giving counsel to members as needed and acting as patient advocate in helping the dying person fulfill strong wishes and desires before death. Two nursing goals in this area are (1) to promote open, honest communication among family members and (2) to promote coping with the grief and sense of loss experienced by the patient and family throughout the period of involvement.

Attributes of the nurse lending counsel and support include empathy, a high level of respect and warmth for the hospice family, sharing of self and experience, passive responsiveness, and active assertiveness in problem solving. Empathy is essential in administering care to those who are suffering. No one may be able to change what is or what will occur, but feeling truly understood can be therapeutic. The hospice nurse is encouraged to become involved, to know the hospice family in all respects and to a depth not normally practiced in other areas of nursing. Sharing of self can help in establishing rapport, as well as foster the sharing of thoughts and feelings among family members. The nurse learns with experience when to be passively responsive versus actively assertive. At times, listening to the patient and family members may be the best intervention possible. One must never underestimate the family's ability to help themselves. And by portraying a caring attitude and behavior, the nurse stimulates more supportive communication among members of the hospice family.

As mentioned earlier, the hospice family is dealing with a major life crisis. Central to their crisis is an overwhelming feeling of not having control over the situation. Normal coping methods begin to fail and anxiety pervades the household. Crisis points for hospice families include the issue of death itself; uncontrolled symptoms, such as pain; and the period shortly before death.

Each patient and family will work through their grief and periods of crisis in a unique way, but the assistance provided by the hospice nurse can make the process easier and less painful. While acknowledging the validity of distress experienced, the nurse positively emphasizes the family's strengths and abilities in coping with their problems. The nurse intervenes by helping the family to use their problem-solving skills to adapt to changes. The nurse strives to help the patient and family gain a less threatening perception of each event as it occurs and redefine problems into a solvable form. Once this is accomplished, the family can focus their efforts on finding solutions. The nurse can reinforce the coping methods that seem to be working and introduce new methods. For example, encourage family members to accept respite care; taking time out, away from the patient, can be rejuvenating and allow a better perspective on return. The nurse also assists the family by providing situational support through friends, volunteers, clergy, or other external resources.

SPIRITUAL CARE

The care rendered by the hospice nurse is completed by acknowledging the spiritual aspect of the hospice family's life. The subject of spirituality is common to all hospice situations but is highly individualized and personal within each family. The need for support in this realm is as important but less easily defined than in the other areas of care.

Spirituality encompasses a variety of meanings. It can be defined as the belief system held by a patient and family. Such belief systems are as varied as the people being served. Spirituality can be viewed as a means of coping with the decline before death and working toward relinquishment of life. It also provides a way for family members to adjust to their inevitable loss.

Many people accept a conventional means of faith through an organized religion. Each religion offers its beliefs about life, death, and afterlife. In addition, a congregation of believers offers group support, consolation, and spiritual guidance through the grieving process. For those of a particularly strong faith, the issue of spirituality may encompass a greater part of the family's life earlier in the course of an illness. It can prove comforting and provide a way of answering the unavoidable questions about death and the meaning of life.

For others, religious beliefs are less firm, and spirituality may be related more to existential concerns. Most people do contemplate the basic issues and questions of life, death, and destiny. There is often a search for personal meaning, hope for good and comfort, and concern for what lies beyond, as well as for what will be left behind.

In the delivery of spiritual care the goal of the hospice nurse is to assist the patient and family in attaining their personal, spiritual preparation for death. Nursing interventions are intended to help those served to achieve a sense of completion in life. The nurse accomplishes this through continued care and support in all areas of hospice care.

Spiritual support is rendered by the hospice nurse through a continuation of the functional roles discussed throughout the chapter. By continuing to give direct care to the patient, teaching the family, counseling, supporting, and advocating for all involved, the nurse gives the care needed by the hospice family to achieve a feeling of acceptance toward death. The nurse helps to create an atmosphere of openness and concern for all areas of need, including spirituality. The nurse must first listen to the patient and family as they share their beliefs. Through the expression of feelings of uncertain destiny or unfinished business, the family will define their own spiritual requirements. It is appropriate for the nurse to inquire as to the needs or desire for further support through spiritual counsel and to initiate such involvement if requested, according to individual and family preference. The hospice nurse should be prepared to respond to and share in a personal request in providing comfort and support. For example, if asked to participate in a family prayer on behalf of the dying member, it is appropriate for the nurse to participate respectfully. By doing this the nurse shows sensitivity to the needs and desires of those served.

Last, the hospice nurse intervenes by attending to the patient and family at the time of death. During this time the support given continues to encompass all aspects of care for the hospice family. Nursing interventions are intended to confirm the family's efforts in providing complete, optimal care to their loved one. The nurse attends to after-death activities and may assist the family in notifying the physician and the mortuary. The nurse also ensures proper, dignified handling and removal of the deceased's body, thus promoting and validating the meaning of life to the very end.

CONCLUSION

I would like to focus briefly on the hazards and rewards of hospice nursing. As detailed within the chapter, the role of the nurse is a demanding one. The working atmosphere is often one of uncertainty and conflict. The nurse must cope with seemingly endless problems, many of which can never totally be dispelled. Personal needs may be put aside in order to provide for others. And there can be the tendency to feel as though one must be all things to all people. The hospice nurse often feels the need to be optimistic in order to instill hope to those served, to be resourceful in finding solutions for unsolvable problems, and to be able to answer the unanswerable questions concerning life and death. The constant drain and strain of all of this can lead to personal distress and a sense of failure. In addition, the hospice nurse experiences a series of relationships and losses and therefore experiences grief. Inadequate handling of grief, added to the other emotional pitfalls of the job, can lead to burnout.

In order to reap the rewards of hospice nursing one must be prepared to meet the hazards openly. First, one should examine one's own beliefs and attitudes toward death before sharing concerns with the terminally ill. It is beneficial to develop a sound philosophy of purpose. It is important to be aware of personal needs and gains desired in working for hospice. Several motives common to hospice nurses may be the need to nurture others, the need to win approval and respect, and the desire to feel that one is doing something worthwhile. It is also important for the hospice nurse to remember that ultimate responsibility for good grieving and coping lies not with the nurse, but with the hospice family members. Last, the nurse should use the support offered by others working in hospice. A cohesive, caring staff can make up for the frustrations experienced and assist one in learning and growing on both a personal and a professional level.

The rewards of hospice nursing come primarily through the satisfaction of being a part of something very special. Hospice is an area of work in which good will, compassion, common sense, and honesty are highly valued. The hospice nurse is witness to a part of life many do not experience. Working with a hospice patient and family that do cope well replenishes one's sense of purpose and achievement. Knowing that the effort given has made a difference in someone's life and has been truly appreciated instills a wonderful feeling of well-being. And finally, experiencing the love and cohesiveness involved in a good death reaffirms one's faith in humanity and hope for good in life.

NOTES

1. National Hospice Organization, *The Basics of Hospice*, pamphlet, 1984.
2. Sen. Edward M. Kennedy, "Preface," in *A Hospice Handbook*, ed. Hamilton and Reid (Grand Rapids, Mich.: William B. Eerdman's Publishing Company, 1980), p. vii.
3. National Hospice Organization, *The Basics of Hospice*, pamphlet, 1984.
4. Avery D. Weisman, *Coping with Cancer* (New York: McGraw-Hill, 1979), p. 99.

REFERENCES

Gibbs, Earl C. *Caring for the Grieving*. San Rafael, Calif.: Crystal Press for Omega Books, 1976.

Kavanaugh, Robert E. *Facing Death*. New York: Penguin Books, 1972.

Keleman, Stanley. *Living Your Dying*. New York: Random House/The Bookworks, 1974.

Kübler-Ross, Elisabeth. *To Live Until We Say Good-Bye*. Englewood Cliffs, N.J.: Prentice-Hall, 1978.

Stoddard, Sandol. *The Hospice Movement: A Better Way of Caring for the Dying*. New York: Vintage Books, 1978.

Chapter 14

Rural Home Health Nursing Care Delivery

Joy E. Buehler

The notions of the antiquated farmhouse standing with modest grace among the expansive fields of grain and quiet afternoons spent sipping tea, hearing yarns of yesteryear, are the romantic realities of rural home health nursing. The other side of the coin is the reality of the privation and desperation of a hand-to-mouth existence. Both scenarios manifest themselves in the rural setting, where the mode and characteristics of nursing take on an added dimension.

The following is a synthesis of feelings, observations, and events I have experienced in the delivery of rural home health nursing. My goal is to illustrate the dynamics and impact this form of nursing has on the patient and the nurse. The concepts are not limited to rural health nursing. The uniqueness comes from the content of the experience.

DEMOGRAPHICS

When discussing the concept of rural home health nursing and delivery of services, it is important to recognize and assess the area's unique cultural circumstance and the geographic constraints.

I work with the Butte Valley—Tulelake Rural Health Projects in north central California. This area boasts a population density of 6.4 persons per square mile, only 4 percent of the statewide average.[1] It has been described as California's last frontier. There is one major thoroughfare on each side of the service area. These roads are subject to closure during hazardous winter storms. The area is surrounded by high valleys, mountain peaks, and national wildlife refuges. Agriculture, lumber, and tourism are the major contributors to the economic base.

The closest major population center is Klamath Falls, Oregon (population approximately 40,000), 30 miles from each of the major rural communities.

Residents in these outlying areas must travel the distance for many of their goods and services.

A study of the area was undertaken to provide the Butte Valley—Tulelake Rural Health Projects with the necessary data for making long-range service plans. The study demonstrated that 65 percent of the population lived outside the city boundaries.[2] Census data from the two major towns (population approximately 800) in this area indicate that 16 percent of the population is over age 65—5 percent higher than the state average.[3]

Another major population group residing in the area is the migrant agricultural worker and his family. Estimates suggest that as many as 2,000 are here on a seasonal basis.[4] Many of these people are monolingual in Spanish and have multiple medical needs.

The majority of medical and social services are in the western portion of the county. Access to these services is poor. The distance for some residents is 100 miles one way, through what can sometimes be treacherous mountain conditions. Because of these obstacles most consumers elect to either use the services made available by two rural health clinics, one in each of the small rural communities, or travel the distance to Klamath Falls. For some, even travel to the clinic sites is difficult. In-home nursing accommodates that need.

SERVICE DELIVERY

My nursing career began in the cloistered environs of a hospital. In that setting there is a sense of being part of a tangible and ever-present system. Feedback is a plentiful commodity. Staff are well rehearsed in their medical roles. Laboratory data are readily available. Members of the code team know their specific duties and can be at the patient's bedside within minutes. The patient's activities of daily living are easily monitored and assessed. Nutritional needs are assessed and modified as needed. And these features are available and operating 24 hours a day.

Rural home health nursing is the antithesis of the institutional setting. I may see my clients once every two weeks or, for some, only once a month. Laboratory data are far from being readily available for homebound patients. The code team consists of family or friends, who may or may not know CPR, who may or may not have a telephone to call for medical assistance, which may or may not, because of considerable distances, arrive in time. As for nutritional needs: "Hell, I've been eatin' like this for pertnear 70 years—if you think I'm gonna change now yer crazier than I am!"

The scenario of Myrtle, an 80-year-old retired nurse, is illustrative of this contrast. Already suffering from physically compromising ailments, she incurred a fall, fracturing several ribs. At the time she was living many miles from any medical service, in a rural community she had called home for many years. On experiencing chest pain and shortness of breath she became frightened. A call was placed to her physician requesting transport to the hospital. It was not a good day to be in need of an ambulance! The highways between her rural home and the hospital, a distance of 50 to 60 miles through a hazardous mountain pass, were closed because of blizzard conditions. Her physician made a cursory assessment over the phone and determined that a closer look was warranted. Enter the rural health nurse.

In the warmth and safety of the clinic I was analyzing the storm clouds to the west when the doctor's call came in to the clinic. My supervisor explained Myrtle's situation, adding offhandedly that the ambulance would have trouble coming in from the other side because of road closures and could I "run on out there and evaluate her." "No problem!" Ebullience at the thought of performing frontier nursing and smugness over having an opportunity to challenge my first set of studded snow tires blunted my ability to appreciate that I was about to have a new life experience.

After the highway patrol gave their OK on road travel south, I headed out. The storm was moving in my direction. Buffeted by 80 mph gusts of wind, I gripped the steering wheel in an attempt to keep the car from going off the road.

About midpoint between the clinic and Myrtle I realized just how formidable the storm was. With 15 miles remaining, I began to experience a whiteout—swirling, blowing snow causing all points of reference to blend together. Somehow my old '67 Volvo kept on going. Specific thoughts relevant to my decision to make this home visit began to surface. Topping the list was "Why am I doing this?" "Myrtle needs me!" "Was this in my job description?" (Provide in-home nursing services to patients living in and around the Butte Valley/Tulelake areas, at the request and under the direction of their physician and under the auspices of the BVTL Rural Health Clinic.[5]) This would probably qualify as "other duties as required to maintain patient at his/her maximum level of health."[6]

I plodded on, maintaining a vigilant eye for any recognizable and familiar landmark. Just as my death grip on the steering wheel was beginning to impede blood flow to my hands and fingers, I recognized the general store! Then, feeling a real sense of relief, I paused a moment to ponder my situation. I had made it to the general store, the snow plow's whereabouts remained a mystery, the snow was falling at a phenomenal rate, and the wind continued to blow. I would not be leaving by the same route by which I had arrived. In fact, there was a good chance I would not be leaving at all. And I was going to see a sick and injured woman.

Myrtle was anticipating my arrival, and when I finally got there she cordially invited me in. We briefly discussed the weather—she reminiscing of winter storms past and me describing the journey to her home. With the appropriate salutations behind us I proceeded with my assessment. She was snuggled down in bed, resting with a moderate degree of comfort. Her manifestation of pain and associated symptomatology occurred during minimal movement and did appear to be related to her fractured ribs. From her guarded respiratory effort she was beginning to develop bibaselar rales. She also had a moderate elevation in blood pressure. All other parameters were within reasonable limits. Through telephone consultation, a health-promoting regimen was prescribed by her physician. With the prescribed regimen carried out, additional health teaching to accommodate the healing process administered, a neighbor recruited to monitor her condition, the cats fed, and the fire stoked, my mind was free to unriddle the dilemma of my return to the clinic.

The local residents recommended the "old road" as my return route. Their recommendation was much appreciated and was soon to be seen as anticlimactic. Strangely, there were geographical pockets that experienced only moderate accumulations of snow. The "old road" was one such pocket, resulting in a fairly uneventful trip home.

My biggest obstacle became my conscience. With my basic survival no longer threatened, my narcissism was supplanted by the realization I had blown it in recognizing Myrtle's more subtle, yet equally important, needs. She was scared, lonely, and losing impact on her environment, and I basically paid little heed. It was a difficult but important awareness for me. Fortunately, I had numerous follow-up visits in which to rectify my negligence. Another lesson indelibly imprinted on the heart and mind of this rural health nurse.

Many residents in rural areas are hard-working country folk, who often use practical methods of problem solving and trouble shooting. A strong reliance on self is a way of life. Maintaining their independence within the familiar environment of their community is their fervent wish.

Mrs. Westerfield is the epitome of such self-reliance. Wearing the demeanor of a proper Englishwoman, she declares: "The only way I'll ever go to the hospital is if I am unconscious. And the only reason I'll go then is because I won't know I am going!" She spends her days attending to the needs of a small dog, a big cat, and treasured chickens. At age 85 she maintains her own modest home. Typical chores include stacking wood, minor carpentry and electrical repairs, and meal preparation on a beautiful old cookstove that doubles as a heat source. Her yard and vegetable garden are maintained with immaculate standards. The chronic phlebitis and stasis ulcers that have plagued her for years express their malevolent nature as she endeavors to meet these normal activities of daily living. Rarely will she request outside intervention for any malady she may be suffering. And when she does it is not of a superfluous nature. She will have exhausted all home remedies available to her and be chagrined for "imposing on your day" when finally asking for a "second opinion." Mrs. Westerfield provides a totally refreshing experience for me.

In light of these expressed desires for independence and self-reliance, the rural home health nursing service becomes an acceptable alternative to any mention of an institutional placement.

CLIENT PARTICIPATION

Participation by the client is the central theme of delivering any health-related service. The amount of energy and effort a person is willing to invest is directly related to his or her perception of the amount of change it will effect. We all want to know if it is worth the effort. Nursing is familiar with the ill client who experiences the frustrations of hopelessness and futility, immobilized by believing he can effect no change. The client may be covertly encouraged to become a passive recipient of medical care. He becomes swallowed up by the technical ingenuity of modern medicine, mesmerized by complicated jargon, and reinforced for relinquishing his individuation. Others are shrouded from the decision making process, the seeking of alternatives, and the discovery that there are choices.

These experiences effect a heavy toll on the patient's ability or desire to participate in a health maintenance or health-seeking process. The client in the rural areas is further challenged by being far removed from the support of his medical provider and the expeditious resolution of medical needs and concerns.

A rural location prohibits easy and ready access to goods and services. Communication is accomplished by telephone or the postal system. Compared with the urban community, procurement time of a requested item doubles. Again, the delays only reinforce the "what's the use?" feeling.

Agnes, an 85-year-old widow living alone, has had a debilitating degenerative bone condition for a number of years. Her mobility is compromised to the point of requiring a variety of mechanical aids for basic activities of daily living. She is reluctant to participate in a health maintenance process. "What can I do? My doctor says it's only going to get worse, so what's the use?"

In doing my initial assessment I had to agree with Agnes; it was a difficult situation. Her comfort level appeared to be in rapid decline. Therefore, I directed my energies to identifying and acquiring aids to improve the quality of her life and her comfort level. We collectively decided on her first priority need, and I set in motion the process of acquisition. The item, an elevated toilet seat, arrived 35 days after the initial request. "Oh, it shouldn't take that long." And fortunately, it does not always take that long. But in Agnes's case

I was anxious to reduce her discomfort in hopes that she would become an active participant in a health-seeking process.

The experience clearly demonstrated the importance of recognizing the geographical constraints of the service area and reminded me that patience is a virtue. I am glad to report that Agnes and I persevered; we did not crumble during our first encounter with "the system."

PRIVATION

Privation is a reality. The most lucid examples are from some of the area's monolingual migrant workers. In search of a better life they come to the Basin to work in the potatoes. The work is hard: long hours and minimal pay. Many bring with them a sundry of medical problems. Because of their illegal status and their cultural norms they are reluctant to seek treatment until these problems interfere with basic living requirements.

Angela, who speaks only Spanish, has reached the 38th week of her fifth pregnancy without any prenatal care. She was brought to the clinic by an acquaintance who, through a series of events, became aware that Angela was experiencing symptoms of preeclampsia: swelling of hands and feet, dizziness, and blurred vision. With the aid of two bilingual women I made a follow-up visit to Angela's rural home. On the day of our visit the forecast was for snow, and it was cold outside: we soon discovered that it was also cold inside. On entering the home we felt a draft blowing through a broken window. Three children bundled up in little jackets, with hoods tied snugly around their faces, were standing at the kitchen table eating. The children, pausing in their meal to investigate the strangers, graciously offered us their only two chairs. Angela, wearing two heavy sweaters, lay on the family's communal double bed in order for me to assess her. Fortunately, all parameters were found to be within acceptable limits. Through interpretation, Angela agreed that the house was cold. Working late hours, her husband had not been able to fix the window or get oil for their small diesel stove. Considering this brief moment in their existence I could not help but wonder if this was their dream of a better life.

During the drive back to the clinic I pondered their situation and wondered what, if any, difference I could make in their lives. I recognized the limitations of services available to families who may be in the United States with a somewhat tenuous status and felt a deep concern for their well-being.

The experience was an explicit illustration of privation and one I will not soon forget. Yet, in order for the scenario to have some balance, I must, as a service provider, recognize that privation, or any other subjective interpretation, is in the eye of the beholder. To impose my values on clients and families is to invalidate who they are. Problem identification and patient advocacy are better transacted through dialogue with the client rather than muddled with shoulds, musts, and "if it were me, I would" monologues.

In working with families that I see as existing at subsistence levels, I continually have to keep in check my expectations for their lives. Part of me wants to rush in and make everything OK.

Believing that I have been to the room with all the answers I occasionally establish my own very reasonable expectations of how the client should live his or her life. When I become angry because "they are not doing what they are supposed to," I am reminded, number one, that I have not been to the room with all the answers and, number two, of whose expectations I want them to meet.

What helps me to remain in check is to first recognize my rescuer tendencies and then begin to assist the client in the identification and prioritization of problems and the establishment of goals as he sees appropriate. From there we can begin an active course toward problem resolution. For some clients there will be a positive outcome, and their lives will be more satisfying.

LONELINESS AND ALONENESS

For me, in the rural setting, the concept of loneliness and aloneness have become an ever-present, although not debilitating, theme. I have had the opportunity to develop an intimate relationship with both.

When I was working in a hospital I enjoyed collegial discussions about patient care, simple existential bantering about theoretical concepts, even catching up on the hospital goings-on while waiting in line at the time clock. These were some of the ways my affiliative needs were met. Now I am in a situation that cannot coequal that interaction. Number one, there is no time clock, and number two, there is only one rural home health nurse in the clinic—me! After spending a day interfusing with some of life's vexations and tribulations, I occasionally have a need to debrief and collaborate with a colleague.

For a time that loneliness successfully disguised itself as a vague sense of doubt, feelings of desolation, and a need for connecting with other people. Several months of feeling that void passed before I could identify what was missing. Once I was able to recognize the professional isolation and label it loneliness, the intensity and mystery abated.

Now when those old feelings creep back into my awareness I am not caught off guard.

I recognized the necessity to augment and accommodate my professional and affiliative needs. In doing so I address my professional needs by aligning myself with several groups and organizations whose primary interests are home health nursing. My affiliative needs are affirmed on a more social level. My good friend and neighbor and I throw on our walking shoes, gather up our respective dogs, and off we go, walking and talking ourselves into exhaustion. These affiliations have proved themselves invaluable in the assuagement of those feelings of disquiet. They also serve to replenish and validate me as a worthwhile person.

On the other hand, the being alone, which to me is different from loneliness, has given me a new sense of freedom. It gives me the opportunity for independent decision making. Traveling between clients, in the sole company of my car, I enjoy the opportunity for contemplation, self-study, and meditation. The self-reliance and independence expressed by my clients must be a natural byproduct of the hidden riches of this rural existence.

CONCLUSION

I have shared the experiences that illuminate the fundamental essence of nursing care delivery in the rural setting. The rural home health nurse delivers services to the pioneer family who, through generations, has derived life's bread from the land. She sees the families who gave up the hectic city life to raise their children in the solitude of the rural community. The migrant worker searching for a better way of life is familiar to her. Three unique and distinct groups of people with one common thread: a fervent desire for independence and self-reliance. It is important for the nurse to recognize and respect these values. Cultivating a dependency would be presumptuous and counterproductive to their life style.

Having grown up in an area of similar demographics I understand the challenges of rural life. And with the passage of time I am developing an expanded appreciation of its hidden beauty and simplicity.

If you are tantalized by the notions of rural home health nursing care, I invite you to consider the professional challenge and the concomitant satisfaction that are its indelible rewards. It is a very human and direct way to impact some people's lives positively and remember, it is quiet out here.

NOTES

1. Rosenburg Associates, *Butte Valley Rural Health Project Market Analysis: Home Health Services, Adult Day Health Care, Hospice Care* (Bolinas, Calif., February 25, 1984).

2. Ibid.

3. Ibid.

4. Ibid.

5. Butte Valley—Tulelake Rural Health Projects, Inc. *Policy and Procedure Book*, June 1984.

6. Ibid.

Chapter 15

A Conceptual Overview of the Health Care Needs for a Quadriplegic in the Home Setting

Michael Parker Cashman and Ronald Atwood

The increased effectiveness of the emergency medical system has led to dramatic saving of quadriplegics' lives. Some 5,000 quadriplegics have been treated at the 17 regional spinal cord centers throughout the United States from 1973 to 1981. These clients are discharged from the hospital soon after their injuries occur, to continue treatments and therapies at home.

The fact that a spinal cord injury requires specialized treatment limits both the number of source persons for consultation and the amount of updated information that are available to the visiting home health care nurse.

These clients present a challenge to the visiting home nurse, inasmuch as every major system in the body is affected. Quadriplegics need care providers who are attuned to their special needs and who understand the physiological and psychological changes that occur as a result of a spinal cord injury.

This chapter was developed using a system-oriented problematic approach to the special needs of the quadriplegic. The material is based on ten years of personal experiences working with patients who had acute spinal cord injuries at the northern California regional spinal cord rehabilitation center.

NEUROLOGICAL CARE

Quadriplegia is defined as any spinal cord injury with neurological deficit above the first thoracic vertebra. Such injuries can be complete or incomplete. In a complete injury, there is no motor or sensory function below the

This chapter is dedicated to the regional spinal cord injury center at Santa Clara Valley Medical Center in San Jose, California. Special thanks to Sally Manalo, R.N., M.S.N.

Assistance was provided by the Northern California Regional Spinal Injury System, Grant No. G008435010, Project No. 128EH40013, from the National Institute of Handicapped Research, U.S. Department of Education, Washington, D.C., at Santa Clara Valley Medical Center in San Jose, California.

level of injury. In the incomplete injury partial sensory or motor function might be retained below the level of injury. Symptoms vary from client to client.

The quadriplegic may receive all of his or her rehabilitation either in a hospital center or as an outpatient living at home. In either case the client may require the services of a visiting home nurse for care and advice. The nurse, on referral, should record base line motor and sensory neurological levels in order to assess any change in the client's neurological status.

If the quadriplegic is being seen as an outpatient or has been discharged early, she or he may still be maintained in an external support system, either a halo and body cast or a cervical brace. Care for external stabilization varies from one hospital to another. The visiting home nurse should become familiar with such equipment. This may necessitate contacting the discharging hospital for information and assistance as to the specialized care that will be required for a client maintained in one of these specialized support systems.

The amount of care required by a quadriplegic is determined by the level of injury. A client with an injury at the level of the first through third cervical vertebra will require complete care and mechanical ventilation. Neurological-ly, this client will not retain motor or sensory function below the deltoids. At the level of the fourth cervical vertebra, mechanical ventilation is, in most cases, unnecessary; however, there will still be no useful function of the upper extremities. Function of the upper extremities does not occur until the level of the fifth cervical vertebra. If injured below this level, the quadriplegic begins to gain useful function of his or her upper extremities. Below the level of the seventh cervical vertebra hand function begins to return. At these levels, below the fifth cervical vertebra, the client can assume greater independence in his or her daily care and may require only minimal home assistance.

Neurological problems the visiting home nurse should be aware of in the quadriplegic are autonomic dysreflexia, poor regulation of body temperature, hypersensitivity, and the ascending lesion. In the case of autonomic dysreflexia, there is a sympathetic response that leads to vasoconstriction of blood vessels below the level of injury. Without the brain being able to transmit nerve impulses below the level of injury, this vasoconstricting process can develop into an increasing hypertensive condition, producing blood pressure high enough to cause a stroke.

Symptoms of autonomic dysreflexia consist of diaphoresis, restlessness, headache, peripheral vascular changes, bradycardia, and an elevated blood pressure. The cause of dysreflexia usually can be traced to a reflex in the spinal cord that is stimulated by overdistension of bowel or bladder. The following steps should be followed if a client develops symptoms of a dysreflexic state. First, blood pressure needs to be monitored frequently. To reduce the blood pressure, place the client in a sitting position and remove antiembolitic hose. This will decrease the blood pressure by allowing the blood to pool in the abdomen and lower extremities. The client's bladder should then be checked by catheterization for overdistension. Urine volumes greater than 500 ml can cause this reaction. As a reminder, too-rapid decompression of an overdistended bladder can lead to hypotension and shock. This can present a life-threatening situation.

If the blood pressure remains elevated after catheterization, the rectum should be checked, using 2% Xylocaine jelly as a lubricant to prevent overstimulation of the bowel. Manual evacuation of the lower bowel may be necessary to empty the lower colon. In some cases of autonomic dysreflexia a simple repositioning of the client can alleviate this problem. A headache may persist after the blood pressure is reduced, and a mild analgesic may provide relief.

Another problem encountered by a quadriplegic is the inability to regulate body temperature. This results from the body's inability to perspire below the level of the injury and to dilate or constrict peripheral blood vessels. Thus the quadriplegic cannot release or conserve heat.

It becomes the nurse's and the client's responsibility to monitor body temperature and adjust the environment as needed. When the client is outdoors a thermometer should be present to monitor body temperature, especially when there are extreme climatic changes. In the winter months extra clothes may be required, to meet changing weather conditions. During the summer months a spray bottle with water can be used to simulate perspiration.

The fragility of the thermoregulatory systems causes other problems when the quadriplegic becomes too hot or cold. Under this situation the time it takes to lower or raise the client's temperature is greatly increased, compared with the time it takes to lower or raise a normal person's temperature. This may require such measures as ice packs and sponge baths for an elevated temperature. In the case of hypothermia, warm blankets can be used to raise the temperature.

Hypersensitivity is a common occurrence in the quadriplegic, involving the neck, shoulders, and upper extremities. Nerve roots entering at the level of the spinal cord injury are often traumatized and produce a hypersensitive response from nerve impulses traveling to the cord. This state is often misinterpreted as a painful sensation in the brain. Treatment for this condition consists of analgesics, warm packs to affected areas, and biofeedback techniques.

An infrequent but devastating condition occurs when the level of injury ascends and the quadriplegic loses additional motor or sensory function. This can be caused by infarcts in the spinal cord, by bone pressing on the cord, or by a syrinx. Any changes in neurological condition should be reported immediately.

CARDIOVASCULAR CARE

Homeostasis of the circulatory system is altered in the quadriplegic, resulting in a loss of vascular tone. This occurs because the quadriplegic does not retain the neuropathways from the brain to the blood vessels below the level of injury, resulting in lack of control over vasoconstriction. Blood vessels dilate and venous return is poor, especially in the extremities.

The first difficulty one encounters with a quadriplegic is orthostatic hypotension. When the quadriplegic is placed in a sitting position, blood tends to pool in the lower extremities and in the abdomen, resulting in decreased blood flow to the brain. The client may feel lightheaded and faint.

Several measures can be taken to prevent orthostatic hypotension when placing the quadriplegic in a sitting position. The use of antiembolitic hose and an abdominal binder can help prevent blood from pooling in the lower extremities and the abdomen. Placing the client in a sitting position slowly allows the body time to adapt to postural changes. In extreme cases, medications can be used to cause vasoconstriction and prevent hypotension. If the client becomes hypotensive while in a wheelchair, pressing on the abdomen and tilting the chair back can alleviate the problem.

Because blood tends to pool in the extremities when the client is in a wheelchair, edema of both hands and feet occurs. The quadriplegic may need to have his or her legs elevated several times throughout the day to alleviate postural edema. Hands may need to be elevated to improve venous return. It is recommended that at night the client's extremities be elevated on pillows.

Potential problems that quadriplegics can develop as a result of poor vascular tone in the lower extremities are deep vein thrombosis and phlebitis. A thrombosis may not be detected, owing to a lack of sensation in the lower extremities, placing the client at risk of pulmonary emboli.

Daily physical assessment of the lower extremities is a simple method for detecting vascular changes. Lower extremities should be inspected for swelling, redness, and excessive warmth. These symptoms, however, are not inclusive, and measurement of the thigh, knee, and calf can detect deep thrombosis by enlarged leg circumference. Base line measurements should be recorded and repeated every week at the same time of day, with the client in a supine position. A 3-cm difference in circumference from the opposite extremity or from previous measurements should be reported.

RESPIRATORY CARE

Pulmonary vital capacity is decreased in the quadriplegic owing to the lack of innervation to the intercostal muscles. With an injury above the fourth cervical vertebra the client is dependent on ventilatory assistance; with an injury below the fourth cervical vertebra the diaphragm becomes the sole driving force. Poor respiratory drive exposes the quadriplegic to various complications associated with an ineffective cough and low vital capacity.

Adequate pulmonary hygiene often requires the assistance of the nurse, especially in the ventilator-dependent quadriplegic or any client with a tracheostomy. Quadriplegics, especially those who are smokers or who are elderly, have trouble expectorating their secretions. Thus it may be necessary to place the client in Trendelenburg's position and use gravity to help them expectorate their secretions. Percussion and vibration may also be required if the secretions are tenacious. If the client is maintained on a ventilator, the visiting nurse will need to instruct the family on care of the tracheostomy site, the ventilator, and the suctioning techniques.

Another useful technique to remove secretions is the "quad cough." This procedure consists of maximizing the client's expiratory force and volume through the use of abdominal thrusts. This procedure can be beneficial for quadriplegics with or without a tracheostomy. However, in the client who is ventilator-dependent, bagging with an AMBU bag should be done just before the "quad cough."

Quadriplegics should be advised against smoking, as this will compromise their respiratory status and increase their risk of developing pneumonia.

GASTROINTESTINAL CARE

A quadriplegic develops a neurogenic bowel after a cervical injury. As a result, there is no conscious control over the anal sphincter and lower bowel. This manifests itself in the inability to control bowel movements.

Quadriplegics are routinely started on a bowel training program while in the hospital or rehabilitation center. The client needs to understand the procedure and rationale behind the implementation of the bowel training program. It is the visiting home nurse's responsibility to provide feedback on care and follow-up education on the procedure.

The purpose of the bowel training program is to stimulate a reflex evacuation of the bowel through the use of physical and chemical stimulation of the rectum. The bowel training program is best done when the client is in a sitting position on a commode chair or on a toilet with a seat adapter. This allows for gravity to aid in the evacuation of the lower bowel. When the quadriplegic is confined to bed, the procedure is best done with the client positioned on the left side. The bed should be padded with protective material.

Physical stimulation consists of digital dilation of the anal sphincter and digital stimulation of the rectum lasting approximately three minutes. Physical stimulation is followed by chemical stimulation with either a glycerine or Dulcolax suppository. After insertion of the suppository, digital stimulation of the rectum should be repeated every 15 minutes until the rectum is clear of stool. Depending on the quadriplegic's level of injury, this procedure may be done by the visiting home nurse or by the client. With special adaptive appliances, quadriplegics who have the use of their arms can be taught to do their own bowel programs.

As the name implies, the bowel training program is reeducation of the bowel to evacuate on command. This process can take months to accomplish. Timing is important in the success of the bowel training program. It should take place at the same time each day. In most cases, clients are placed on an every-other-day schedule. The best time for this procedure is 30 minutes after eating, while peristaltic action is at its peak. Clients usually start their bowel programs after either breakfast or dinner, with most opting for a morning program. A program at this time is preferred, as it empties the bowel before the start of the day, thus reducing the chance of an accident occurring.

Constipation is often a problem and may require special adjustments to the program. When the results of the bowel program are absent or poor, the program should be repeated the next day. In some cases a mild oral laxative may be beneficial when given six to eight hours before the start of the program.

UROLOGICAL CARE

With the neurogenic bladder, the quadriplegic requires specialized treatment in elimination of urine. As with the neurogenic bowel, the client has no conscious control over the urethral sphincter and the emptying of the bladder. Without catheterization, the bladder will distend with urine and reflux into the kidneys. Immediately on admission to the hospital, in the acute stage, the quadriplegic will have an indwelling catheter inserted to a closed drainage system. While in the hospital the client will undergo complete urodynamic studies, with routine follow-up tests done to monitor bladder and kidney function.

Kidney damage is a major concern in the quadriplegic. Increased risk of urinary tract infection and reflux of urine into the kidney place this client in a high-risk category for kidney damage. Once the client is discharged home, follow-up on bladder care is imperative.

Most quadriplegics will be discharged home on one of the following bladder maintenance programs: indwelling or suprapubic catheters, intermittent catheterization, reflux voiding, or sphincterotomy, with an external catheter in the male client. The quadriplegic with a spastic bladder or incontinence may be discharged home with an indwelling catheter. To prevent reflux of urine into the kidneys during bladder spasms, an indwelling catheter will be used to prevent excessive pressure from developing in the bladder. If medication cannot control incontinence in the female client, an indwelling catheter may be an option.

Intermittent catheterization decreases the risk of urinary tract infection, which is commonly associated with indwelling catheters. Clients on this type of regimen are catheterized at various intervals throughout the day. The time span is determined by fluid intake and urine output. Urine volumes should not exceed 600 ml, as bladder stretching and reflux into the kidneys can occur. To prevent urinary tract infection with this program, the client is usually placed on prophylactic antibiotics.

The bladder can be triggered to void by reflex in certain quadriplegics. Such individuals can stimulate an evacuation of the bladder through the use of external stimulation. Clients can trigger urination by tapping on the abdomen or by Credé's maneuver over the bladder.

The male quadriplegic may decide to have a urethral sphincterotomy as an alternative to intermittent or indwelling catheterization. This procedure then forces the client to wear an external catheter to prevent incontinence. Several problems develop with this method. First, the penis can become irritated from adhesives used to hold the external catheter in place. Second, the adhesive used is not 100 percent effective in preventing urine from leaking around the catheter. This can result in an embarrassing situation.

The visiting home nurse needs to be knowledgeable on the various types of bladder care. The nurse should be able to instruct the client and family on the various procedures and care of the equipment. High costs of medical equipment may discourage clients from using disposable supplies. Thus the visiting home nurse should be aware that reusable equipment will often be utilized. The equipment may require special care and cleaning.

INTEGUMENTARY CARE

The nature of a spinal cord injury eliminates the conscious control of movement in response to sensation. This places the victim at high risk for skin breakdown.

Bony prominences are prime sites for skin breakdown owing to the limited amount of fatty and muscular padding between the bone and the skin. Prolonged pressure on these areas will compress the tissue to such a degree that the blood supply is greatly impeded or absent. A decrease of oxygen and nutrients to the tissue causes cellular injury, and necrotic areas may develop.

A simple test for cellular injury is the "blanch response." This is done by pressing a finger into the reddened area and rapidly withdrawing it. A white area can be seen where the blood was pressed away by the finger pressure. The area should become red again as the capillary beds refill with blood. This is a positive blanch response, and the skin should return to normal within an hour. If the area remains red and does not blanch, even after several attempts, then it is a negative blanch response, and the doctor should be notified. The client must not be allowed to put any pressure on that area until normal skin color returns. If the skin breaks down and an open bedsore develops, the doctor must be notified. The resulting wound should be treated according to orders prescribed.

The prevention of a bedsore is much easier than the treatment of one. Ensuring that the skin is clean and dry while turning the client regularly, according to skin tolerance, is the best way. Skin tolerance is the amount of time the client can remain in one position without damaging the skin. Padded boots and the use of sheepskin or egg-crate padding over the mattress are helpful in building skin tolerance and preventing skin breakdown.

If the quadriplegic uses a wheelchair, weight shifts need to be done frequently. The purpose of the weight shift is to ease the pressure on the ischial tuberosities and the sacrum. If the quadriplegic has functional use of his upper extremities, a depression weight shift can be done by the client pushing his or her body up and off the seat.

If this is not possible, the weight can be shifted by leaning the client forward and shifting the buttocks so there is no pressure on these areas. A side weight shift can be done after the side arm has been removed by leaning the client over the side of the wheelchair onto a soft surface the same height as the wheelchair. Again the buttocks should be shifted to relieve pressure.

To improve circulation, circular massage and gentle patting to the affected bony areas are useful. Whichever weight shift is used, make sure the client is comfortable, and hold the position for at least five minutes. These weight shifts should be done every hour, or more frequently if skin tolerance is low.

If the client is in an external support system, with a vest, cast, or brace, the base should be checked where it contacts the skin for possible pressure areas. If the client is maintained in a hard collar or brace, the chin, clavicles, and scapulae should not be overlooked as possible sites for pressure-related skin breakdowns.

A complete skin check should be done in the morning before dressing the client and in the evening on returning the client to bed. If the client is on bed rest, skin checks should be done with each turn. If the client is able to hold a hand mirror, either with or without support straps, encourage her or him to do the skin checks. Remember, pressure sores can be prevented.

Careful skin and peri care should be done twice a day, and more frequently if the client has an incontinence problem that's not being treated successfully by special supplies or medications. Urea cream or a good lotion should be massaged into any area of skin that is dry and cracking and applied regularly to the hands and feet.

Because of the circulatory impairment of the quadriplegic, absorption of intramuscular injection is poor when given below the level of lesion. The physiological response is such that an injection could abscess, or there could be a toxic build-up of the substance injected. If injections are necessary, they should be given above the level of lesion, in an area where the client has sensation. The client may protest, wanting the injections to be given in an area of decreased sensation; this should not be done.

If the client has any skin openings or has halo pins to the skull, these areas must be kept clean and infection-free. Follow the doctor's directions concerning their treatment. To promote rapid healing and healthy skin, the quadriplegic should be encouraged to follow a high-protein diet.

Routine turns, bridging, padding, and massage of bony areas, along with careful positioning, should prevent skin breakdown for the quadriplegic in bed, while frequent weight shifts and vigorous gluteal massage should keep the client who is in a wheelchair free of pressure sores.

MUSCULOSKELETAL CARE

The quadriplegic has, at best, limited function of arms and hands and nonfunctioning legs. Therefore, the client will require passive range-of-motion exercises at least twice a day. These should be done to maintain functional joint flexibility and prevent contractures.

Splints may be prescribed for hands or arms to combat contracture or to mold a contracture into a functional position. When splints are applied or removed the skin should be checked for possible pressure areas. Pillows should be positioned to allow a bend in the legs when the client is supine.

Often there will be complaints of neck pain related to muscle tension. Range-of-motion exercises to the shoulder, massage, and repositioning of the arms often relieve the discomfort.

Quadriplegics frequently manifest uncontrolled muscle spasms as spinal cord swelling decreases. These spasms can affect all parts of the body below the level of lesion. Spasms are caused by a reflex in the spinal cord. These spasms can be so severe as to draw the client violently into a fetal position or stiffen him or her out like a board. This places the quadriplegic at risk of falling if left unrestrained in a wheelchair or unsecured in bed. Such spasms can be painful or uncomfortable and are often relieved by repositioning the affected body part.

Another condition that affects the adolescent or elderly quadriplegic is decalcification of the long bones. This is mentioned as a warning to the visiting home nurse that stress fractures can easily develop. This decalcification in the adolescent can also lead to heterotopic bone ossification, in which calcium is deposited in soft tissue around joints, usually in the lower extremities.

The visiting home nurse should be knowledgeable in body mechanics and single-person transfers. Quadriplegics require assistance in wheelchair transfers; therefore, special care needs to be taken when transferring clients to prevent injury to the client or the nurse.

PSYCHOSOCIAL CARE

To assist you in developing a context from which you can relate to your client's wants and needs, imagine being dependent on others for food preparation, getting dressed, or something as simple as opening a can of beer. Psychologically, this is an extremely devastating type of injury. This type of client may seem difficult to relate to at first, demanding and difficult to please, especially in the early phase, shortly after injury.

The coping mechanism used by a quadriplegic is an individualized form of the grieving process that one goes through with loss or the death of a loved one. In a sense, this is a loss of a loved one inasmuch as the body image and former life style are concerned.

This response to loss has been well documented and will be reviewed here in terms of three phases: (1) denial and protest, (2) despair and depression, and (3) acceptance and reinvestment.

At first, the quadriplegic is concerned with what has been lost and spends a great deal of time trying to regain this. During this period the quadriplegic feels anxiety and deep sadness. The client attempts to make deals with God, the doctors, nurses, and therapists in order to bargain back from the loss. During this period the client thinks and says such things as, "Just you watch, I'll walk," "Why me?" "I've never done anything that bad." To assist the quadriplegic through this phase the nurse must answer many questions involving denial and protest with complete honesty. Answers should reflect the reality of the situation and be delivered with reassurance of what is realistically possible.

Allowing for effective expression of anger is difficult indeed. At times the anger is directed at the treatments that the client must undergo. Naturally, nurses can expect some anger to be directed at them. Becoming defensive or angry in return is not an appropriate response. Instead, the nurse should acknowledge the anger and allow expression of the client's feelings. This type of acceptance will allow clients to express themselves and work through their anger.

Denial can be used by the quadriplegic to such a degree that it interferes with treatments. Nursing intervention is that of a sounding board, allowing the client to express feelings while maintaining the reality of the situation. This allows the nurse to assist clients in accepting themselves as worthwhile.

One of the biggest causes of despair and depression is the abrupt transition from independence to dependence in almost all activities of daily living. These are periods of time in which the loss is realized and the ramifications are felt. Once again, the visiting home nurse should encourage the expression of feelings, create a space of acceptance, and actively support the client.

Assisting the client in moving from shock and disbelief to an awareness that the loss is, for the most part, irreversible is done by keeping communications oriented to the reality of the injury. With this in mind, the nurse should allow the client to make decisions concerning activities of daily living. The visiting nurse should stress that the client do the maximum amount of activities and self-care that is possible. Outside activities should be considered in light of the client's physical wellness. Whenever appropriate opportunities arise, the client should be encouraged to make choices that will lead to participation. This allows a sense of independence to develop, which can lead to acceptance of loss and reinvestment in life.

The higher the level of the injury, the greater the dependence on assistance. Regardless of the level of injury, involvement in activities and relationships should begin as soon as possible. For it is through this process that the quadriplegic is able to start reinvesting time and energy into life.

Family, friends, and significant others also suffer from the shock of loss caused by the cervical injury. They, too, go through a grieving process, although it is usually shorter and less severe. The visiting nurse must be prepared to assist them through the grieving process as well. That is, encourage and accept their expression of feelings, clarify the various situations that arise, and advise any constructive changes.

Socialization should be encouraged as soon as the quadriplegic is out of the critical care phase. This is a time of social rehabilitation for both the client and visitors. When it is time for the client to receive treatments of the type that can cause embarrassment, the visiting nurse should provide the maximum amount of privacy to reduce situational stress. This may present itself as having to remove the client to another room.

Encouragement by family and visitors is a powerful tool in motivating the client to accept the loss and reinvest in life. It is an equally powerful tool for the family working through the loss as well.

Under no circumstances should the visiting nurse allow the client to escape mentally through the use of drugs or alcohol. Visitors should be advised of this also.

The key points are being able to listen to what the client is communicating and respond appropriately and realistically and encouraging decision making on all levels, thus enabling the client to participate in life.

CONCLUSION

This chapter has been written as a general overview of problems to stimulate the visiting home nurse's interest in the care of the quadriplegic.

This particular type of client requires not only maintenance nursing but also treatment with dignity and encouragement to become as independent and productive as possible.

In summation, the quadriplegic should be treated with a holistic as well as a problematic approach. Unlike the terminal patient, the quadriplegic has an ongoing need to contribute to society as well as live the good life.

REFERENCES

Bedbrook, G. M. *The Care and Management of Spinal Cord Injuries.* New York: Springer-Verlag, 1981.

Haber, J., et al. *Comprehensive Psychiatric Nursing.* New York: McGraw-Hill, 1978.

Northern California Regional Spinal Injury System. Final Report of the NCRSIS. HEW 13-P-55874/9-0. San Jose, Calif.: Santa Clara Valley Medical Center, 1982.

Pierce, D. S., and V. H. Hickel. *The Total Care of Spinal Cord Injuries.* Boston: Little, Brown & Co., 1977.

Chapter 16

Chronic Obstructive Pulmonary Disease

Kathi Santoro

Approximately 16 million Americans suffer from one or more chronic pulmonary diseases. These include chronic obstructive pulmonary disease (COPD; emphysema, bronchitis, asthma), lung cancer, tuberculosis, and bronchiectosis. Sooner or later you are going to encounter someone with lung disease in the home who requires home care. In this chapter home care specifically for the COPD patient is addressed. Because these people have a chronic illness, authorization for home care will generally be for only a few visits. You will have a lot of questions to answer and a lot of teaching to do in a short period of time. Some practical approaches you can use when caring for the COPD patient are covered in this chapter.

The most valuable tools you have are your understanding of what the illness is doing to the person and your attitude toward the patient. Many times this group of patients can be difficult to deal with. If you understand the various coping mechanisms—the denial, anxiety, isolation, depression, anger, and dependency—you can then determine the locus of control.

Let's take locus of control first. You can determine this within a few minutes after questioning the patient about his or her illness. Ask how did it start, what were the causes, and what is the prognosis. From the answers you can determine whether the patient is externally controlled or internally controlled. The externals allow things to happen to them and prefer to have decisions made for them. The internals like to be in control and prefer to assist with any decision making. Once you have made this assessment you know how to begin your teaching and which approach to take. You can imagine how you would be received if you tried to make an external make all of the caretaking decisions; you would get nowhere. You would know that you would have to make the decisions and give specific directions. It would be equally difficult if you tried to tell the internal what to do. You would know that the best approach is to consult and offer directions and guidance.

245

After the locus of control has been determined the coping mechanisms must be understood. Most patients have used denial for a long time. For years, leading up to the present they have probably said, "Oh it's nothing, I'm just short of breath, getting older you know." But what you shouldn't accept is that getting old doesn't necessarily mean getting short of breath. You might also hear: "I seem to have developed a fear of water. Someone has to be close by before I can take a shower. It takes all of my will power to finish showering. It's terrible; I used to love it." The fear of taking a shower was a displacement of the anxiety caused by fear of shortness of breath. A shower stall is an enclosed area, and the steam produced by the water can give the feeling of suffocation. When people develop phobias they sometimes think they are being foolish or childish. This is not the case. The phobias or other defense mechanisms used are based on real concerns. Once you can understand the basis of the phobia, you can help them deal with it.

The feelings of isolation are strong with such patients. Many times they have few friends left because they have been unpleasant and demanding with them. They have lost friends over the years because they have lost their ability to do what they used to. They can't just get up and go anymore. Imagine how it must feel to have a loose, moist cough that causes you to hack and expectorate frequently, causing heads to turn to stare at you. COPD patients may find it less embarrassing to stay at home. They cannot keep up with others because of shortness of breath. They feel claustrophobic in crowds and are unable to walk any distance because of fatigue, so they choose to stay at home.

Depression, which is anger turned inward, is frequently a problem for these patients. Many are depressed because they begin to realize that they may have had some control over acquiring their illness. Smoking is the classic example. Or perhaps it was related to their employment, and they found out that they had worked for years under unsafe conditions. Many are depressed because they have lost their independence and maybe even their position as the family breadwinner or the keeper of the house. Many begin to lose their will to live and feel that they have nothing to live for.

They become increasingly dependent because it's easier than trying to do things for themselves. Along with this loss of independence comes the anger at the caregiver and others who can still come and go as they please. The anger directed at the caregiver and others only causes more anxiety, isolation, and depression. Sometimes this is the only control they have over their environment. Try to imagine how frustrating that must be for the patient. Picture the father, husband, ex-breadwinner of the household, who is used to being in control and running his family, now confined to one spot, unable to do much for himself without having others help him. If you can understand some of these basics of the commonly used coping mechanisms, then you can successfully care for COPD patients. If you have difficulty understanding or accepting these mechanisms, then you will find taking care of COPD patients difficult and frustrating. They will manipulate and anger you, and you will take their anger personally.

With this understanding you can prepare yourself and address some of the commonly encountered problems that the person with COPD faces daily. The role of the home health nurse is not to foster the patient's dependence, but rather his or her independence. Such patients need to be given some tools to use to regain some control over their environment and their lives. They need to feel that they are valuable, contributing members of the family, society, the world.

I will begin with the alarm clock awakening them in the morning and take you through to bedtime. You will see what obstacles occur for these people in trying to do activities of daily living that we take for granted.

Morning is generally a difficult time for COPD patients. They awaken to the frustration of knowing they can no longer jump out of bed, shower, dress, grab a cup of coffee, and leave. They must get up to a sitting position with feet on the floor. The mucus has just been displaced that has accumulated all night. They will begin coughing and try to expectorate to clear their airways. Coughing spells can make one feel tired, frightened, and short of breath. A useless hacking cough happens when they keep coughing because of a tickle in the throat or because of irritating mucus, but they don't have enough air to move the mucus. They are unable to control their coughing and they feel helpless. When they learn to cough from deep in the lungs, they put air power into the cough. You can teach them to cough properly. If they are coughing out of control, then no one has taught them this technique. A useful cough should not tire them or take their breath away. Tell them to follow these steps when they feel a cough coming on:

- Breathe in deeply.
- Hold your breath for a few seconds.
- Cough twice; first to loosen the mucus and then to bring it up. (This usually can't be done with one hard hack, but rather with the two-step method.)
- Afterward, breathe in by sniffing gently.
- Get rid of the mucus with strong tissues. Swallowing mucus can upset your stomach. The best position for coughing usefully is to sit with the head slightly forward, feet on the floor.

Do not allow the COPD patient to keep from coughing; this is the body's way of trying to keep the airways clear. Check with the doctor before administering any cough medicines. You do not want the patient to stop coughing, but to use the cough to clear the airways whenever it is necessary. Expectorants are usually preferred.

If the patient uses a free-flow nebulizer or inhaler, it is wise to keep it at the bedside to use the first thing in the morning. It is important that everything be assembled and ready to use. Having to get up and find parts, or clean them, would only add to the frustration and would not be an energy-efficient approach.

The next project the patient may attempt is to shower. Let the patient know that the phobias associated with this activity are not uncommon. Offer some suggestions to make showering easier. The most important thing to do is to plan ahead and allow plenty of time, to avoid being rushed. Because showering is energy expensive, it may be best to save showering for nighttime, before bed. Before showering, gather all the items that are needed—soap, towels, washcloth, deodorant, shampoo, razor, and so on.

The water should be tepid. Hot or cold water has an adverse effect on energy consumption. Extremes of temperature are a shock to the circulation, which results in an increased heart beat and breathing rate. Hot water produces steam, which may add to the fear of suffocation, and increases the amount of effort it takes to breathe. If the cold water is turned on first, there will be less steam than if the hot water is run first.

Use of a shower chair or bath bench decreases the amount of energy required. Another energy-saver is a hand-held shower head. Such devices are relatively inexpensive and easy to install. Teach the patient how to save energy by drying off while remaining seated, draping one towel over the shoulders and the second over the lap and legs. The towels will prevent chilling and absorb most of the moisture. Remove remaining moisture by just patting dry with the towel. Another way to save energy when drying off is to put on a terry bathrobe to absorb the water. If the patient is to use oxygen either continuously or with exercise, she or he should have the oxygen-delivering device on in the shower, using either a portable tank or the stationary source with extension tubing. Many patients are afraid that water will get into the oxygen canister. This is not possible. Encourage them to wear the oxygen *during* the activity of showering. They will harm themselves if they take it off or wait until they are short of breath and unable to finish their activity.

Dressing is the next task at hand. This activity can be fatiguing. It is so important for COPD patients' emotional well-being to be dressed each day. They are not going to want to get dressed if it wears them out for the morning. They should avoid dressing when they are tired from a previous activity, such as showering. If the tasks of bathing and dressing are too fatiguing when done in sequence, they can be separated by rest periods or by an activity that is less taxing, such as eating breakfast. All of the clothing should be conveniently arranged and easy to reach. Front-closure clothing and slip-on shoes are the easiest to put on. Over-the-head clothes or clothes with buttons or zippers in the back can be difficult. The new Velcro shoes are easier to manage, and there are elastic shoelaces for tie shoes that can be left tied, thus avoiding the difficulty of bending over.

I will digress from the daily routine to address the benefits of pursed-lip breathing. Many patients don't understand why they need to know that air comes into the lungs easier than it goes out; therefore, breathing too fast traps air in the lungs. Then there is less room for fresh air to come in because the stale air cannot get out. This causes a feeling of tightness in the chest, called "shortness of breath." Pursed-lip breathing helps to slow down respirations and helps to keep small airways from closing down and trapping the air inside. If patients get out of breath, are exerting themselves, or feel a tightness in the chest, don't panic; have them follow these two steps to do pursed-lip breathing:

1. Breathe in slowly through the nose.
2. Then pucker (purse) the lips like you are going to whistle, and let the air fall out slowly through the pursed lips.

Remember: Slow, easy, and relaxed in and out . . . until control is regained. Pursed-lip breathing should be used whenever they do anything that makes them short of breath, such as climbing stairs, bathing, doing housework, bending, or walking.

Good food, like good medicine, works to heal, repair the body, and make it stronger against disease. Because eating is hard work when one is short of breath, you may find that the patients are not eating the best foods. If they are overweight, the extra body fat may be interfering with their breathing and demanding more oxygen. COPD patients should eat six small meals a day instead of three big meals. This will cut down on the extra oxygen that is needed to chew and digest each large meal. It need not mean extra work to prepare extra meals. Foods like salads, fruit, bread, milk, and desserts can be eaten between the cooked meals. Encourage patients to wear their oxygen, if ordered, to chew foods well, and to eat slowly. Instruct them to breathe evenly while they chew. They may stop if necessary, relax, and take a few deep breaths. If they are very short of breath in the morning, they can have a liquid breakfast but should never skip a meal. Some foods produce gas, which causes the stomach to become distended and to push the diaphragm against the lungs, making it more difficult to breathe. Some gas-forming foods to avoid are beans, broccoli, cabbage, cauliflower, turnips, cucumbers, onions, peppers, pimentos, radishes, raw apples, soybeans, rutabagas, sauerkraut, scallions, brussel sprouts, and corn.

As the morning progresses, patients may have some tasks to do, but they seem impossible to accomplish. You can encourage them and assist them to use certain principles of work that will help to conserve energy. Help them to break down the task into smaller parts. Is the task necessary? Do the results pay for the time and effort they have spent doing the task? Are they the ones that should be doing it, or should another person or member of the family share the task? Sometimes tasks are done out of habit, and they should really be jobbed out. If the task must be done, collect all tools and equipment, eliminate unnecessary details, combine details when practical, simplify all tasks. Whenever possible, patients should work sitting down, at a comfortable countertop, where they aren't stretching and reaching. Things that are stored but used frequently should be within easy reach. Suggest using a portable table with wheels to assemble and transport things from one room to another. Duplicate supplies in various work areas will decrease the number of items to be transported. For example, duplicate stores of cleaning supplies in each bathroom and the kitchen can eliminate several trips.

Vacuuming is a job that should be assigned to another family member. It is an extremely fatiguing, energy-expensive activity using the shoulders, the arms, the back, and the leg muscles. It is one of those activities that is almost never worth all of the effort.

Making the bed is another difficult task. Help patients to organize their steps. If they are to wear oxygen, they should definitely wear it when attempting bedmaking. They should not walk around the bed more than once. They should begin on one side and complete it before walking slowly over to the other side. This is another instance when pursed-lip breathing will help to keep them from getting so short of breath and out of control.

Many COPD patients are on an exercise regimen. The better conditioned their muscles are, the less oxygen they will require, and they will feel stronger and be able to do more before tiring. Help them to set aside specific times each day for their exercise. Perhaps they can make two daily appointments with themselves. They should pick their best times. Walking is one of the most useful and enjoyable ways to strengthen their muscles. They should start out with short daily walks. Never allow them to set their goals too far ahead. To have unrealistic goals can be harmful and frustrating. They should begin by walking with their arms hanging loosely at their sides and their shoulders relaxed. If they need to use oxygen for exertion, they should have it on now. Many types of portable oxygen sources can easily be taken along on a wheeled cart or carried with an over-the-shoulder strap. Find an easy, even speed, and have patients take the same number of steps for each breath. They can try to walk a little farther each day, even if it's only a few feet. If they become short of breath, have them stop and rest. They can walk inside or, on nice days, outside. Enclosed shopping malls are a terrific place to walk and pace themselves. They've got a controlled environment and, generally, benches to use for rest periods, shops to look in, places to get refreshments, and many, many people. Some malls have measured walkways; the mall is marked off in ⅛- to ¼-mile increments that are posted on the wall or floors. This can be a great place to meet others and socialize while exercising.

To relax tense, tight muscles, have patients perform this relaxation exercise: Sit upright in a chair and let your arms hang loosely at your sides. Breathe slowly, deeply, and evenly. Next, clench your fists, shrug your shoulders, and tighten your arms for a count of two. Then let your shoulders relax, the hands open, and the arms hang loosely for a count of four. Next, tighten your feet and legs for a count of two. Then relax for a count of four. Alternating these simple tightening and relaxing techniques will create a sense of relaxation and calmness.

Sexual intercourse is exercise. It should be treated as any other form of exercise. COPD patients, because of their age, may not inquire about sexual activities, so you, as the professional, may have to bring it up and offer some energy-conservation techniques. Because sexual activity involves a certain amount of energy, they should avoid combining stresses that could make intercourse fatiguing. Reassure them that some shortness of breath is natural and can be tolerated within limits. Remind them that anxiety and fear may contribute to shortness of breath. If they become anxious, they should stop, try to relax, cuddle, and start again. You can suggest positions to them that do not require that they support their entire body weight with their arms and legs. Some suggestions might be to have both partners lying side by side, or in a lying position with the non-COPD partner on top, or in a sitting position in an armless chair with the non-COPD partner on top. Some of the factors that may contribute to sexual dysfunction include monotony, boredom, anger with the sexual partner, mental or physical fatigue, overindulgence in food or drink, and fear of failure. Help them to understand and then to overcome or avoid these problems.

Certain environmental concerns need to be brought to the patients' attention. When dirt and dust land on their skin they can wash it off, but not so when it is inhaled into their lungs. Much pollution comes from industrial smokestacks and automobiles; this they have little control over. Some household products, such as cleaners, paints, glues, and aerosol sprays, add to the air pollution. And, of course, cigarette smoking is among the most dangerous. Help them to become aware of these pollutants, and offer suggestions on how to avoid them. They should avoid places with dirty air, such as traffic jams, parking garages, dusty work areas, and smoke-filled rooms. They can ask smokers to respect their need for clean air. Avoid the use of all aerosol sprays, such as hair spray, deodorant, and cleaning products. Listening to the weather reports for the smog alerts is important.

On smoggy days they should stay indoors with the windows closed whenever possible.

The weather can affect their breathing. Cold air puts an extra strain on the lungs and can cause bronchospasms. Hot dry air can dry out mucous membranes and make breathing difficult. Some people are affected by damp weather.

Infection is the most common cause for readmission to the hospital. We, as home health nurses, can't be with them all the time, so it is important that they be able to recognize the signs and symptoms associated with problems. They need to know when to call the doctor. Offer them these guidelines, and they will know what to watch for:

- fever
- increased shortness of breath (more than usual)
- increased coughing (more frequent and severer)
- increased sputum production
- change in consistency (thicker) or color of sputum to yellow, gray, or green
- swelling in ankles, legs, and around the eyes
- sudden overnight weight gain (3 to 5 lbs)
- palpitations
- chest pain or tightness
- unusual dizziness, sleepiness, headache, visual disturbance, irritability, or trouble thinking
- loss of appetite (more than usual)
- dehydration, evidenced by concentrated urine and dryness of the skin

Remember, a great deal of what we see depends on what we are looking for.

If patients have oxygen in the home, they will have many spoken and unspoken concerns. Assume that this is the case, and answer some of the unasked questions, for example, Is this oxygen going to explode?

Explain that they must have a healthy respect for the oxygen but not a fear. Oxygen does not burn, but it will support combustion. It will not burn but will make any flame or fire much hotter or more intense. You can use an example of dropping a lighted paper match in a dish of liquid oxygen. The flame will shoot up to the ceiling, but as soon as the match has burned out the fire is gone. The oxygen did not burn—it merely made the small match fire more intense. Patients will have concerns about the pilot light, the fireplace, and electrical appliances. Reassure them that the oxygen would have to come in direct contact with the spark or flame. Electrical appliances should be in good working order so that there is no possibility of sparking. When patients are in a room with a fireplace, they should be at least ten feet away; a screen should be placed in front of a wood-burning fireplace to prevent sparks from jumping out.

Many times patients have the misconception that if they have a long extension tubing on their oxygen, they needn't turn the liter flow up. This is not the case. It is of utmost importance that they realize oxygen is a drug and that it must be used only at the liter flow that has been prescribed for them. More is not necessarily better. If you have a patient who changes his liter flows inappropriately, you can consult with his physician to see whether the regulator can be preset at the appropriate liter flow. The oxygen vendor can do this for you.

Sometimes patients think that they will become addicted to the oxygen if they use it continuously, as directed. Reassure them that it is not possible. You can equate it to water and thirst; if they were in the desert and were very, very thirsty when they got to the oasis, they would drink lots and lots of water until they had replenished the deficit. It would not occur to them that they would become addicted to the water because their body needed it at the time. It is the same with the oxygen; as long as there is a deficit owing to emphysema, bronchitis, or infection, the body will need the oxygen. When the cause of the deficit has been corrected (if possible), then the body will no longer require the oxygen. It is a normal element found in the body, not an outside element to become addicted to.

Patients may tell you that they can't stand the smell of the oxygen. It is, of course, odorless. What they are smelling is the cannula. Several brands are available, and you can try out different brands to find one that doesn't have an odor. You can also offer this unscientific suggestion that does work: On opening a new cannula, place it in the freezer for 24 hours. Take it out and allow it to thaw, and presto—the smell is gone! Another problem associated with cannulas is that they can be uncomfortable on the ears and cause sores in the nose. Rather than trying to stick cotton balls over the ears, you can offer patients the use of moleskin. This is found in the foot care section of the drugstore. It is soft and fleecy on one side and sticky on the other. They can cut it and shape it around the cannula to cushion the ears. The nasal sores should not be treated with Vaseline, a petroleum product. If the solution from the inside of a vitamin E capsule is applied to the sores several times a day, they will be soothed and heal quickly.

COPD patients' most common unspoken comment is that they must be dying if they are on oxygen. Let them know that you realize that this is one of their fears. This is not necessarily the case. Many people live for years on oxygen. Many work or go to school, and still others no longer require the oxygen if they have a reversible disease process. People have lived quite normal lives with oxygen once they have learned to accept it. They can travel, go on cruises, work, volunteer, and do the things they want to do even with the oxygen.

These patients frequently will have breathing treatments. If you are not familiar with the various respiratory treatments, the proper technique, cleaning and storage, then know that you can call on the vendor who supplied the equipment to visit, to ensure its proper use, and to refresh your knowledge.

You really have your work cut out for you when you care for COPD patients at home. You must help them understand their disease process and how it relates to their environment and their lives. You need to have the valuable tools to show them how to accept it and live with it. It can be a rewarding experience.

Chapter 17

Future Trends in Home Health Care

Judy Willingham Hansen

A number of reasonable predictions can be made concerning future trends in home health care. These include growth in number and size of home health care agencies, growth of other industries related to home health care, changes in the education of health care professionals to accommodate the needs of home health care, a diversity of new jobs in the home health care field, higher salaries for home health care professionals, a broader spectrum of services offered through home health care, a new focus on preventive medicine, and changes in the Medicare system as it relates to home health care. Let's consider these areas individually.

GROWTH IN HOME HEALTH CARE

In considering the future of home health care, one overwhelming trend is evident. The popularity and magnitude of this industry will continue to grow. There are a number of reasons for such a prediction. Predicasts, a firm based in Cleveland, Ohio, and Kent, England, gives four major reasons for the expected growth of home health care: (1) the pressure on hospitals to lower costs through reducing lengths of stay and by limiting bed growth; (2) the rapid growth of the elderly market; (3) the emphasis of private business on cost containment by using new health plans, such as health maintenance organizations (HMOs); and (4) a trend among general consumers that emphasizes self-care and independence for the elderly and a more prevalent emphasis on prevention, self-testing, and self-diagnosis.[1]

I certainly would not argue with Predicasts' evaluation and consider these factors well worth discussion; however, there are two overriding reasons for future growth in home health: (1) it's cheaper and (2) it's preferred by the patient.

255

How much cheaper is home health care? In 1982, Medicare patients cost the U.S. government an average of $350 per day for hospital stays. The average stay was 10.5 days, resulting in an average annual cost of $3,675 per patient. By contrast, the cost for home health care services averaged $39 per visit and 21 visits, resulting in a cost of only $819 per year.[2] The difference may be illustrated even more graphically through consideration of a single procedure. The cost of intravenous feeding averages $35,000 per year when performed in the home, compared with an annual cost of $74,000 for the same procedure in a hospital setting.[3] One need not be an expert prognosticator to predict that savings of this magnitude will appeal not only to the government, but to private insurance companies as well.

Thus the amount of money spent on home health care may be expected to rise dramatically in the foreseeable future. A study conducted by the Berkely V. Bennett research group estimates that expenditures by the government and private groups will rise from an estimated $5.9 billion in 1982 to $16.2 billion by 1990.[4] This study closely correlates with a 1983 survey by Frost and Sullivan, which predicts that the market for home health care will triple by 1990. According to Frost and Sullivan, expenditures for home health care products and services will rise from $5.9 billion in 1982 to $18.2 billion by 1990.[5]

There is a contrary view to home care's being a cost-saving movement for the government. Some experts believe that home health care will eventually cost the government more because of increased participation. They point to the "woodwork" effect, which refers to the possibility of new patients "coming out of the woodwork" as they realize that they are eligible for benefits. Opponents point out that Medicare was designed originally as an acute care program, rather than a long-term care program, and therefore is not designed to deal with the increasing responsibility for long-term care.

For a number of years Medicare has been spending more than it takes in, and that trend will continue. There will be more elderly Americans and fewer taxpayers. The largest group among the population of elderly will continue to be women because they live longer, and yet women contribute the least in terms of tax revenue. By the year 2030 there will be more than 7.7 million persons over age 85 and the number of persons over age 65 will have doubled.[6] Furthermore, medical technology is becoming more expensive, and if Medicare expands home care benefits, this would result in many more patients, which would drive up the costs of care even further.

These are convincing arguments against the government's being a willing participant in the growth of home health care. However, regardless of the difficulties involved, the need and demand for health care will still exist, and a government of, by, and for the people cannot ignore such a need, even if revolutionary changes in the Medicare program are required to meet it. The medical needs of the citizens must be met, and they can be met more cost effectively at home. If health care costs are escalating—and they are—then they would escalate more rapidly without home health care.

Solutions to the rising costs of health care will have to be found. Perhaps a partial solution to these escalating costs would be to use people who are either already on the government's payroll or who are receiving tax money in the form of welfare payments. There are probably many welfare recipients who could be trained at minimal cost to perform valuable services as health care aides. In fact, some pilot programs in various parts of the United States are attempting to move in that direction. Such programs would not only help to defray the cost of home health care, but would also provide a means by which the former welfare recipient could attain the sense of dignity and self-worth one gains from being a productive member of society.

Similarly, the vast multitudes of unemployed people might provide a resource. Among them are surely people who could perform many of the more pedestrian tasks associated with home health care, such as transporting equipment or providing transportation, and perhaps others who could be trained for tasks requiring more skill. Some programs of this sort are emerging. One such program is in my home state of Alabama, although the program is still in the developmental stage and its potential for success has yet to be realized. At this point an effort is underway to match unemployed individuals with homebound patients requiring services that those individuals might be able to provide. The patient, however, has to make and be responsible for financial arrangements.

The matching of jobless people with a societal need is certainly sensible and has proved to be successful in the past. There are those among us who remember well the success of the WPA programs, which helped to bring the United States out of economic depression, while bringing to fruition many projects still benefiting us today. If the need for home health care outruns our resources for meeting that need, then perhaps forward thinking, like that responsible for the WPA, could be applied again.

Volunteer agencies may provide an option for those in need of home health care who don't fit into the existing health care structure or have funds to pay for health care services. Volunteer groups, both secular and religious, will no doubt continue to seek causes to support and needs to meet. Consider the number of church-sponsored missions to aid people in foreign countries. Surely these philanthropic people will be willing to do as much for equally needy people at home. Or consider the VISTA and Peace Corps volunteers who are now providing services, among them health care, to Third World people in need. Such outwardly directed resources will surely be turned inward when the need arises.

Another possible solution to the rising burden of health care costs could be prepaid health care programs. According to an article in the *New York Times*, 2 August, 1984, the Robert Wood Johnson Foundation of Princeton, New Jersey, has undertaken a $15.6 million grant to enroll 450,000 lower-income people in its Pre-paid Managed Health Care Program. The program, which is being introduced at 13 institutions in ten states, involves the prepayment of doctors and hospitals for services at a fixed price, rather than the current practice of billing for each medical service as it is rendered. Medicaid will provide anywhere from $500 to $1,000 per patient annually, depending on prevalent costs in each of the ten states. Any unspent funds could be used to defray the deficits incurred by providing care for the indigent. This experiment is in its infancy, but it seems to have promise. Not only could the eventual widespread adoption of prepaid health care save money for the government and private insurance companies, but it could also benefit hospitals by assuring them of a stabler and more predictable source of revenue.

Aside from being cheaper, home health care will grow because it is the type of care most wanted by the public. A survey by National Research Corporation, as reported in *Modern Healthcare*, 1 May, 1984, indicates that two thirds of the 1,000 consumers questioned want more home health care services in their communities. In contrast, only 39 percent of those surveyed think that there is a need for more nursing homes, and less than 50 percent perceive a need for more emergency facilities.[7]

These and various other studies and surveys indicating a general desire for more home health care merely illustrate a fact that our common sense tells us. People would rather be at home than in an institution. The growth of home health care represents a new, more technologically advanced approach to an old idea. There was a time—most of human history in fact—when virtually all health care services were provided in the home. Many of us remember when physicians routinely made house calls. Such a system seems infinitely more sensible than does one requiring sick people to get out of their homes and go to where the doctor is. The comfort and convenience of our homes, the presence of our loved ones, means much to us when we are well and even more when we are sick, or elderly and disabled.

One of the principal reasons cited in the Predicasts study for the expected growth in home health care is the pressure on hospitals to lower costs through reducing lengths of stay and by limiting bed growth. As employment in more traditional branches of health care, especially hospitals, declines, proponents of institutional care are understandably defensive. They fear that the change from a Medicare policy based on actual cost to one using predetermined rates might lower the quality of care. The chairman of the American Hospital Association, for instance, sees this change as serving "primarily the federal government's interest" and warns that it could result in "a big clash between costs and quality."[8] It is understandable that hospital officials are concerned with these changes in the Medicare system of coverage designed to shorten hospital stays. Shorter hospital stays are good from the point of view of the patients, who prefer to be treated at home, but bad if you happen to work in a hospital. Already this incentive for doctors to keep patients out of hospitals has forced many hospitals to terminate employees, cut back working hours, or close altogether. Meanwhile, home health care is being used increasingly as an alternative to hospitalization. This trend seems inevitable owing to social and economic factors, but it is not necessarily an issue of cost versus quality. Home care is quality care too.

Of course, the plight of hospital employees is an important issue as well, and their concerns deserve serious consideration. Many hospitals are opening their own home health care agencies and will likely continue to do so, perhaps staffing these agencies with laid-off or terminated employees. This trend, along with the general growth of home health care agencies, community-based clinics, and other responses to the need for lower-cost care, may help to absorb the displaced health care personnel. After all, the need for health care will be just as great or greater in the future, and good people will be needed to provide that care in whatever system is being used to meet it.

The second factor cited in the Predicasts study as being causal in the growth of home health care is the rapid growth of the elderly market. As mentioned earlier, the number of U.S. citizens over age 65 is expected to double by 1990. What are some of the implications? Well, for one thing it means that older Americans will be wielding unprecedented political and economic power. Thirty years from now the baby boomers of the 1940s will be responsible for another boom: a geriatric boom. The elderly will be a political force of considerable strength and hence able to influence legislation.

Another factor to consider is that as the population shifts toward the upper end of the age spectrum, the elderly will become more sophisticated in terms of their medical knowledge. More literature on health care will be aimed at them because they will make up a bigger part of the consumer market. As the older American gains more influence, we will probably see at least a partial reversal of the youth orientation of our present culture. We are already beginning to move in that direction. People like Jane Fonda, Shirley MacLaine, Linda Evans, and other popular women over 40 in our culture are imparting a new vitality to the image of the woman who is approaching middle age. I use examples of women because aging, in terms of loss of self-image, has been more of a female problem. The future image of older people, women as well as men, will be enhanced, and growing old will lose some of its negativity. Old age is, after all, something we all strive to attain. We may as well view it in a more positive light. As far as the future of home health care is concerned, increased influence of the elderly is favorable. The largest population of home health care patients is the elderly, and as we have seen, they prefer to remain at home.

The emphasis of private business on lowering costs by using new health plans will certainly be a factor in promoting the future growth of home care. Many businesses pay full insurance coverage for their employees as part of their benefit packages. The rising cost of health care, particularly in a time of economic lethargy, is seriously cutting into their profit margins. Thus they are faced with the necessity of either encouraging the use of lower-cost forms of medical treatment, such as home care, or cutting benefits in their insurance programs. Most American workers could ill afford any loss of insurance coverage. Wise business and industrial leaders know that the welfare of their companies depends on the welfare of their employees, so they are likely to encourage the use of home care and other lower-cost health care alternatives. And we know what a powerful political force the business lobby is in the United States.

We have considered some of the reasons why we might expect a general growth in home health care. There are other reasons, such as the emphasis on self-care and independence mentioned as the fourth factor in the Predicasts study. A book could be written on this subject alone. But let us move on to a consideration of some of the other trends we might expect in home health care, beginning with a look at the growth of industries related to home care.

GROWTH OF RELATED INDUSTRIES

As the home health care industry continues to grow, those industries related to home health care will also grow and new industries may be born. Medical supplies for home use are already in great demand and will be even more so in the future, as the number of patients being cared for at home goes up. More portable equipment will no doubt be developed to facilitate the implementation of more complex procedures in the home, and medical equipment companies will be involved in research and development in a competitive effort to be first with such equipment.

The home health field may spawn its own support service businesses, such as credit unions, special insurance companies to deal with the complex needs of health care agencies, and fleet rental car companies offering industrywide group rates. What would you think about the idea of a special car for home health care nurses? Don't laugh. Some of us remember the "business coupes" of the 1930s and 1940s, the cars with just a front seat and a huge trunk. Well, those cars were designed in response to the needs of traveling salesmen.

One can easily visualize accounting firms specializing in the unique, specific financial needs of home health care agencies, particularly if one is familiar with just how complex the whole system is. Or what about lawyers who deal with the legal aspects of home health care as their sole practice? It's already happening. And why not? Uncle Sam created the need for tax lawyers, and there were no divorce lawyers until divorce became so widespread. Similarly, the legal situation, as it pertains to health care in the home, is a whole new ball game. The creation of such new specialties will require the addition of new areas of study to universities and professional schools, hence stimulating further growth in those institutions.

The number of spin-off industries one could imagine is quite large. Home health care involves a number of specialties, such as respiratory therapy, physical therapy, medical social work, and nutritional service, and each of these disciplines requires various types of support industries that will benefit from a home health care boom. It's good to contemplate widespread growth in a number of interrelated industries at a time when so many businesses are struggling to survive. Perhaps growth of home care is part of the larger shift in the United States from a production- to a service-oriented economy. The effect that home health care will probably have as a social and economic force could be staggering, and it is good to hear an optimistic note.

Before leaving the general topic of growth in home health care, we should consider some precautions that need to be taken seriously. Rapid growth always causes problems, and we are already seeing some in home health care. One problem area is that home health represents a terrific business opportunity, and there is a danger that the rapidly expanding number of new agencies will include many who may be in home health for the wrong reasons. Home health care is a business, and because health care is so much affected by legislation, it is a business in which politics plays a big part. Those of us working in the field must never lose sight of the fact, however, that the main purpose of health care, home-based or otherwise, is the delivery of service and that self-serving business and political considerations should never be allowed to interfere with that purpose.

Another factor requiring attention is the need to provide what one of my colleagues has referred to as "care for the caregiver." History has taught us that in times of rapid growth and change there is a tendency for people involved most directly in these changes to experience a kind of culture shock. It happened on a grand scale during the industrial revolution and more recently with the high-technology revolution. When one's points of reference are changing so rapidly, feelings of instability and insecurity are sure to follow. If we in home health care don't take steps to avoid this problem, some good people may fall through the cracks, and good people are a valuable commodity. Therefore, attention to such details as good working conditions, adequate vacation time, respect for the individual dignity of employees, and sympathetic attention to legitimate grievances will go far in ensuring the success of individual agencies.

A shift in emphasis from institutional to home-based health care will result in changes in the traditional roles and education of many health care professionals. Let's consider some of these changes.

FUTURE ROLES AND EDUCATION FOR HOME CARE

As a nurse, I am most sensitive to a view of home health care from the nurse's perspective. The reader will, I hope, forgive my biases, but I see nurses as the people who are most essential to the delivery of home health care services. Nurses are the home health care team leaders, and it is through them that services are funneled.

Not every nurse is suited for home health care work. In fact, in examining the profile of the successful home health care nurse, we see that such work takes very special people indeed. For one thing, home health nurses are on their own most of the time, and they represent the only link that the patient or his family has with the health care network. Therefore, these nurses must be independent, self-motivated, and innovative. There is no one for them to consult with in the field, and no one to appeal to when a decision must be made. A home health care nurse must be decisive and authoritative in order to earn the confidence of the patient and the patient's family. Simultaneously, home health nurses must be patient and tactful. They are, after all, guests in the patient's home, which is essentially a reversal of the situation we find in institutional care.

Home health care nurses who work in rural settings must be even more endowed with the qualities of self-assurance, as they are more often than not cut off from assistance and in a more primitive environment. Nurses working in the community must be as familiar with that community as hospital nurses are with their hospital settings.

The rapidly growing and changing field of home health care requires that all who work in this field, especially nurses, be flexible. Technological advancements in treatment methodology are coming fast and furious, and people who are inclined to be inflexibly set in their ways and comfortable in a routine will probably not find home health care to their liking. We will reserve our discussion of technology in home care until later, but on this topic I will mention that home health nurses, particularly those in supervisory and administrative positions, are faced with the need to be as familiar with the computer as with the stethoscope.

In the past, home health care nurses have been viewed as generalists. However, the rapid emergence of home health care as a field with its own separate and distinct identity has created a tendency to make home care nurses into specialists. No other field of nursing truly prepares one for the tasks and circumstances that are unique to home health care. The need to prepare individuals who wish to enter this challenging field cannot be ignored by colleges of nursing. Nurse-educators are not unaware of the need to include in their curricula those skills that are pertinent to the field of home health care. The need for knowledge in such areas as documentation for Medicare and Medicaid reimbursement and other procedures will have to be accommodated in the future nurses' education.

Dr. Lynne Faulk and Susan Randall, professors in the college of nursing at the University of South Alabama, were most helpful in sharing their opinions with me concerning the future direction of nursing education. They believe that in the future, colleges of nursing will need to emphasize high-technology nursing procedures and that home health care will have a definite impact on the future development of nursing curricula. According to these educators, nursing students will have to be taught to adapt the acute care skills currently taught in the hospital setting for use in the home environment. They feel that the current, strong emphasis on acute care will likely diminish in favor of a more balanced curriculum, incorporating those attributes essential to home health care with the traditional approach.

Regarding the preparation of student nurses for the specialized documentation used in home health care, Dr. Faulk points out that good documentation and writing skills are closely related. At the University of South Alabama, there is currently a strong emphasis on improving the writing skills of nurses, a trend that is widespread among colleges of nursing in the United States.

Another concession to the need for home health care preparation in the student nurse's curriculum, according to the educators, involves the home health care nurse's role as teacher. Unlike the hospital nurse, the home health nurse must teach many techniques for self-care to the patient, as well as the use of whatever equipment might be involved in the patient's treatment. The nurse working in the patient's home must be more attuned to the psychological and social needs of the patient than does the nurse in a traditional setting. The nurse who wants to work in the home health care field will require a more sophisticated educational background in the areas of sociology, psychology, business, and the law.

Both Dr. Faulk and Professor Randall point out that nurses in home health care are going to have to be more politically astute than their institutionally based counterparts. They will require a knowledge of political and legal issues that have not been of much concern to nurses who work in hospitals, as the hospitals have taken care of such matters for them. Universities have a responsibility not to thrust graduates into this new situation totally unprepared.

Another possible trend in nursing education could involve the routine release of university faculty members to participate, under contract, with home health care agencies in treating patients. Such an arrangement would be mutually beneficial. The home health care company would benefit from the expertise of these highly trained and educated nurses, and the faculty members would gain an opportunity to stay abreast of the latest developments in the home health care field while keeping their practical skills sharp. There is an advantage in teaching procedures when the teacher has practical as well as theoretical knowledge of those procedures. Such a coalition between educational institutions and home health care agencies would enhance the quality of patient care, afford the teacher more practical experience to share with students, and add to the credibility of the home health care industry.

Respiratory therapists, physical therapists, nutritionists, and others who are more accustomed to being based in the hospital are also moving into home care in greater numbers. Provisions will have to be made in the education of these professionals to prepare them for work in the home environment as well. They will need the same interpersonal skills that are required of the home care nurse and will therefore need more knowledge in psychology and sociology. They will, in many cases, be using more portable equipment than their counterparts in the hospital are used to. As the field of home health care becomes an increasingly more viable option for these professionals, additional courses will have to be taught to better prepare them for possible entry into this field.

Besides the need to educate increasing numbers of health care professionals in traditional occupations who are moving into the home health care field, there will be a need to prepare for home care duties people who are in occupations currently extraneous to home health care, because there will be a diversity of new jobs available in the future.

NEW JOBS IN HOME HEALTH CARE

Another trend that seems inevitable in view of the rapid growth of home health care is the availability of a variety of new jobs in the future. This field is still in its infancy, and it is likely that agencies will expand the types of service available. In the years to come, positions may exist in areas of treatment that do not even exist yet. Are home repairs related to health care? Is companionship for lonely, elderly people related to their health? The World Health Organization, in its charter, defines "health" as "complete physical, mental and social well being, not merely the absence of disease." If we adopt this view of health, then the number of jobs that could be related to the maintenance of health becomes enormous. Of course, whether or not many of these jobs are accepted as legitimate aspects of home health care will depend on the willingness of the government and private insurance companies to accept a broader spectrum of home health services as reimbursable. Clearly, if we are to treat the patient in terms of his or her "complete physical, mental and social well being," then sweeping changes in the Medicare system will be needed.

THE NEED FOR MEDICARE REFORM

Medicare support of home health care is not new, according to Richard Douglas, former regional director of Medicare for the Atlanta region. Payments to home health agencies have been made since day 1. For Medicare to pay for home health visits, under present regulations, the patient must need part-time skilled nursing care, physical therapy, or speech therapy. The patient must be confined to his home, and a doctor must decide that he needs home health care and set up a treatment plan. Medicare will pay for part-time skilled nursing care, physical therapy, and speech therapy. If a patient qualifies under one of those categories, Medicare will also pay for occupational therapy, part-time services of home health aides, medical social services, and medical supplies and equipment provided by the home health care agency.

Medicare does not cover full-time nursing care at home, drugs and biologicals, meals delivered to the home, homemaker services, or blood transfusions. It doesn't cover general household services, meal preparation, shopping, providing transportation, or other home care services that are designed mainly to meet family or domestic needs.

It almost seems certain that an expansion of home care services covered by Medicare will occur in the future. One of the most attractive aspects of the experimental, prepaid managed health care programs mentioned earlier is an emphasis on preventive medicine. It is essential that the government, as well as private insurance agencies, see the value of reimbursement for preventive care, rather than just for the treatment of existing conditions. There is movement in this direction. The reduced rates that many insurance companies already offer for nonsmokers or for those involved in physical fitness programs demonstrates that the insurance industry believes that the old adage "an ounce of prevention is worth a pound of cure" applies to health care as well. Prevention is cheaper than treatment, so the government will lean toward preventive medicine in time.

THE NEED FOR PREVENTIVE MEDICINE

One of the most exciting aspects of new programs like prepaid health care is that they focus on preventive medicine and therefore could potentially lower the cost of health care significantly. If such programs prove successful, they could herald the beginnings of a commitment by the government to the support of preventive medicine. The current system used by Medicare reimburses only for the treatment of existing conditions, despite the fact that measures to prevent those conditions in the first place would have been much cheaper. In fact, knowing what we do about the value of prevention and maintenance, we must conclude that a commitment to preventive medicine is one of the most sensible ways to cut costs. Recognition of this fact seems inevitable in light of the evidence that our society is becoming more health conscious. We are exercising more and trying to exclude unhealthy and toxic substances from our diets and our atmosphere. People are becoming more concerned with staying healthy and not just getting treatment when they are ill. The attitudes of the people always filter up to the government eventually.

All of us who work in the home health care field are dedicated to the promotion of preventive medicine. Many of the acute illnesses we are called on to treat every day could have been prevented with proper health care management, and we would rather spend our time and efforts preventing suffering than treating it.

Of course, before we can practice preventive medicine to an effective degree, changes in the regulations for Medicare and insurance reimbursement will be needed. As a nurse, one of the major problems I see at the present time is that I am not allowed to focus on the psychosocial needs of the elderly because this kind of nursing activity is not considered medically related and therefore is not reimbursable. Even social service visits are, of late, being disallowed at an alarming rate because the focus of the visit is such that *any* disease process could be the cause. Such visits are therefore not covered. As long as these activities are nonreimbursable, important interventions pertaining to the psychosocial needs of the elderly cannot occur and an important part of the total health care needs of the elderly will not be addressed. It is therefore imperative that those individuals who write the reimbursement guidelines keep pace with what is proper and acceptable care in light of today's knowledge, instead of using guidelines from the past. Those who write the new guidelines should study the aging process and gerontological concepts in order to write enlightened guidelines. Only then can nursing and other health care disciplines be reimbursed for activity that is appropriate and reasonable in light of the true health care needs of the elderly.

The revision of admission criteria, especially under Medicare, is certainly in order for the future if preventive medicine is to be practiced. "Homebound" is a criterion that has long been interpreted in as many ways as anyone chose. Much clarification and some system of objective uniformity is needed. Criteria for admission have never used the patient's rights as a foundation. If a terminally ill Medicare beneficiary can elect hospice over other types of service, then why can't any Medicare beneficiary elect, with assistance from his or her doctor, how care is to be given? Does it make sense to force our aging society into certain medical care molds we may not fit into and to pass the cost of that poor fit on to the taxpayer? In the future the beneficiary of any insurance program may be allowed to choose the care he or she wants or believes to be the most helpful.

Preventive medicine has long been a proper focus for health care, whether it be home or hospital based. We can all benefit from the generally healthier society which will result from an emphasis on preventive medicine. The prevention of illness will also shift some of the focus in home care from just treatment of the elderly to treatment of the general population.

A BROADER SPECTRUM OF HOME HEALTH SERVICE

It seems almost certain that an expansion of home care services will occur in the future. We are accustomed to thinking of home health care as primarily care for the elderly, and this has been chiefly true. In the future, however, home care will be seen as appropriate for people of all ages. There are a number of reasons for such a trend.

To begin with, we are beginning to see an overabundance of doctors in many large metropolitan areas and even in some smaller cities. And more people are going to medical school than ever before. This situation is resulting in stiffer competition for patients, as can be seen by the recent abundance of community-based family practice clinics and one-day surgery centers. Medicine, as some have jokingly suggested, is taking on a fast-food look. If the current trend toward higher enrollment in medical schools continues, the abundance of doctors may become an actual glut, and competition will become stiff indeed. Add to this the facts that as a nation we are becoming healthier and more interested in self-treatment, and the result will be a buyer's market for health care. And where would most sick people rather be treated? At home. Ambitious, competitive doctors will be coming after patients the way sellers of other services have had to do all along. Perhaps we may even see doctors advertising the way lawyers have begun to do. The house call will once again become a routine occurrence, and not just for treatment of the elderly. Every sick person, unless in need of equipment that is not yet portable enough, will have the option of being treated at home. Doctors will become a direct part of the home health care team, rather than just a part of the team through referrals.

If this situation comes about, it will be the catalyst for another trend: the education of physicians for home health care. Already a push is on, chiefly through home health care agencies, to acquaint physicians with home health services, techniques, and referral procedures. When doctors themselves become a direct part of the home care team, they will need many of the skills already required of other home health professionals. Not every doctor currently has a good bedside manner, yet when people are in a position to pick and choose their doctor, they are likely to consider personality an issue. Would you buy a sofa from a foul-tempered furniture salesman? The ability to deal effectively with people and to manage situations away from their bases of operations will become essential to physicians, as it is now for all home health care personnel. The future doctor's education may include more courses in sociology, psychology, and communication arts. In addition, the doctor's legal situation will change, and he or she will need some knowledge of that new situation.

As competition for patients gets tougher, a broader spectrum of services will be offered by home health care companies in an effort to win more of those patients.

Although it may seem like a strange prediction, considering this view of the competitive nature of home health care in the future, another trend in home health care will be higher salaries.

HIGHER SALARIES IN HOME HEALTH

Higher salaries will represent another trend for the future in home health. Initially, as with any booming industry, there will probably be many new companies jumping on the bandwagon. They will be competing for staff, particularly nurses. The overall situation will be in a state of flux initially, partly because of the decline in employment in other areas of health care, but in the long run a leveling off will occur, and it will be the good agencies that last. To attract and hold the talented people needed to make a good agency, competitive salaries will have to be paid.

Another reason pay for home health care employees will rise is because doctors will be more directly involved. While doctors, because of increased competition, will not make the extraordinary incomes they have enjoyed in the past, they will nevertheless command respectable salaries. The more direct involvement of doctors will exert an upward pressure on the average incomes of home health care workers.

Home health care professionals are becoming more specialized and therefore more valuable. Home health is at the forefront of the technological revolution of medicine.

HIGH TECHNOLOGY IN HOME CARE

One might argue convincingly that the need for special equipment and surroundings will continue to make institutional care essential in many cases. I do not, for example, envision traveling surgeons performing bedroom organ transplants. However, the list of procedures once requiring hospital stays that can now be done in the patient's home is growing, largely because of the use of high technology. Chemotherapy and other kinds of treatment that only recently required hospitalization are now being performed routinely in the home setting.

Technology will, in fact, play a big role in the future of the home care industry. Computers are being used widely today for such purposes as billing and personnel management. In the future their use will probably include the management of the logistics of visiting, thus maximizing the use of field time. The growth of home care will no doubt provide the impetus for development of new high-tech devices designed specifically for the purposes of home health care. More compact equipment may, in the future, turn the patient's bedroom into the equivalent of a hospital room and the health care specialist's car into a rolling laboratory.

I hope that my enthusiasm hasn't left the impression that I think home health care is the only health care. For the sake of balance, I should say that home care will never be appropriate for every situation. One should take into account issues other than just the patient's preference in deciding whether or not home care is appropriate. For instance, the effects on other family members of having a prolonged illness in the home should be considered. Aside from the more obvious physical demands of caring for a patient at home, there is also the inevitable psychological stress that arises. Some assurance that such stress will not work an inordinate hardship on any other members of the family is needed before considering home care. The patient isn't the only member of the family whose needs must be taken into account. Does someone at home have the time, skill, stamina, and emotional maturity for the job? Can adequate plans and provisions be made for any emergencies that might arise? These are questions to be considered seriously before plans for home care are finalized. Indications are, however, that more and more people will find home health care to be appropriate for their needs. The future of home health looks bright.

NOTES

1. "Facts About the Elderly," *Homecare*, National Association for Home Care, Research Division, January 1984, pp. 1–2.

2 Spencer Rich, "The Old Folks at Home," *The Washington Post*, 19 July 1984.

3. Phyllis Wesley, "Health Care Is Taking a Homey Approach," *The Birmingham News*, October 1984.

4. Rich, "The Old Folks at Home."

5. "Home Health Market Trends," *Homecare*, National Association for Home Care, Research Division, January 1984.

6. "Facts About the Elderly.

7. Bill Jackson and Joyce Jensen, "Home Care Tops Consumers' List," *Modern Healthcare*, May 1984, p. 88.

8. "AHA Chief: Medicare Change Pits Cost Against Quality," *The Birmingham News*, 19 August 1984.

Index

quality care and, 124–129
supervisor roles and, 105–107
wages and, 129–132
Employee projections, 150
Employment discrimination, 17
End-stage renal disease, 27
Equipment
home medical, 194, 195
quadriplegic, 234
technological development and, 98
Equipment suppliers, 118
Ethnicity, 169–170, 173
Evaluation. *See* Assessment;
Performance evaluation
Exchange relationships, 138
Exercise, COPD and, 250
Expenditures. *See* Costs
Expenses, 10

F

Fair Labor Standards Act (FLSA),
131
Family
cultural variances and, 122, 167
home care environment and,
179–187
hospice care and, 219, 220
involvement with, 114
liability and, 89
multiproblem, 166
nurses' interaction with, 156, 160,
161, 164, 166, 167, 176,
179–188
patient assessment and, 163
patient assessment case study and,
168–171
case example of, 171–176
performance of nursing activities
by, 90
provisional visits of nurses and, 86
volunteerism and, 148
Faulk, Lynne, 263
Federal government. *See also*
Medicaid; Medicare
health insurance participation

conditions and, 36–48
licensing and, 4–9, 22
Financial issues, 9–11, 22
Fingerprint cards (licensing), 7
Firing of employee, 119, 121
Fiscal intermediary, 5
Fluids, IV therapy and, 210
Food, COPD and, 249
Fraud, 13
Free-standing facilities, 27, 102
Fringe benefits, 130

G

Gastrointestinal care
(quadriplegic), 237–238
Governing body, 42
Grief, hospice care and, 219, 220
Guidelines for Staff Development
(ANA), 116

H

Hall, Edward T., 185
Handel, Gerard, 168
Health agencies, 21
competition and, 93–102
hospital-based, 24, 26, 27, 99
not-for-profit, 25–26, 95, 99, 101,
102
SNFs, 24, 26, 27
VNAs, 25, 95, 99, 102, 146, 147
voluntary, 25, 257
Health behavior, 168–169, 171
family case study and, 174–176
Health Care Financing
Administration (HCFA), 5, 12–13,
27, 29, 32, 139, 151
cost reporting process and, 32–33
Health maintenance organizations
(HMOs), 26, 137, 138, 140, 142,
194, 213, 255
Health-manpower-shortage area
(HMSA), 150, 151
Health teaching, 143, 186–187
Heparinizing (IV catheter
procedures), 203–204, 212

About the Editor

Sandra Stuart-Siddall is the Director of the Rural Clinical Nurse Placement Center, housed on the campus of California State University–Chico. She has taught nursing at the diploma, AA, and BSN levels. She has had a number of nursing articles published, and has edited-authored several books. She has spoken on the local, state, and national level concerning the maldistribution of RNs. She was the first editor of the *Home Health Care Nurse* journal, having designed the departments and philosophy of the journal, as well as founding the editorial board.